W9-CXT-086

Mercy Otis Warren

Twayne's United States Authors Series

Pattie Cowell, Editor

Colorado State University

TUSAS 618

MRS. JAMES WARREN (*MERCY OTIS*), ABOUT 1763, BY JOHN SINGLETON COPLEY. COURTESY, MUSEUM OF FINE ARTS, BOSTON.

Mercy Otis Warren

Jeffrey H. Richards

Old Dominion University

Twayne Publishers
An Imprint of Simon & Schuster Macmillan
New York

Prentice Hall International
London Mexico City New Delhi Singapore Sydney Toronto

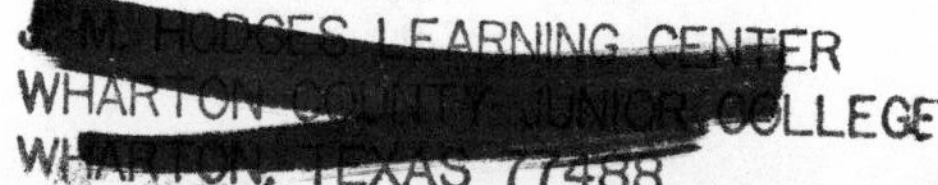

Mercy Otis Warren
Jeffrey H. Richards

Twayne Publishers
An Imprint of Simon & Schuster Macmillan
866 Third Avenue
New York, NY 10022

Library of Congress Cataloging-in-Publication Data

Richards, Jeffrey H.
Mercy Otis Warren / Jeffrey H. Richards.
p. cm.—(Twayne's United States authors series; TUSAS 618)
Includes bibliographical references and index.
ISBN 0-8057-4003-1
1. Warren, Mercy Otis, 1728–1814—Criticism and interpretation. 2. United States—History—Revolution, 1775–1783—Literature and the revolution. 3. Literature and history—United States—History—18th century. 4. Women and literature—United States—History—18th century. I. Title. II. Series.
PS858.W8Z88 1995
818'.109—dc20 94-49327
CIP
AC

The paper used in this publication meets the minimum requirements of American National Standard for Information Sciences—Permanence of Paper for Printed Library Materials, ANSI Z39.48-1984.∞ ™

10 9 8 7 6 5 4 3 2 1

Printed in the United States of America.

For Stephanie,
who asked for Mercy and found her home

Contents

Preface

When I first proposed writing a book on Mercy Otis Warren, some people discouraged me because of the subject's alleged obscurity. In recent years, however, several articles on Warren have appeared that are bringing renewed attention to her work, and a number of books about her are apparently in progress. If she is not yet a household name, she and her writing will no doubt gain a wider audience as scholars continue the act of recovery of American women writers.

But for anyone doing research on her writing, many barriers await. Much of her work, particularly letters and some poems, remains unpublished, and other texts are available only in facsimile reprint or microform. A bigger problem is finding reliable information. Many of the earlier studies on Warren were written at a time when women's literary accomplishments were devalued and consequently give her little credit for what she actually wrote; others contain significant gaps or errors of fact, many of which have been repeated by later scholars. As a result, even some of the best new work is flawed in its reliance on outdated biographies or studies.

I have tried, within the limits of this book, to correct the record or to add information not otherwise conveniently accessible concerning Mercy Warren the writer. The first chapter gives a brief biography that focuses largely on the events and influences of her life as an author of poems, plays, letters, and a major history of the American Revolution—not simply as an interesting historical figure. I have also said more about Warren's religious beliefs than many previous commentators. This chapter does not supplant the need for a modern, full-scale biography, but it does suggest some newer ways of thinking about Warren.

The remaining chapters take individual genres, but follow in something of a historical progression, from her beginnings as a writer in letters and poems to the modes she worked in later—plays, history, and political writings. These chapters draw on and develop ideas suggested in the biographical sketch, but take as their first task setting the material in an accurate historical framework. Through notes or brief statements, I have tried to identify Warren's correspondents and the people to whom she refers in her plays and other work. I have also suggested some influences behind certain works or tried to identify some themes in work otherwise ignored or only occasionally discussed in the critical literature. Thus, I conceive this book as a basic source, a beginning point for scholars who wish to pursue more elaborate analyses of individual works than I have space to provide here. At the end, following an afterword that gives a brief assessment of Warren's importance, I provide scholarly notes and a selected, annotated bibliography.

One is mindful, of course, that in correcting the old record, something newly wrong might be introduced. If that is the case, none of the following are to blame: the several people and institutions I have to thank for their help in the making of this book. Among the former, I must first cite Pattie Cowell of Colorado State University, a field editor for the Twayne United States Author Series and an expert on early American women writers, who gave her unflagging encouragement to this project. Without her labors and her belief that Warren deserved scholarly treatment, this book would not yet be launched in the world. Another who shared his belief in the worth of this project is Everett Emerson, whose kindness and previous example as a Twayne author I benefited from in many ways. I would also like to thank my department chair at Old Dominion University, Philip Raisor, for lending his support to the writing and completing of this work.

Much of the research was supported by a Faculty Summer Grant from the Old Dominion University Research Foundation; this grant enabled me to travel to collections to look at Warren papers and provided writing time. Among the libraries where I gathered material, the Massachusetts Historical Society, the principal repository of Warren manuscripts, generously allowed me access to a number of collections and materials. Director Louis L. Tucker, librarian Peter Drummey, and reference librarians Virginia H. Smith and Catherine Craven deserve special mention for their consultation and assistance. Likewise, at the Boston Public Library and the Houghton and Schlesinger libraries at Harvard, my visits to examine Warren letters and papers were made pleasant by able staff members. Manuscripts and books curator Peggy M. Timlin of the Pilgrim Society in Plymouth was most efficient and helpful during my stay there. James H. Hutson, chief of the Manuscript Division at the Library of Congress, kindly answered my inquiries concerning the Library of Congress holdings. I wish additionally to acknowledge those institutions above who granted permission to reprint passages from manuscript collections.

I am grateful for the constructive words of many English department colleagues at Old Dominion; the persistence of Diana Ballin and the interlibrary loan staff at ODU; the efforts of Lynda Erickson in the acquisitions department at the ODU library; the word-processing skills of Elaine Dawson; and the help of Marsha White with almost everything. Bob and Marilyn Danner, the folks at Churchland Challenge, and Dorothea M. Anderson had their roles to play, all positive, as did my editors at Twayne, Mark Zadrozny and India Koopman. I also benefited greatly from an Internet exchange with David Shields of the Citadel on Warren and the bluestockings.

Those who had to deal with the book on a daily basis merit special recognition. My children, Aaron and Sarah, suffered my time in the study with good humor, and my wife, Stephanie Sugioka, allowed me not only to regale her with details of Warren's life but even to drag her to Plymouth in search of Warren's traces. I thank them all.

Chronology

1581 John Otis I, paternal great-great-grandfather of Mercy Otis Warren, born in Glastonbury, England.

1620 Edward Dotey (Doten), maternal great-great-grandfather, arrives in Plymouth on *Mayflower* with Richard Warren, paternal great-great-grandfather of James Warren (husband of Mercy Otis). John Otis II born.

1630–1632 John Otis I and family arrive in Hingham, Massachusetts from Devonshire.

1657 John Otis I dies; John Otis III, son of John II and Mary, born.

1662 John Otis II, wife Mary, and family move to Scituate.

1677 In January Indians attack Scituate in King Philip's war, but Otis properties escape damage.

1678 Otis family moves to West Barnstable.

1683 John Otis III marries Mercy Bacon 18 July. John Otis II dies.

1702 Son James Otis born 14 June.

1724 James Otis marries Mary Allyne and settles in Barnstable.

1725 James Otis, Jr., first child of James and Mary, born 5 February.

1726 James Warren born 28 September.

1728 Mercy Otis born 25 September in Barnstable, third of 13 children.

1743 James Otis, Jr., receives B.A., Harvard.

1745 James Warren receives B.A., Harvard.

1754 Mercy Otis marries James Warren 14 November; earthquake hits New England 18 November.

1757 James Warren inherits Clifford Farm from father; Warrens move to North Street, Plymouth, in July; son James Warren, Jr., born 18 October.

1759 Son Winslow Warren born 24 March.

1762 Son Charles Warren born 14 April.

1764 Son Henry Warren born 21 March.

1765 Stamp Act mobs attack homes of Peter Oliver and Thomas Hutchinson in August; Stamp Act Congress called in New York in October; Stamp Act repealed by Parliament in December.

1766 Son George Warren born 20 September.

1769 James Otis, Jr., attacks John Robinson, commissioner of customs, on 5 September and is beaten and injured in return.

1770 Boston Massacre occurs 5 March.

1772 *The Adulateur* appears in *Massachusetts Spy* 26 March.

1773 Mercy Otis Warren extends friendship with John and Abigail Adams. *The Defeat* appears in *Boston Gazette* 24 May; Boston Tea Party takes place 16 December.

1774 Mercy Otis Warren writes "The Squabble of the Sea Nymphs" and "To the Hon. J. Winthrop, Esq."; Thomas Hutchinson sails for England in June.

1775 *The Group* published; Battles of Lexington and Concord 19 April; Gen. Richard Montgomery killed in assault on Quebec 31 December.

1776 Mercy Otis Warren writes "To Fidelio"; Declaration of Independence.

1777 James Warren appointed to new Navy Board for the eastern department, headquartered in Boston, in May. As only major general left, appointed command in August of one-month militia to repel British fleet off Massachusetts coast; refuses orders, resigns commission, but accepts Navy Board appointment. Gen. John Burgoyne surrenders to Gen. Horatio Gates in Saratoga, New York, 17 October.

1778 James Warren fails to win election to General Court in May; Mercy Otis Warren writes "The Genius of America" 10 October; her father dies 9 November.

1779 Death of John Winthrop, science professor at Harvard,

subject of poem "On the Death of the Hon. John Winthrop"; Mercy Otis Warren has case of "trembling nerves" in June, causing husband James to refuse possible delegacy to Continental Congress.

1780 Hutchinson dies in England 3 June; Winslow Warren, after detention in Newfoundland, arrives in England on 5 October.

1781 Winslow arrested in London, then allowed to go to The Hague. Warrens move to Milton Hill in Milton, Massachusetts, 1 June; among the visitors there over years are Marquis de Lafayette, Thomas Jefferson, Francisco de Miranda. Lt. James Warren, Jr., wounded in knee 9 June; leg amputated. Gen. Charles Cornwallis surrenders at Yorktown in October.

1783 James Otis, Jr., killed by lightning bolt while watching storm 23 May; Winslow returns to Plymouth in September.

1784 Winslow sails back to Europe (Lisbon) in April; Catharine Macaulay Graham visits Mercy Otis Warren at Milton in November.

1785 Sans Souci controversy; John Hancock steps down as Massachusetts governor; James Bowdoin elected during time of bankruptcies; Mercy Otis Warren works on *The Sack of Rome* and *The Ladies of Castile*; Charles Warren dies at St. Lucar, Spain, 30 November.

1786 Winslow arrested in New Haven, Connecticut, 1 March for debt to Dutch bankers, the Van Staphorsts; Shays's Rebellion begins in September; Winslow tried, found guilty, and jailed for debt in New Haven but escapes to Massachusetts.

1787 James Warren, despite being accused of sympathizing with Shays, elected to General Court in spring and is made Speaker of the House; Constitutional Convention meets in Philadelphia in May.

1788 Mercy Otis Warren publishes *Observations on the New Constitution*; Warrens move back to Plymouth in June; Washington elected president in fall.

1789 Washington and Adams administration begins in April.

1790 Death of Hannah Winthrop in May. Mercy Otis Warren readies *Poems, Dramatic and Miscellaneous* for publication in June (she travels to Boston); book published in September. U.S. Circuit Court opens in November; one of the first cases tried is *Nicholas and Jacob Van Staphorsts v. Winslow Warren.*

1791 Catharine Macaulay dies 22 June; Winslow joins regiment in New Jersey in July; Henry Warren marries Mary Winslow (called Polly) in November; Gen. Arthur St. Clair's army annihilated 4 November at Wabash River, where Winslow is killed.

1792 Marcia Otis Warren (grandchild) born to Henry and Polly in October.

1796 Abigail Adams visits Mercy Otis Warren in Plymouth in August, first face-to-face encounter in 12 years.

1797 John Adams announces electoral victory for president 8 February.

1799 Washington dies 14 December.

1800 George Warren dies in Maine 5 February; Jefferson wins election in fall.

1804 Jefferson reelected.

1805 Mercy Otis Warren's *History* begins to appear.

1806 Third and final volume of *History* appears.

1807 John Adams reads *History;* Adams sends first of 10 long letters to Mercy Otis Warren citing errors in *History.*

1808 James Warren dies 27 November; James Madison elected president.

1812 War with England declared 18 June; Abigail Adams visits Mercy Otis Warren in Plymouth during August and September with daughter and granddaughter; friendship renewed and locks of hair exchanged.

1813 John Adams renews correspondence with Mercy Otis Warren in September.

1814 Brother Samuel Allyne Otis visits Mercy Otis Warren in Plymouth in spring, then dies in Washington, leaving Mercy Otis Warren the last surviving member of the family of her birth; John Adams goes to Boston Athenaeum in August to certify that the library's copy of *The Group* was written by Mercy Otis Warren; British capture Washington and burn Capitol in September. Mercy Otis Warren taken violently ill 14 October; dies at 2 A.M. 19 October.

1821 James Warren, Jr., dies.

1828 Henry Warren, last of immediate family, dies.

Chapter One

A Revolutionary Life

Among other notices in a Boston newspaper for 22 October 1814 was this terse statement: "DIED— . . . In Plymouth, Madam M Warren, AET 86."[1] The fact was correct; Mercy Otis Warren, aged 86 years, 3 weeks, and 3 days, had died at 2 A.M. on 19 October, attended by her two surviving sons, Henry and James, Jr.[2] But hidden behind the screen of a death notice was a life full of American history. Though still known to a younger generation, Mercy Warren had outlived most of her compatriots and immediate family; when she died, a war was going on, filling the papers with its often ominous news. Tastes had changed with the years and names. For this active patriot; this political consultant to the leading figures of the Revolution; this passionate mother of five sons; this devoted wife and equal partner in a marriage of 54 years; this firm and demanding friend; and this author of plays, poems, essays, a three-volume history of the Revolution, and hundreds of letters, there was hardly anyone left to do her the justice of a proper public eulogy.

But she did leave papers. If anything, Mercy Warren wrote her own life, sometimes boldly, sometimes with what seems now to be a frustrating modesty. She wrote even during times when good paper was scarce, and when she could not see well enough to put pen to leaf herself, she dictated to her son James or whoever was available. She was many things to many people and has been characterized in a number of ways, good and bad, by historians and biographers; but as one examines the documents that contain her name, one cannot help but see this woman foremost as a writer—one of the most important American writers of her generation.

Scholars in recent years have been paying renewed attention to Warren's works, and of course most of this book—the first full-length study of her writing—will be devoted to the manuscript and printed pages that remain from her considerable output. First, however, we need to place her in the context of a life lived during significant political and cultural change, when the colonies became a new country and when radical republicans emerged to argue for a new ordering of society. In this light, it is crucial in examining Warren the author to consider the question of a woman writing in eighteenth-century America. How did this particular woman, contrary to many of the expectations for females of her time, come to imagine herself and finally create herself as one whose written words mattered to a world larger than her domestic circle?

Warren's biographers make much of her family history, and on the surface one can see why.[3] As the great-great-granddaughter of settlers who arrived in New England at the beginning of English colonization and later as the wife of another *Mayflower* descendant, she would have as great a claim to familial priority as any English-speaking white person north of Virginia. Although she acknowledged the Pilgrims in general, however, Warren almost never referred to her particular ancestors in her writing. She was attached to her immediate family and no doubt felt affection for surviving members of earlier generations, but aside from observing the new holiday of Forefathers Day, a celebration of the 1620 landing in Plymouth, Warren more assumed her place in America than claimed it by family background.

At the time Mercy Otis was born—14 September 1728 by the old style calendar (O.S.) then in use, 25 September by the calendar we use now—her family was comfortably established in the New World (Hutcheson, 380). Her mother, Mary Allyne (1702–67), came from Connecticut, though Mary's family had roots in Plymouth; Mary's great-grandfather, Edward Dotey (or Doten), was a *Mayflower* passenger, alleged mutineer, and the first New Englander to fight a duel (Fritz 1972, 6–8). Of Mary herself there is little record, although a portrait by John Singleton Copley (who also painted Mercy's father and husband and Mercy herself) shows an unsmiling, heavy-set woman.[4] Mary's husband was James Otis (1702–78), the fourth son of John Otis (1657–1727) and Mercy Bacon (the woman after whom Mercy Otis Warren was named) and the inheritor of mantle as family leader. The emigrating Otis (1581–1657), who had lived in Glastonbury and Barnstaple in England's West Country, and his wife, Margaret (d. 1653), settled first in Hingham, part of the new colony of Massachusetts Bay, sometime between 1630 and 1632; his son (1620–83), also named John, moved the family to Scituate in Plymouth Colony. John III, Mercy's grandfather, established himself in Barnstable on Cape Cod. The Otis farm in Barnstable would be Mercy's home until she married.[5]

The third of 13 children, most of whom after the fifth died in infancy, Mercy was also the first girl (Anthony, 25). When her older brothers James, Jr. (1725–83), and Joseph (1726–1810) were sent to Rev. Jonathan Russell's house to be tutored, a prerogative limited almost exclusively to boys, Mercy went, too, taking the same college preparatory curriculum as her brothers with the exception of formal study in Latin and Greek.[6] Since her intellectual avidity lasted her entire life, we can surmise that she was an apt pupil. A manuscript biography in the Mercy Warren Papers by an unknown writer notes that one of the books she read at Russell's was Sir Walter Raleigh's *History of the World,* a work that obviously gave her a taste for both historical and global thinking. That same biography also makes clear that Mercy learned the usual domestic arts, such as cooking, sewing, and needlework, required of women at the time. Thus at a young age, Mercy Otis learned to move easily between an intellectual world inhabited primarily by men and a household world run largely by women, and emerged into adulthood relatively but not entirely free of the self-consciousness that intellectually and artistically ambitious women of her time felt about deviating from established patterns. She somehow also conceived the idea that she could and should have opinions and that those opinions would be intellectually sound, worth expressing in speech and writing, and right.

Certainly, her being tutored with her brothers was important; she also stayed close to her oldest brother, James (Brown, 19). He graduated from Harvard in 1743, and the commencement in Cambridge may have been Mercy's first trip away from Cape Cod. It is also possible, as some biographers aver, that she met her future husband, James Warren, Harvard class of 1745, through James Otis, Jr.; James Warren's father, however, had business and legal dealings with James Otis, Sr., "as early as 1734," and it is just as likely that by the time of her brother's graduation, Mercy Otis already knew James Warren through their fathers (Brown, 33; Fritz 1972, 23; Waters, 71).[7] But her brother's more significant values to Mercy lay elsewhere. He was exceedingly bright, apparently encouraged Mercy's studies, and wrote to her as a confidante and intellectual equal. Later, when he resigned his government position to argue the famous Writs of Assistance case (1761) in opposition to the almost unlimited search powers of customs officials, Mercy would have learned in one way or another that her brother had challenged the authority of England to set American policy—an argument that many believed later to be the opening salvo in the rhetorical war against parliamentary policy in the colonies. Though little of their mutual correspondence survives—James, during the prolonged period of mental instability that marked his later years, burned nearly all his papers—one letter from brother to sister tells a great deal. Replying to a letter from Mercy that told of the death of their sister-in-law Rebecca Sturgis Otis

(d. 1766), Joseph's wife, James reflects on "the vanity of things under sun" (a frequent theme in Mercy's later life) and speaks candidly of the cost of his activities in defense of American liberties:

> Dear sister, for near two years I have not had it in my power to spend any time for myself; it has been taken up for others and some of them perhaps will never thank me. The time however I hope is at hand when I shall be relieved from a task I shall never envy any man who in performing it shall pass the anxious wearisome days and nights which I have seen. This country must soon be at rest, or may be engaged in contests that will require neither the pen nor the tongue of a lawyer.[8]

The matter of sacrifice for cause Mercy may not have learned entirely from James, but he certainly gave the abstraction a concrete and dramatic reality. There is something else, too: a shared sense that the Whig view of history, one that attacks the restrictions of rights to a privileged class, must prevail: "If we are to be slaves the living have only to envy the dead, for without liberty I own I desire not to exist here. I think I have written you diverse letters within the period you mention and will write you many more." As much as Otis appeals to his sister's political acumen, he does not omit the source of his attachment: "This you may depend on, no man ever loved a sister better, and among all my conflicts I never forget that I am endeavoring to serve you and yours" (*WAL,* 1:2).

On 14 November 1754, Mercy married James Warren (1726–1808) of Plymouth and settled in that town for most of the remainder of her life (Hutcheson, 380). Judging from the testimony of letters from each and from poems by Mercy, they were a loving, supportive, compatible couple, who, if they quarreled, never did so in public. "Never man Loved a wife with sincerest [*sic*] affection," wrote James to Mercy in 1770; "The fond and affectionate friend of my heart," Mercy would write to James, in one form or another, almost every time they were apart long enough to correspond (1770, MWP2; 22 April 1772, MWP2). The couple set up housekeeping in Plymouth proper, but on the death of James's father, they inherited the original Warren estate, Clifford Farm, created at the first division of *Mayflower* landholders, on the Eel River.[9] There James would farm and Mercy would retreat to write. Five sons were born to the couple: James, Jr., 1757; Winslow, 1759; Charles, 1762; Henry, 1764; and George, 1766. Since James, like Mercy, was secure in his identity as an Old Colonist, and was moderately successful as a merchant and public official (he was for a time high sheriff in Plymouth), and because she took her roles as wife and mother with all the seriousness of a career, Mercy could well have looked forward to a modestly prosperous and fulfilling life (Brown, 38–46).

The period of the 1750s and 1760s is critical in determining Warren's identity. We know that by 1759 she was already writing poems, still early in her childbearing years. Despite giving birth to five children in a space of nine years, her relatively late start (James Jr. was born when his mother was 29) may have saved her from the fate of her mother, whose 13 pregnancies over a period of more than 20 years would have left her little opportunity for other forms of creative self-expression. With two homes, including a country place, sufficient economic means so that her labor was not required for moneymaking (she would never take to farming like her friend Abigail Adams), and a large number of female relatives as well as a housekeeper (Ann) to assist with child-care responsibilities, Mercy Warren had opportunities as well as an education that many women did not have.

Still, even these advantages do not fully explain how Warren would come to think of herself as a writer. Indeed, for many women, the only way to secure any social independence was through the economic sphere, that is, in work such as running taverns or other businesses assumed on the deaths of husbands. During the eighteenth century, as Barbara Berg has shown, there was some acceptance of women as workers outside the domestic realm.[10] Women were also seen often as "helpmeets," sharing fully in family responsibilities with their husbands, not as figures relegated to a secondary status in the household. Nevertheless, women whose family income or estate left them with much leisure time could simply become "ornaments" whose function would have been more decorative than vital.[11] Warren's economic status was never so exalted in any case, but she clearly believed that she had duties beyond the minimally acceptable household chores that most people publicly assumed belonged to women.

Part of her freedom certainly came from the encouragement of her husband. James was often a vehicle for her literary productions, sometimes sending poems and plays to friends like John Adams who were in a better position than James himself to find the right outlet for them. But he also actively promoted her self-esteem as a person of accomplishment. Writing to Mercy in the dark days just before hostilities between England and the colonies turned into military battles at Lexington and Concord, James reassures her of his belief in all the aspects of herself she held dear: "God has given you great abilities; you have improved them in great Acquirements. You are possessed of eminent Virtues and distinguished Piety. For all these I esteem I love you in a degree that I can't express. They are all now to be called into action for the good of Mankind, for the good of your friends, for the promotion of Virtue and Patriotism."[12] James Warren was a political radical, a man of democratic sympathies whose ideas extended into his own home and whose respect for his wife's abilities was bound up with his love. And if at times he also called his wife a "Scribler," she seems not to have taken it amiss (MW [Mercy Warren] to JW [James Warren], 22 April 1772, MWP2).

He was not alone among men in recognizing that women had an important role to play in the coming conflict with England. As Stephanie Coontz argues, using Mercy Warren as one of her examples, the period of the Revolution produced a climate that allowed women to be more freely involved in political matters (145–46). Other women, through letters or poems, used writing as a means to advance political goals, although few were as widely known and eventually as feared as Warren.[13] In addition, a changing "ideology of woman's sphere" in the late eighteenth century seemed to be reducing the gaps in the hierarchical relationships between men and women.[14] Nevertheless, gains in status did not mean full equality for women, especially those who entered into the arena of public discourse. As Mary Beth Norton observes, any woman who asserted herself in intellectual or political matters ran the considerable risk of having her work diminished solely on gender grounds.[15]

Besides an encouraging spouse and a relatively favorable cultural attitude toward the contributions of women to public debate, two other factors need to be considered in assessing what enabled Warren to write what she did. One is her religious views. Like her Puritan forebears, she believed in a providentially guided universe, ruled by an inscrutable God, but she departed from Calvinist tradition by seeing that God as ultimately reasonable.[16] Like the Roman Stoics, she accepted that she would have a role, a divinely assigned part in a cosmic drama. In this synthesis of nonconformist Protestantism, Roman Stoicism, and an eighteenth-century belief in an orderly, well-regulated universe, she developed a creed that sustained her in periods of comfort and in times of loss or even doubt. Neither orthodox nor freethinking, Warren identified herself as a Christian but expressed herself in a language that almost never mentioned God or Christ by name. Firm in her faith and active in its expression, she felt required to exhibit a sometimes reluctant passivity—to use words well-known to her generation, a resignation or submission—which amounted to a bending to divine will. At the same time, in her stoicism she thought herself called to participate in events of great moment, to fulfill duties that would be rewarded in the right end toward which all things work. Thus by acquiescing in the role chosen for her by the Great Director, she became an activist committed to a just cause.

Writing to her close friend Abigail Adams in 1774, shortly after the Boston Tea Party, Warren aligns herself to the sweeping changes of the time by adopting both the conventional language of gender position and the Stoic belief in God as a kind of grand puppeteer:

> But however dark the aspect has heretofore appear'd I think we now have a Brighter prospect, and hope the united Efforts of the Extensive Colonies will be able to repel every Attempt of the oppressor and that peace and Fredom will be restored at a less Costly Expence than the sacrifice of the Bleeding Hero.
>
> But as our weak and timid sex is only the Echo of the other, and like some pliant peace of Clock Work the springs of our souls move slow or more Rapidly: just as hope, fear or Courage Gives motion to the Conducting Wiers [wires] that Govern all our movements, so I build much on the high key that at present seems to Animate the American patriots.[17]

However much the words "weak and timid" may have been a standard description of her gender, they have little to do with the actual woman who wrote them; she would have seen in all persons, male or female, a connection (by "wires") to divine agency. Everyone has a role to play in world affairs, but for her that role could not be separated from a relationship with an eternal guide and corrector. Although one can see this doctrine of having a part to act in many of her works, it can be observed especially well in a prayer she composed later in life, a text suffused with the essential tenets of her theology:

> Almighty Being! on whom depends the existence of the Universe, and by whose providence I have been supported to this moment in the enjoyment of many undeserved mercies; graciously accept my grateful sense and acknowledgment for all thy benificence [*sic*] towards me; deliver me from the consequences of all my transgressions and follies; [endow] me with such dispositions and powers, as may carry me innocently and safely, through all future trials. Enable me on all occasions, to behave myself conformably to the law of reason, piously and wisely. Suffer no being to injure me—no misfortune to befal me, nor me to [hurt] myself, by any

> misconduct of my own. Oh! vouchsafe to me, clear and distinct perceptions of things, with so much health and prospects as may be good for me, that I may, at least, pass my times in peace with contentment and tranquillity of mind; and having faithfully discharged my duty to my family and friends, and endeavoured to improve myself in virtuous habits and useful knowledge, I may at last make a decent and happy exit, and find myself in some better state.[18]

As thoughts of last things grew more pronounced, she grew frustrated with theological discourse, fearing that the Unitarian-Trinitarian debates then raging in New England would only undermine people's beliefs in the divine. In the last year of her life, she gave vent to these worries over the debates and gave a final summary of what she held to be all that anyone could assert in this world:

> We know there is only one self-existent, infinitely wise, and adorable Being, possessed of all possible perfection; we believe that he has sent a person styled his *beloved Son,* to redeem a wretched Race. Him, he has commanded us to hear. To him who was with Him before the World began, he has given all power in Heaven and on Earth. Of his essence, of his equality with the Father, it becomes not us to decide. He has said, "my Father is greater than I," but that, "my Father and I are one." I lay my hand on my mouth and silently bow, not doubting, if we sincerely and devoutly desire to know God and Him whom He hath sent, we shall have light sufficient to lead us safely through this valley of Night, and introduce us where we shall see and understand more of the true meaning of St. Thomas's expression, "my Lord and my God," as well as more—infinitely more of the nature the essence of both the Father and the Son, than can possibly be discovered or comprehended, while in this probationary state.[19]

This belief in the face of doubt, bowing silently when one most wants to stand and question, and demanding that action in the world be tied to faith in the divine became the hallmarks of Warren's religious identity.

The other major factor contributing to her need to write was politics. Warren's political beliefs—as strong as her religious beliefs—were forged in the family rivalries of provincial Massachusetts. As an articulate and forceful member of the prominent and sometimes contentious Otises, she adopted many of the causes of her father and brother. Colonel James, a lawyer and merchant with political ambitions, serving at one point as Speaker of the House in the Massachusetts General Court, often butted heads with Thomas Hutchinson (1711–80), son of another Thomas and direct descendant of the expelled, excommunicated, and murdered antinomian, Anne Hutchinson. The rivalry between Mercy's father and the then lieutenant governor for a position on the superior court reached a head in 1760 when Hutchinson—already serving as a "councillor, . . . commander of Castle island, and judge of probate in Suffolk County" in addition to holding a high-level post in the royal administration of Massachusetts—was appointed chief justice by Gov. Francis Bernard.[20] A series of conflicts over freedom of trade and the government's rights in pursuit of alleged customs violations encouraged the formation of a popular party, allied with the Otises and prominent merchants, and an administration party, tied to Hutchinson, Bernard, and associates. In essence, the arguments shaped up as provincial and individual liberties versus royal and parliamentary control over provincial affairs or, perhaps more directly, as who would benefit most from the prerogatives and preferments of political power.[21] Beneath the political debates, however, were personal enmities so powerful that Hutchinson became for Mercy Warren a bogey of almost satanic magnitude.

How much Warren, in the middle of her childbearing years, spoke out on these matters is not fully known, although the forcefulness and knowledge with which she speaks about them in the 1770s suggest she had been doing so for a long time. Nevertheless, certain events from this decade become grist for her poetic and dramatic mill in the next. As the split between the Otises and Hutchinson widened, and as parliamentary laws designed to increase customs revenue from America—such as the Stamp Act of 1765—were enacted, creating divisions between a popular faction and the political elite, the familial and provincial struggles began to take on the shape of a neoclassical drama in Warren's mind.

But perhaps two events, both having to do with her brother, fixed Warren's belief in Whig ideals and the power of the pen. One was the cruel mocking of James Otis, Jr. (called Jemmy by family and friends), in Tory papers, especially in a satiric song called "Jemmibullero." Appearing in the 13 May 1765 issue of the *Boston Evening-Post* and presumed to have been written by a customs official named Samuel Waterhouse, the gibe against the seemingly quixotic Otis may have had a reverse effect, galvanizing popular feeling on his behalf. Nevertheless, Warren must have seen acutely the power of satire to wound or to rouse. She had no doubt read, and would continue to read, the attacks on Hutchinson in such Whig vehicles as the *Boston Gazette*. But this was different; this was family and a righteous cause. When news of the Stamp Act reached Massachusetts shortly thereafter, Mercy and James Warren, along with the Otises, held a session in the Warrens' home that led, according to contemporary historian William Gordon, to the formation of a Stamp Act Congress to resist the parliamentary measure.[22]

The other event, occurring four years later on 5 September 1769, was a beating James received from customs commissioner John Robinson, an attack that Mercy memorialized in a poem and that she forever after blamed for James's erratic behavior.[23] In fact, so frequently does she refer to this fight that one might see a portion of her career as a continuing attempt to keep Otis's name and early reputation in the public eye. By the time James entered Mercy's plays, he was past being effective in person, but "The Patriot," as contemporaries called him, took on new life as the Roman rebel against imperial authority, Brutus. Later on, she would ask that her writing be judged on its artistic merits, but in the beginning, fierce family loyalty coupled with fast republican principles provided the stimulus not necessarily to write, but to write for the public.

There was one other inducement to Warren's writing that was more particular than religious and familial-political duty. Just a few months before the Robinson beating, James Otis had received a letter from an Englishwoman, Catharine Sawbridge Macaulay (1731–91), author of a controversial multivolume work on the Stuart kings.[24] Macaulay had heard of Otis and, a Whig herself, took pleasure in his opposition to the Tory administration against which she herself contended. Praising his "patriotic conduct," she compares her literary efforts with his actions: "The principles on which I have written the History of Stewart Monarchs are I flatter myself in some measure correspondent to those of the great Guardian of American Liberty" (27 April 1769, *WAL,* 1:7). Here was a woman, a historian no less, whose fame through writing had aroused strong feeling in British political circles, both condemnation and adulation.[25] As a woman with a strong sense of history and a commitment to politics, Warren would naturally be drawn to this model of a woman unafraid to enter the lists and take both heat and praise for her written words. Through her possible prior knowledge of Macaulay, this letter to her brother, and her subsequent correspondence with Macaulay through the agency of John Adams, Warren had all the stimulation and encouragement she needed to pick up the pen not only for private poems but also for public political debate.

The 1770s proved to be momentous times for the country and for Warren. With the Boston Massacre on 5 March 1770 and the formal accession of her political enemy Thomas Hutchinson to the governorship on 14 March 1771 (he had served as acting governor during the leave of absence of Francis Bernard), she and her husband were fixed in their opposition to administration policies (Bailyn 1974, 169). As James became increasingly involved in political activities, Mercy found herself even in the relative obscurity of Plymouth often at or near the center of controversy. For one thing, the Warren fireside "at the North West Corner of Liberty square Plimouth" became famous as a gathering place for those most strongly opposed to the Hutchinson-Oliver clique.[26] It may have been at their hearth, for instance, in October 1772 that the idea of the committees of correspondence was born (Gordon, 207; Anthony, 76–78). The committees were groups formed in many Massachusetts towns to share dissatisfactions with and opinions about the administration's policies (Middlekauff, 216). Though it was their friend, the radical Samuel Adams (1722–1803), who promulgated the idea, the Warrens certainly must have contributed to the scheme. Several months earlier Mercy had published in the *Massachusetts Spy* her first dramatic work, a satiric play called *The Adulateur.* Using code names for political figures—Hutchinson was Rapatio, for example—Warren provided for American Whigs just what the movement needed, a mocking attack on political figures whose power was "out of the reach of popular influence."[27] It also gave her friends names they could use in their correspondence with each other.[28] And though in the custom of the time the work was published anonymously, she earned enough fame as a writer of political plays and poems from the people she respected to give her voice a weight perhaps as great as that of the then admired James Warren.

The 1770s were years not only for increased participation in the rhetorical battles that preceded the literal war but also for Warren's development of a series of relationships through correspondence. She wrote to a number of men who were involved in the politics of the time, and although she was sometimes self-conscious about her unusual position as a woman engaging in public debate, Warren as often felt confident that her views would be heard. Correspondents with James Warren frequently received in letters from him additional greetings from Mercy, as in this revealing postscript to Samuel Adams: "Mrs. Warren, one of the Choicest Gifts of Heaven, sets by att the writeing this Postscript and desires her regards to your Honour" (26 October 1775, *WAL,* 2:425). In return, writers to James asked to be remembered to "Mrs. Warren" or "your good lady," often with compliments attached (JA [John Adams] to JW, 23 October 1775, *WAL,* 1:160). And of course, with James often away on government business, she wrote to her husband, too, as much on politics as on life at home.

One other man stood above all except James in Warren's correspondence—John Adams. John and Abigail Adams lived in that part of Braintree near Boston that is now in Quincy. The Warrens in Plymouth were just south enough from Braintree to make frequent visiting impractical, though visit on occasion they did. Mercy Warren clearly valued John Adams's opinions; in her surviving papers is a separate letterbook (not the so-called "Letterbook" that was written by other hands) in Warren's handwriting that has drafts of letters only to John Adams. As Adams became an increasingly valued member of deliberative bodies, including the Continental Congress, his friend insisted that he provide her with information about rapidly changing events. Yet the relationship during the 1770s seemed to be equally valued by Adams. He begins one letter in early 1775 with the kind of praise that might appear to be excessive, in the mode of the time, were it not that Adams generally wrote with a refreshing, if sometimes pugnacious, honesty:

> I remember, that Bishop Burnet in a Letter he once wrote to Lady Rachell Russell the virtuous Daughter of the great Southampton, and unfortunate Wife of Lord Russell who died a Martyr to English Liberties, Says "Madam I never attempt to write to you but my Pen conscious of its Inferiority falls out of my Hand." The polite Prelate did not write to that excellent Lady in so bold a figure with half the sincerity, that I could apply it to myself when writing to Mrs. Warren.[29]

When her most famous satiric play, *The Group,* first appeared in 1775, Adams in several letters demanded not only that she send copies but that she expand the play itself (JA to JW, 21 May 1775, *PJA,* 3:11).

Many historians and biographers have commented on Warren's writing letters to the better-known patriot leaders, but their remarks are largely derogatory. The accumulation of such biographical "wisdom" has led to an inaccurate picture of the woman doing the writing. Clifford K. Shipton, writing in 1960, typifies the attitude of prefeminist historians toward Warren: "Untroubled by logic, reason, or perspective, furious in her prejudices, she poured upon the leading men of the times a confident and assertive correspondence which caused many a pitying glance to be cast toward her husband" (Shipton, 11:584). There are several problems with Shipton's statement, but two stand out. First, Mercy Warren was no thoughtless virago. Motivated by intelligence, a devotion to reason, family loyalty, political conviction, and religious duty, she used her gift—the ability to write—in what she and many of her male correspondents saw as service to the country. The record shows far more statements of admiration than "pitying" looks directed toward James Warren.

Like the men to whom she wrote, she had her biases, but her commitment to the republican system was far greater—and finally more prescient—than that of many of her more famous contemporaries. Even her rhetorical remarks are based on principles that would have been shared by most Whigs of either gender, as in this statement of encouragement to her friend in the Continental Congress, John Adams: "And may you and your Associates be Directed to those steps which will Redound to the Glory of America, the Welfare of Britain and the promotion of that Equal Liberty which is the Birthright of Man and the only Basis on which Civil Society Can Enjoy any durable Tranquility" (4 April 1775, *PJA,* 2:414). Spoken by any American male reader of John Locke, the English political philosopher whose ideas deeply influenced Warren and her generation of patriots, such a statement would have escaped Shipton's imprecations.

Second, Warren also viewed her correspondence with women to be of great importance. Despite strong evidence to the contrary, biographers have minimized this aspect of her writing. Katharine Anthony declares that without "her friendships with men . . . her life would have been pretty barren. Except for Abigail Adams, she had few friends among the women of her day" (232). Yet throughout the 1770s (and well beyond), she carried on extensive exchanges of letters with Abigail Adams, Hannah Quincy Lincoln, Catharine Macaulay, Janet Livingston Montgomery, and Hannah Winthrop, among others. For a variety of reasons—practical, personal, historical, political—women responded to Warren's overtures or sought her out and expressed gratitude for the attentions given them and their ideas by their friend in Plymouth. In just one example, Hannah Winthrop, married after the death of her first husband, Farr Tolman, to Harvard mathematics professor John Winthrop, often gave Warren lively depictions of life in Cambridge, but she also shared in the strong-willed patriotism of her friend.[30] Responding to an expression of such feeling from Warren, Winthrop says, "I should rejoice to see the Plymothean spirit prevail which discovers such a Noble disinterested Virtue and such a sacred regard to rights" (to MW, 4 January 1773, *WAL,* 1:16). Both Hannah Lincoln and Janet Montgomery were widows at the time of their correspondence with Warren. In fact, it was the death of Gen. Richard Montgomery in the battle for Quebec in December 1775 that inspired Warren to write to Janet Montgomery in the first place—duty, perhaps, but a gesture that meant much to Montgomery at the time and led to letters that were valued by Warren for many years. The establishment of female connections and a female circle of correspondence was vital to Warren's self-image; in her last year of life, when all but a very few of her female friends from the 1770s were dead, she was still willing to begin correspondence with a new and younger generation of women.

With the advent of British-colonial hostilities, Warren often accompanied her husband on trips, once to Rhode Island, other times to Cambridge, where Washington had his headquarters in 1775, or to Watertown, where the Massachusetts provincial government had its seat while the British occupied Boston. Following the Battle of Bunker Hill in June 1775, James Warren became Speaker of the House, replacing the hero Dr. Joseph Warren (no immediate relation), who died in the bloody conflict. This put Mercy in the position of having to entertain, including such notables as George and Martha Washington, with both of whom Mercy conducted correspondence for many years.

But more often, Warren found herself at home during the war, looking after sons and household. Sometimes she could write of home with a good sense of humor. On her return from a visit to Watertown, she sent to James an account of the struggle by one of their sons to appear manly: "Winslow half afflicted that I had delayed coming home so long & more than half happy in the return of his fond mother turned up his smiling cheek to receive a kiss when he failed in the effort to command the graver muscles of his countenance" (21 September 1775, MWP2). She could also give vent to some pretended jealousy of her husband's social state at army headquarters in Cambridge, but still make clear her security in James's love: "I think it will be Highly Sociable at head quarters when so many Ladies of Character appear there. But yet I think you will not be Happier if the Assembly of Ladies should be ever so Brilliant unless one I Could Name is somewhere in the Neighborhood of your Residence" (8 December 1775, MWP2).

Still, it was often during wartime separations that she felt herself to be at her most vulnerable; in letters to James she often betrays the anxieties that plagued her in his absence. She would use code phrases for her feelings, like "rather pensive this evening" or "a Little too Low spirited" (February 1776, MWP2; 24 November 1776, MWP2). For his part, James had frequently to write reassurances: "I feel for my Dear Wife, least her apprehensions should hurt her health, be not concerned about me, take care of your Self" (18 June 1775, *WAL,* 1:60). Whether she was depressive, as her son James may have been, or simply better able to articulate personal feelings than most, these worries had real-life implications. So upsetting were her anxieties that her husband began to decline positions of responsibility, especially those that would take him from home, including that of army paymaster and Superior Court justice (Fritz 1972, 160–61). Indeed, James Warren earned a reputation as a refuser of positions, something that led his friends to plead with him not to absent himself from public affairs. When he declined selection as a member of the Continental Congress in 1779, explicitly citing as one (but not the only) reason Mercy's "Trembling Nerves and . . . palpitating Heart," he may have hurt his reputation not only among contemporaries but also with later historians (*AFC,* 3:208n5; JW to MW, 6 June 1779, *WAL,* 2:101).

James's relative obscurity in our own time, compared with his relative fame during the Revolution, when he was known by his militia rank as General Warren, has been blamed in part on his wife[31]; she was not, however, the only woman to request that her husband devote more time to home and less time to cause. Her friend Abigail Adams, for example, lamented in several letters to Mercy of her husband's long separations from his family. Whatever James's real worries about Mercy's health, the decisions to stay away from politics (which until 1804 were temporary anyway) also suited some aspect of his own farmer's temperament.[32] And it is clear that unlike many men of his era, James's great respect for his wife, whom he styled a "Saint" and whose "good Sense, . . . Exalted Virtue and refined Piety" he often praised, led him to risk criticism from his peers in order to do what he thought was also in her interests (JW to MW, 6 June 1779, *WAL,* 2:101).

Mercy did seem to suffer from one physical complaint—her eyes—even as early as the 1770s. To James in 1778 she mentions her "Wounded optics" and decides it will be "less hurtful . . . to write" than to "Exercise" them in some other way (5 April 1778, MWP2). It is possible, of course, that sore eyes could be associated with migraine headaches, a malady often made worse by stress. In fact, she does complain of "head ach" attacks that come upon her in "greater severity," though she resorts to a Puritan-style explanation that such pain "may be necessary to remind me of the affliction to which we are all hastning" (4 December 1775, MWP2). Whatever the diagnosis, by the early 1800s her eyes gave her so much trouble that she virtually gave up writing letters in her own hand. After one of the few long gaps in her correspondence record, Warren wrote to a friend that "This day counts up twelve months since I have been able to read a page, or take up my pen" (to

Sarah Cary, 7 February 1802, CFP3, box 2). That same friend noted that in her old age Warren was nearly blind (Sarah Cary to Henry Cary, 10 October 1814, CFP3, box 3).

By the time the war was over, James had resigned, then continued in his position on the Navy Board until hostilities ceased. He had also been defeated in the election of 1778 to the Massachusetts House, a setback that led to bitter denunciations of the "Folly, Fickleness, & the Ingratitude of Mankind" by his wife (MW to JW, 2 June 1778, MWP2). James read his defeat more philosophically, declaring to John Adams that "really I am Tired of public Life, tho' I was determined never to desert the Colours I helped to hoist" (7 June 1778, *WAL,* 2:20). Adams, writing back to James from France, commiserated with the desire to be a private person, seeing in the sacrifices of the Adamses and Warrens little personal benefit. But he saw some brightness: "Remember me, Sir, in the most respectfull Manner to your good Lady, whose Manners, Virtues, Genius, and Spirit will render her immortal, notwithstanding the general Depravity" (7 December 1778, *WAL,* 2:73). For Mercy Warren and her immediate circle, sacrifice—the key to immortality—was inseparable from the process of revolution.

While the Warrens could count their blessings that none of their sons had died during the war, one, James, had been wounded in a naval battle. This forced the amputation of a leg, leaving him, as Mercy wrote to another son, Winslow, "a cripple in the vigor of life."[33] Because of this injury and possibly a preexisting tendency to depression, Harvard graduate James never married and for some time remained at home, where he served as amanuensis to his mother. James wrote in an attractive, legible hand. He undertook most of his mother's correspondence during the 1800s and was responsible for copying her poems in the manuscript books now at the Houghton Library at Harvard and at the Massachusetts Historical Society. In addition, he wrote out the final draft of Mercy's three-volume history for the printer, also now housed at Houghton Library. It is unlikely that Mercy could have been as prolific as she was in her later years without the aid of her wounded son.

The 1780s and 1790s did bring their share of drama to the Warrens. In 1781, in what must have struck them as the sweetest of ironies, the Warrens purchased the home in Milton once owned by their nemesis, Gov. Thomas Hutchinson.[34] Others, too, saw the irony in the arch-republicans' strolling the grounds that had been held by the symbol of imperial authority. After hearing of their purchase, Arthur Lee of Virginia, in Philadelphia following service in Europe as a commissioner, wrote to tell them of the "great pleasure" he received from the news: "It has not always happend in like manner, that the forfeited Seats of the wicked, have been filld with men of virtue. But in this corrupt world, it is sufficient that we have some examples of it for our consolation" (Bailyn 1974, 374; Lee to JW, 8 April 1782, *WAL,* 2:171). With war's end, owning the estate of a one-time enemy and being closer to Boston and many of their friends, the Warrens would seem to have reached a state of comfort and content.

For people used to struggle and sacrifice, however, James and Mercy might have guessed that the placid life was not to be theirs. There were the pleasant excitements of famous visitors—Catharine Macaulay stayed and took letters of introduction from Warren to other American luminaries; Venezuelan soldier and future revolutionary Francisco de Miranda ate dinner at Milton, observing that his hostess "reveals great acuteness and knowledge"—but there were problems, too.[35]

In a larger sense, both Warrens worried over what they saw as an overall loss of civic virtue and a lack of respect for the principles that had led to American independence.[36] As early as 1779, Mercy was decrying "the Votaries of pleasure" whose fashion-consciousness and lack of morality were infecting American politics (to JA, 29 July 1779, *WAL,* 2:114). Yet for all her concerns over the direction of the country—concerns that led in 1787 to her writing an Anti-Federalist essay against the constitution then being debated—her sons gave her more than enough to brood over. Her oldest son, James, spent several years at Milton in the gloom of his amputation and shattered prospects before going to Hingham to teach (Anthony, 139–40). Her middle son, Charles, whom Mercy had once thought would surely drown in a storm as he sailed to Plymouth from Boston, contracted tuberculosis; he went to Haiti in the fall of 1784, but the following summer showed signs of worsening.[37] He then left to join his brother Winslow in Portugal, but en route to Cadiz died at Sanlucar de Barrameda, along the southwest coast of Spain, on 30 November 1785 (Anthony, 141; Fritz 1972, 237). Henry, who thought he and Charles would start a trading venture, left Boston immediately on hearing of Charles's death and moved to Plymouth to engage in the family business. Before long, George, the youngest, then living in Northampton, would head off for Maine (then still a part of Massachusetts) to find his fortunes (Anthony 141, 154; Fritz 1972, 221).

One son dominates the written record—Winslow. In sharp contrast to James, whom Warren mentions only occasionally in correspondence, her second son seems to have been the repository of most of her hopes and fears. It was Winslow who first left the family nest for Europe and was promptly captured by a British warship; Winslow who lived in London during the war, was eventually detained and questioned by none other than Lord Hillsborough, the British secretary of state, and talked his way out of trouble; Winslow who cut a dashing figure in France and Portugal and who was situated by Mercy and James with no effort spared; and Winslow again who inspired Mercy to continue with her history of the war, to write more poems, and to create her two verse dramas, *The Ladies of Castile* and *The Sack of Rome.*[38] In fact, this latter may be part of the clue to her attachment, for Winslow had a literary bent. His letters, his journals, all bespeak a polish that his mother both admired and in some ways feared. After all, she too was a literary person; perhaps she saw her son as her personal creative act, as if she could write him into being. Despite his professional failures and legal scrapes, she wanted to turn him into the model republican man by the power of her words. He could then carry on the family pen to greater glory than she would ever allow for herself. In any case, she was less restrained with Winslow, at least in letters, than with any family member save her husband.

This is quite apparent in a letter she wrote on his unexpected arrival in the country after his first European sojourn. For the past three years, he has, by her declaration, dominated her daily thoughts:

> And is my son—my dear Winslow again in the same continent with myself? I nearly cannot express the joy—the Gratitude—the tenderness that permeated my bosom when the tidings reached my ear. let me stop—and adore that Being who has preserved your health and that has guided you through such a variety of dangers—and has brought you back to your native country. . . . It is three years this day since I bid you adieu—since which every evening has wafted a sigh to the shores of Europe, and every morning breathed a prayer for the safety of my son. (19 May 1783, MWP2)

Before long, however, Winslow would be back in Europe, trying to create business opportunities, but whether through lack of initiative or overmuch attention to the good life, he never succeeded. Ironically—or curiously—Winslow sailed for home after the second stay, in fall 1785, when he must have known that his brother was coming to see him. Whatever his motivations, he was not up to the hard work and self-sacrifice that his parents knew almost intuitively as a mode of being.

In 1791, with few prospects, he joined a military regiment as an officer and set out for Ohio. His travels west must have agreed with him, for he sent home several detailed letters and in his exuberance even predicted that they could march all the way to California without hostile interruption (to JW and MW, 22 July 1791, 10 August 1791, 29 August 1791, MWP2). He was unduly optimistic. The troops he was with, under the overall command of Gen. Arthur St. Clair, were surprised by the brilliant strategist Little Turtle and a powerful combined force of warriors from the Miami, Shawnee, Delaware, Wyandot, Ottawa, Chippewa, and Potawatomi tribes. In the rout of the army on 4 November, Winslow was killed.[39] A letter received by the Warrens, and later copied by Mercy, assured them that "your son fought bravely and bravely did he fall in the cause of his country," but that did not change the fact that a second of her five sons, and her favorite, was dead.[40]

Not all the darkness of the 1780s fell from her sons. On 23 May 1783 her beloved brother, the by-now much-reduced James Otis, Jr., was killed by lightning. In the years following the Robinson beating—and even before—Warren and others like John Adams had felt his loss to the cause through mental illness to be tragic. Better for one who had struck the prerogatives of royal administration with the suddenness of a thunderbolt that he go as quickly as he came.[41] For Mercy, his contribution was clear; as she wrote to Otis's daughter, he was the single most important champion of American "rights & . . . Liberties."[42]

Those same liberties also seemed in danger. A revolt by western Massachusetts farmers in 1786 against the financial policies of the postwar government elicited the Warrens' sympathies, at least for the victims of government high-handedness if not the violent means used by the rebels in redress.[43] After the uprising, Shays's Rebellion, was crushed by a force that ironically included Maj. Henry Warren, many family friends turned on Mercy and James, including John Adams.[44] To the Warrens, liberty was liberty; to many of the former revolutionaries now in the business of crafting new governments, disorder was disorder and needed to be suppressed. The proposed constitution for the federal government, which promised strong central powers but did not contain much language of individual rights, struck Mercy as repugnant to the principles of the Revolution; but as with the Shays issue, she was on the losing side. By the time her once closest male friend besides James became vice-president of the United States, the ardor of respect that had passed between them had cooled to a frosty civility, sometimes laced by icy accusations that the other had forfeited his or her integrity.[45]

By 1788, the Warrens, feeling politically isolated and socially snubbed, faced the realities of their financial situation and discovered that they could not keep the Milton house. If, as Arthur Lee had suggested, there was poetic justice in their living where Hutchinson once did, there was perhaps a humbler and more practical justice in returning to Plymouth. Son Henry was there, and just days before his brother was killed, he married Mary "Polly" Winslow (Anthony, 236). The timing was right, to be sure, for in the grief that Mercy felt over her son's death, she could also look forward to the birth of her first grandchild, Marcia Otis Warren, in the fall of 1792. James Jr. would return from Hingham, taking up residence with the Warrens and eventually becoming postmaster of Plymouth (Fritz 1972, 271, 291).

In the summer of 1790, after the move back to Plymouth, Warren went to Boston to oversee the publication of her first book, *Poems, Dramatic and Miscellaneous.* When it appeared in September, the volume put her in rare company, with Anne Bradstreet and Phillis Wheatley, as one of the few women in America ever to publish a book of poems. She earned the further admiration of George Washington, now president, to whom she dedicated the book; he subscribed to six copies. But, more interestingly, she earned the genuine respect of a fellow writer, Judith Sargent Murray, who praised Warren's work and who later helped her sell subscriptions to her history.[46]

The 1790s were a period of change. Party divisions solidified between the Federalists, of whom John Adams was a member, and the more liberal followers of Jefferson. Despite the long-standing but now strained relationship with the Adamses, the Warrens became firm Jeffersonian Republicans. For Mercy, the tenure of Adams as president from 1797 to 1801 was a disaster and the Alien and Sedition acts so many threats to the liberty she prized. Jefferson's election in 1800 brought a grateful letter from James to the new president and renewed hope from Mercy that their battles would be justified (Fritz 1972, 291).

Personal relationships were changing, too. Her close friend and correspondent Hannah Winthrop died in 1790, 11 years after Hannah's husband, John. Abigail Adams paid a visit in 1796, the first since the early 1780s, but political differences between her husband and both Warrens kept the relationship from regaining its former vigor. Other friends, like Janet Montgomery, increasingly found writing to be too much of a chore to do very often.[47] But others found Warren's company, or more usually, her letters, to be valuable documents. An old acquaintance but relatively new friend was Sarah Gray Cary, a younger woman with an increasingly large family. Her husband, Samuel, had plantations in the West Indies, which might have made his patriotism suspect during the Rev olution; but probably for business reasons, the Carys spent the war years in Grenada.[48] Despite a many-years separation and political differences (the Carys were Federalists after the war), the two women engaged in an intense correspondence, often discussing children and childhood education. As early as 1786, Sarah Cary was writing from Grenada to Mercy's sister-in-law: "when you see Mrs. Warren, tell her I very often think of her & always with pleasure" (to Mary Gray Otis, 20 May 1786, CFP3, box 2). By 1793, after the Carys had moved to the Retreat in Chelsea, Massachusetts, letters between the two become more frequent.

As important as Sarah Cary was herself to Mercy, Sarah's daughters were significant, too. As she approached and surpassed 70 years of age, Warren became something of a guide to women of a new generation. Many of her letters seem to have been passed around and copied, often among young women, or from older to younger. Sarah's daughter Margaret engaged Warren's interests, especially in matters of religion and behavior. The call to accomplishment and rectitude that was the Warren code was passed to women of a newer age, even if those of Warren's generation sometimes chose not to listen.

For her own granddaughter, Mercy composed an alphabetical set of maxims, an act that brought pity for young Marcia by one Warren biographer (Brown, 186–87). For "E" is this piece of advice: "Egotism may be a little indulged in old age from its long experience and want of novelty; but in youth it is at once both impertinent and tiresome." And the last entry urges caution in character evaluation: "Zeal to imitate examples of real dignity & worth is laudable—but be careful to scrutinize the model with an unprejudiced and perspicuous eye." As the introductory poem says, the alphabet "is not made for a child / But for refining merit if not early spoil'd." Warren intended her doctrine of duty and moderation to outlive her—if not in her sons then in the figure of her new favorite, Marcia Warren.[49]

On 5 February 1800, a third son, George, the baby, died in Maine (Fritz 1972, 290). As with the deaths of Charles and Winslow, Warren used poetry to mourn her loss and find strength in the resignation to the will of providence. But with the change of administration and the encouragement of friends, she also dusted off her history, worked it to her satisfaction, and sent it to the printer. The process of completing her biggest work turned out to be arduous and frustrating; a series of letters to the printer from both Mercy and her amanuensis, James, Jr., speak of unaccountable delays in press runs.[50] Finally, in 1805 and 1806, this project of three decades was at last out in the world, Mercy Warren's three-volume *History of the Rise, Progress, and Termination of the American Revolution.* It was her last publication and the work by which she hoped to make her mark both on and in history.

For the next few years, much of her correspondence would deal with her magnum opus. Have you read it? she would ask friends. When they had not—as it seems with Samuel Cary—she could be hurt and angry (MW to Sarah Cary, 24 November 1809, CFP3, box 3). Unfortunately for Warren, her history appeared rather late among books written by her contemporaries. She had composed most of it during and immediately after the war, but others had gotten their volumes out ahead of her. Notices of it were mixed, although friends generally praised it.[51] But one friend who scoured it with an eagle eye most certainly hated it—as he had feared he would years before (JA to JW, 9 December 1780, *WAL,* 2:155).

In summer 1807, the first of nine detailed and blistering letters from John Adams reached Mercy Warren in Plymouth. He called her his "ancient friend" but felt obliged to "point out some" of the "several mistakes" relating to himself in the pages of her history.[52] Warren, by now unable to write except through the help of her son James, gallantly answered them, but the critiques often came faster than she could respond individually. By the end, all pleasantries banished by Adams's vigorous repudiation of the picture of him she had painted, she insisted that he apologize for his abuse of her, especially in the lines that closed the ninth letter. This time, only silence greeted her demand.

On 28 November 1808, just two months past Mercy's eightieth birthday, her "friend of my heart," James Warren, died.[53] Already stoic by philosophy if not always by temperament, she seems to have accepted the blow. She had had more than five decades of happy married life, far more than many of the women with whom she corresponded over the years; she still had two living sons nearby and grandchildren through Henry. She yet had friends—Elbridge Gerry, Charles Turner, James Winthrop (son of John), Sarah Cary. And she still had some spark of righteousness or determination or gumption to make people pay attention to her, even in, maybe especially in, her octogenarian widowhood.

"The long silence of my beloved Mrs. Cary is to me unaccountable," she scolded her correspondent 11 months after James's death (and to which Sarah drafted the answer, "I plead guilty my dear Mrs. Warren to your charge of delaying to write you"); she wanted a response to the news of her husband's decease. But she also wanted to reflect on a long life. "When I look back, I see a desolated theatre where, once moved a numerous band of the most worthy friends, now entombed in silence waiting the decisive day that recalls to life and immortality." Characteristically abstracting away the pain of her loss, she says of James, "the venerable head of my own family has made his transit from this vestibule of being to a state of peace and felicity."[54] That said, though, she turned to the future. When can the Carys, mother and daughters, pay a visit?

The visit would not come for some time. Meanwhile, though, there was a life to live and to reflect on. If life so long lived brought many losses, it also brought some satisfactions. A long and extraordinary letter from Charles Turner told Warren all she could have wanted to hear from an old friend—by Turner's count, of 55 years:

> General Warren and yourself, actuated, as I charitably trust, by those noble Christian patriotic principles which *accompany Salvation,* have done, by the help of God, great things in the cause of *republican,* that is to say, *Christian* righteousness freedom and happiness; and (as might naturally be expected in such a case) you have greatly suffered, by the malignity of the aristocratic children of this world; and for your comfort, I recommend it to *you* Madam . . . to contemplate the following passages . . .

among which is "*Blessed are they which are persecuted for righteousness sake.*"[55] No riposte to John Adams could have given her more pleasure.

Though increasingly frail, Warren never gave up intellectual or social activity—or for that matter bridging rifts with one-time friends. With the help of Elbridge Gerry, she reestablished relations with John and Abigail Adams, an act marked by an exchange of tokens that included locks of hair from each. Letters started again in 1812; Abigail and granddaughters visited Plymouth in late summer 1813; and even John Adams himself began to write directly to Warren, signing himself, "your old friend and respectful, humble servant."[56] And if there was any doubt that this renewal was anything more than mere civility, it was put to rest in August 1814 when John, nearly 80, acting on request of his Plymouth correspondent, traveled from Quincy to Boston to write into a copy of *The Group* at the Boston Athenaeum that it was in fact the work of Mercy Warren.[57]

At last, in early October 1814, the promised visit from Sarah Cary came. The two women had not seen each other for 21 years. To Mercy, Cary wrote of the pleasure at seeing her "in the full vigour of your mind,

& altho feeble, yet in good health & retaining your native vivacity." Still, the writer of possibly the last letter received by Warren knew what the visit meant; on the return, Cary tells her friend the company in the coach sang and kept up spirited chatter, "to dissipate every gloomy idea consequent upon parting with a dear friend, whom perhaps I had embraced for the last time" (9 October 1814, CFP3, box 3).

To her son Henry Cary, Sarah added more details of the visit, including one of the most concrete descriptions of Warren we have. While the rest of her company went off to visit local factories, and while all were careful with politics, Sarah sat with Mercy and listened "to her tale of sorrow . . . imparting as well as I was able that consolation, that sovereign [*sic*] balm, which points to futurity."

> She was seated in an old Fashioned easy chair with a crimson damask covering, dres'd in a gown of black sattin a mob cap tied under the Chin & a small snug black Bonnet, with a little green curtain to shade her Eyes, which, have faild her very much of late years, so that she cannot discern objects at a distance, nor either read or write. Her little Hands which are still fair, & almost transparent, were adorned with rings, chiefly mourning ones, but one which she was lately received from the former Pt. Adams with his, & his Wife's Hair, she seems to value most highly. Her form is as thin as you can conceive, and were it not that she takes snuff, more interesting than you can imagine.

Impressed as she was with Mercy's spirit and presence, she knew death was coming soon. Still, her friend "converses on death with the deepest reverence & humility," as if she too knew it was coming (10 October 1814, CFP3, box 3).

Warren may have had a premonition of her death. In the spring, her only surviving sibling, Samuel Allyne Otis, paid a visit to Warren in Plymouth. Shortly after his return to Washington, D.C., where he worked as clerk for the Senate, he died 22 April, leaving Mercy the last Otis of her generation (Shipton, 14:480). In a letter of consolation to Samuel's widow, Mary, Warren speaks of their final parting, she at the window, looking at his "intelligent countenance" and reading in his gaze back at his sister "that he never expected to behold her faded countenance again in this world." Of course, she continues, he no doubt expected to be weeping for her than the other way. But, she concludes, "May we my dear Sister while we tarry be diligent followers of those who through faith and patience are inheriting the promises!"[58]

She apparently never lost that faith. Stricken by an unrecorded ailment, at last on Friday, 14 October, Mercy Warren recovered briefly, then after another episode of pain on Tuesday night, died early on Wednesday, 19 October 1814 (Anthony, 246; Fritz 1972, 320). "And thus the *last* frail reed is broken!" wrote Henry Warren to his aunt Mary Otis; "Your beloved friend & sister left us this morning at 2 oclock & took her flight for Heaven" (19 October 1814, MWP2). There was a funeral on Saturday; she was interred in the same grave as her husband (in the Warren plot on Burial Hill) and would share a headstone with him.[59] Who besides Henry, his family, and James attended is not certain, but one notable absence was Mercy's nephew, Mary Otis's stepson Harrison Gray Otis. Living in Boston, Otis was by this time a staunch Federalist, a politician in the conservative party; the Warrens were still "high Democrats," to use Sarah Cary's phrase (to Henry Cary, 10 October 1814). But as Henry Warren discreetly but pointedly reminded Otis, she had, despite political differences, appreciated his "manners—understanding—talents & powers of mind" and thought of him as "her peculiar favorite."[60] Whatever Otis's reasons for not coming, the episode tells us that to the end, Mercy Warren, passionate in politics, deeply reverent, and literary to her bones, valued loyalty to friends and family no less than to cause or creed.

Thanks to the loyalties of James, who died in 1821, and Henry, who died in 1828 and whose descendants became caretakers of the Warren letters, her papers were preserved and the bulk of them deposited in the Massachusetts Historical Society. These, materials in other collections, and her printed works provide the eulogy and command the audience her corporeal remains could not that 22 October almost two centuries ago. Now the task remains to us, as Janis McDonald rightly demands in her essay on the need for contextual revision, to reconsider and revise our sense of who this woman, this writer, was and is.[61]

Chapter Two

Correspondence

Mercy Warren's correspondence has long been recognized as a significant documentary source for historians of the Revolutionary period. Elizabeth Ellet, writing in 1848, remarks, "Her correspondence with the great spirits of that era, if published, would form a most valuable contribution to our historical literature."[1] Those that have been published—mostly in connection with the Adams family—have been cited by many modern historians in a variety of contexts. But taken as a whole, her letters have not been fully assessed or completely catalogued.[2]

Yet it is clear from the number (over 300) of her letters that have survived, as well as from the presence of draft versions of many of those letters, that Warren took this aspect of her writing seriously. As she remarks in her *History,* "Nothing depictures the characters, the sentiments, and the feelings of men, more strongly than their private letters at the time."[3] Whether or not she meant "men" to be inclusive of women, the sentence applies to her as well. At least one of her letters was printed in her lifetime, her advice to Winslow about Chesterfield, and her contemporaries assumed (though in many cases probably in error) that other pseudonymously published letters on political matters came from her pen. At any rate, she was recognized as both a stylist and a writer of substance, even before she gained much reputation for her poems or plays.

Warren wrote in a thin, linear hand, quite in contrast to the more rounded form used by her husband and many of her contemporaries. Although her letters are readable, those in draft form or to family are sometimes quite difficult to decipher, and some variations in printed letters are inevitable. For the most part, she signs herself in two ways. To her husband James and sometimes to John or Abigail Adams, she ends with "Marcia," but her characteristic signature is "M Warren." This last reflects, even in her familiar letters, a formality of address that runs throughout her correspondence.

Unfortunately, Warren's high style has proven a barrier for later generations of readers. Her first important biographer, Alice Brown, finds much to criticize, at least from the perspective of the late nineteenth century. "[I]n all her voluminious legacy of print and manuscript, I fail to discover one real gleam of humor," says Brown (65); in her letters "she is painfully abstract, and so far as her correspondence bears witness, she lived upon stilts" (67). In the twentieth century, where her letters have often been linked to those of John and Abigail Adams, commentators have continued to find fault with her style. Noting a high-sounding passage from Abigail Adams, the editors of the *Adams Family Correspondence* blame this lapse in the more down-to-earth writer on Mercy Warren: "this sentence is worthy (if that is the word) of Mrs. Warren herself, and that in writing to this correspondent AA [Abigail Adams] tended to take on Mrs. Warren's flowery mode of expression" (*AFC,* 3:290n1). The question remains, then: why did so many people of prominence, men and women, value the receipt of letters from "Mrs. Warren" if she were so humorless, abstract, and flowery?

Regardless of later standards of epistolary taste, letter-writer Warren was held in high esteem by recipients. That such an independent spirit as Abigail Adams felt moved to elevate her prose can be taken as testimony of her respect for Warren's style. Others found her summaries of political events to reflect significant issues of the time; still others thanked her for words of solace, which Warren invariably offered to friends stricken by misfortune or grief. Later in her life, young women especially sought out Warren, many initiating a correspondence with her almost as a badge of honor. The point is that whatever charges of stylistic infelicity or excessive decoration modern readers can lay beside her inkwell, we must remember that her contemporaries regarded a letter from "M Warren" as no mean thing.

It is true, however, that (with a very few exceptions) she rarely presents herself with unguarded lightness or rash outbursts of uncensored candor. She can be passionate, but her passion wears a rhetorically directed garb. In writing to Harriet Shirley Temple, whose conservative husband Robert fled to England before hostilities had advanced too far, the radical Warren closes the gap between the politics of the families with an appeal to a Romanized image of impending war: "Heaven grant that the Civil sword which now hangs over us, may be resheathed before it is again dipped in human gore!" (30 July 1775, MWP1, 91). Purple prose it may be, but she cannot—or will not—say, "I fear for myself and family." Instead, she writes herself out of the expression, casting the potential frightfulness of battle in universal and high sentimental terms.

At some point, no later than the early 1770s and possibly before that, Warren must have become self-conscious about her writing. Knowing full well her abilities with both complex syntax and spelling; finding her expression of philosophical and political ideas meeting with approval; and identifying herself with what Linda Kerber has called the Republican Mother,[4] Warren understood that every expression had the potential to be read by history and by her five sons, and she must have desired to appear well to posterity. Thus, for example, in a letter to John Adams that describes the arrival of a French fleet in Boston, we can see that her wartime paragraph to a friend who was becoming a major political figure has all the earmarks of being constructed for the ages:

> The squadrons of the House of Bourbon, fortifying the Harbour, Riding in the port of Boston, and Displaying the Ensigns of Harmony, are Events which though precipitated by the Folly of Britain, have out run the Expectations of America. And as there has not yet been time to prove the sincerity of Either party, I think most of those officers who Remember the late War, (when we Huged ourselves in the protection of Britain) look as if they Wished, Rather than beleived ancient prejudices Obliterated, and half doubting our Friendship: Reluctantly hold back that Flow of affection which in Reallity we are Ready to Return in full Measure, while the younger part unconscious of injuries, Discover an Honest Joy Dancing in their Eye, and Every Feature softned by the Wish of Mutual Confidence, Extend their arms to Embrace their New allies.[5]

This passage is prolix, even by eighteenth-century terms; yet Warren handles a number of issues and situations within the context of two syntactically correct sentences: the uncertain relations between the Americans and their new near-allies, the French; the reversal of connection between Americans and their protectors-turned-enemies, the British, from the time of the French and Indian War to the present; the hopes of a country that heretofore has had little to celebrate militarily; and the differences between generations in response to the presence of the French ships. In an age that values "personal writing"—novels and peccadillo-laden autobiographies—one might regret the absence of detail about French officers and American ladies at a party held by the French commander, D'Estaing. But this passage is not just "flowery" padding or language on stilts; rather, Warren means through style and impersonal address to convey the historical significance of an event that others might read only as an "Entertainment" (*PJA,* 7:142).

Though the issue of style will come up again, it may be more useful to consider to whom Warren sent letters. With many individual writers, Warren concentrates on certain themes that become peculiar to their mutual correspondence, but it is instructive to consider her correspondents in groups. Among those to whom she wrote letters, three large categories emerge: immediate and extended family; men in the professional class, especially politicians, ministers, military officers, and intellectuals; and lettered women of the same class, often wives or daughters of professionals.

Family

Letters survive from Warren to (among others) her father, her husband James, each of her five sons, her brothers James and Samuel Otis, her nieces Elizabeth Otis Brown and Sally Sever Russell, her nephews James Otis III and Harrison Gray Otis, her sister-in-law Mary Gray Otis, and her daughter-in-law Polly Winslow Warren. Taken together, they bespeak Warren's deep sense of individual responsibility, her love, and her belief in the efficacy of the personal letter as a medium for giving advice to the young and comfort to the afflicted. Whig though she may have been, she was an ardent family loyalist and proclaimed her feelings as explicitly as her Augustan taste would allow. Nevertheless, as can be observed in the passages quoted in the first chapter, only with husband James does she release herself at all from exacting standards of formality that characterize nearly all of her correspondence.

The few remaining letters between Mercy and brother James Otis indicate a strong attachment, as her biographers have all pointed out. One of the most traumatic events of the first half of Warren's life was the beating of James in 1769; her letter to him shows Warren's ability to display passion even in the abstracted diction of the time: "You know not what I have suffered for you within the last twenty four hours—I saw you fallen—slain by the hands of merciless men—I saw your wife a widow, your children orphans." But hers or others' suffering are secondary to larger forces; thanks to "the unering [*sic*] hand" of God, the wound is not fatal. "You have long and painfully struggled to promote the interest of your country, thousands are thanking you therefor, and daily praying for the preservation of your life."[6] Yet at some deep level, Warren absorbed this beating almost as intensely as Otis received it; although three years younger, she viewed James almost as a twin. She would never forgive Robinson or Hutchinson and never forget the loss to the country of her brother's talents.

This is quite clear in a letter to James's daughter on Otis's death by lightning, as mentioned in chapter 1. Elizabeth had married a British officer and moved to England. But that act of conservative defiance gets only minimal attention in Warren's letter. Her task is to inform and to comfort but also to remind her niece from whence she sprang. First, she recurs to the Robinson affair: "Little has he enjoy'd & less has he desir'd life since the barbarous assassinating hand of Violence gave that irreparable wound which broke the energetic power of reason, & almost shook from the throne that distinguishing Characteristic of the human Soul" (that is, reason). Next, she places James in history: "While the pen of a sister, agitated by the tenderest feelings can scarcely touch the Out Lines, history will doubtless do justice to a character to whom America is more indebted for the investigation of her rights & the defence of her Liberties than perhaps to any other Individual." Finally, she reinforces Elizabeth's relation to this paragon: "His amiable Daughter, born to more brilliant prospects, weeps with resign'd dignity her disappointed Expectations.— Her chearful & filial attention was the only Comfort of a distress'd father;—the same Virtues are still the solace of a mother broken by Age, infirmity & affliction."[7] In the letter's progress from Mercy's personal wound to James's role in history to Elizabeth's filial duty the author transmutes and transfigures private experience into a nearly public testament.

Like Elizabeth Brown, other young women in the Warren-Otis family received Mercy's admonitory epistles. Much of the advice dispensed has to do with being a woman. In a letter to niece Rebecca Otis, she prescribes rather conventional nostrums for dealing with the misleading attractions that society holds out. Pay attention to the "faithful monitress in every bosom" and control passions; cultivate "Sweetness of temper, and gentleness and delicacy of manners" if you lack "briliancy of talents" (1776, MWP1, 57). Later letters, however, offer more far-reaching advice; one from the "Letterbook," to "A Very Young Lady," brings together different pieces of advice offered to Sally Sever before her marriage in 1784 and Polly Winslow before hers in 1791.

To marry well, Warren says in this letter, "there should be a minute similarity of sentiment, in order to [create] a friendly union of hearts." At the same time, a woman of intelligence must confront "the general aspersions so often thrown on the understanding of ours by the illiberal part of the other sex." Despite this long-standing prejudice against women, she implicitly argues to her young correspondent that feminism, in the sense of taking up the single cause of advocacy for women, is not the answer. Better to rise above what she calls in other letters "party spirit" and take the larger, rational view: "I think I feel no partiality on the female side but what arises from a love to [*sic*] justice, and freely acknowledge we too often give occasion (by an eager pursuit of trifles) for reflections of this nature."

Still, like Judith Sargent Murray, who in her essays of the 1780s was arguing for a new style of upbringing for women, Warren makes clear that her cautions and suggestions to young females are based on a firm principle of essential equality: "Yet a discerning and generous mind should look to the origin of the error, and when that is done, I believe it will be found that the deficiency lies not so much in the inferior contexture of female intellects as in the different education bestowed on the sexes; for when the cultivation of the mind, in the early part of life, is neglected in either, we see ignorance, stupidity, and ferocity of manners, equally conspicuous in both." Indeed, like Murray, Warren affirms the value to men as well as women of an education that gives women some preparation for the world—a preparation that is based on the ideal of rational, mutual marriage. Nevertheless, women must develop "œconomy as well as other female virtues" in order to be "the rational companions to men of understanding and taste"; and they ought to adopt the form of "the appointed subordination" to men if only "for the sake of order in families." But in the final analysis, women must never relinquish the belief that they can be "equal in all mental accomplishments" to men and reach "the most masculine heights."[8] Indeed, with few guideposts to female behavior except those that encourage domestic accomplishment, Warren's letters provide a valuable alternative for the young women of her family circle.

To her sons, she delivered a steady diet of epistolary advice. Letters to James Jr. and to Charles while they attended Harvard warn against submitting to temptation and ignoring studies: "May the Great Gaurdian [*sic*] of Virtue, the source, the fountain of everlasting truth watch over and ever preserve you from the baleful walks of vice and the devious and not less baneful track of the bewildered sceptic" (MW to JW2 [James Warren, Jr.], c. August 1772, MWP2); "Cultivate every worthy principle" (MW to CW, 29 August 1780, MWP1, 350). Other letters express concerns over prospects or pass on news of their father or other family members.

But in the correspondence with her sons, the largest body of letters is that to Winslow.[9] Something of a dandy, a young man whose easy acquisition of the social graces would have marked him as a rising star in the urban social scene, Winslow was both his mother's pride and her fear. One letter of advice to her son, written when Winslow was 20 and living in Boston, was so admired by friends, including Abigail Adams, that it was eventually published three different times; this was her attack on the pernicious effects of *Letters Written by the Late Right Honorable Philip Dormer Stanhope, Earl of Chesterfield, to His Son, Philip Stanhope,* just published in Boston.[10] Originally dated 24 December 1779, Warren's letter seeks to dissuade the handsome and susceptible son from admiring the much-cited author more than his due. For many Americans, Lord Chesterfield became synonymous with Europeanized corruption; in his advice to his son, Chesterfield argued for an amoral conduct of individual self-interest, made palatable by style of dress and address, not by devotion to moral or religious principle. Warren's letter seeks to save her son from becoming a devotee to soulless civility.

In providing advice of her own, Warren acknowledges Chesterfield's elegance in writing and the completeness of his "code of politeness." But her response—in balanced cadences and precise diction—demonstrates that refinement need not exclude principle:

> But when he sacrifices truth to convenience, probity to pleasure, virtue to the graces, generosity, gratitude, and all the finer feelings of the soul, to a momentary gratification, we cannot but pity the man, as much as we admire the author; and I never see this fascinating collection of letters, taken up by the youthful reader, but I tremble, least the honey'd poison, that lurks beneath the fairest flowers of fancy and Rhetoric, should leave a deeper tincture on the mind, than, even his documents for an external decency and the semblance of Morality. (quoted in Hayes 1983, 618)

Warren detects Chesterfield's aim—"to arouse the corrupt passions in the bosom of his son." She also attacks his attitude toward women, expressed in his philosophy of pleasure, whereby a man uses whatever witticisms and charms he can concoct to get a woman into bed: "I think his trite, hackney'd vulgar observations, the contempt he affects to pour on so fair a part of the creation, are as much beneath the resentment of a woman of education and reflection, as derogatory to the candor and generosity of a writer of his acknowledged abilities and fame."[11] Far from being elegant, Chesterfield betrays his "cloven foot" in both morality and style. As a mother, as a woman, and as a person of faith in divine justice, Warren uses the opportunity of a personal letter to expound a republicanism that encompasses more than one son.

During Winslow's absences from the country, Warren wrote long letters to him, not only expressing her concern over his welfare but also portraying the situation in America in the 1780s. On his first trip to Europe, after Winslow had been arrested and transported to England, his mother had many anxious moments. At finally receiving several letters from her son, she writes of her relief: "I, at times, apprehended everything. I fear the enemy, the sea-sickness and imprisonment, but above all the dread influence of vice cloathed in the specious disguise of politeness and pleasure and backed by the example of the most splendid and brilliant characters." Happy that he has survived the first dangers, she warns him further of the second, telling him especially to "beware of the smiles of beauty and the deceptive allurements of female art, where gallantry is the spontaneous growth of the soil and intrigue the great business of life" (28 September 1781, MWP2). Thus however much his physical endangerment might cause her distress, Warren—as in the Chesterfield letter—worries more about Winslow's soul.[12]

In a letter to Winslow of 17 July 1782 she also expresses her general fears of the corruption of American virtue in the postwar era. He can be assured, however, that there is one place of safety: her home at Milton Hill:

> there are in the country, courts and courtiers, sycophants, flatterers, and pimps, and all the necessary train of danglers, who usually wait at the levee of power, ready to attend the embryo monarchy about to be reared in America. Your father with all the principles of uncorrupted patriotism, a firm, independent private gentleman, is above paying homage to men in high office—much less to those who by several fortunate circumstances are possessed of power without dignity, and who are both in point of ability and integrity, generally below the standard of merit which marked the early opposers of British tyranny. (MWP; quoted in C. Warren 1932–36, 262–63)

Already contemptuous of a new generation of leaders, Warren both politicizes family (unsullied patriot father) and familializes politics (monarchy in utero). Winslow must resist temptation now in order to take his rightful place, as principled Warren, in due season. It is clear that Warren imagined Winslow to be her voice into the next generation, the son who would shine most gloriously in the new republic. Though his failure to find his niche did not deter her, his death did, and letters to other correspondents after 1791 show a greater disinclination to make sweeping political and historical comments than she possessed while Winslow lived.

Professional Men

To some extent, a list of Warren's male correspondents reads like a who's who of Revolutionary America: future or sitting presidents George Washington, John Adams, and Thomas Jefferson; notable politicians or officeholders Jabez Bowen, James Bowdoin, John Dickinson, Elbridge Gerry, Alexander Hamilton, and James Lloyd, Jr.,; Unitarian ministers James Freeman and Joseph Tuckerman; military figures John Thomas, Benjamin Lincoln, and Henry Knox; and writer-intellectuals Joel Barlow and James Winthrop.[13] If there is any common thread among this diverse group, it is their avowed respect for Madam Warren.

Many of her letters are perfunctory: requests for favors, greetings, or matters related to her books. Concern for a niece leads her to ask General Thomas, the commander at Dorchester Heights during the siege of Boston, to secure safe passage for the daughter of James Otis to Plymouth.[14] Worry for her sons prompts many letters to men in government or the military for recommendations or appointments—a tactic that would hasten the alienation between the Adamses and the Warrens. But even beyond the requests themselves is the power of association, a private woman to a public man. This can be seen in her letter of dedication to George Washington (whom she had met in 1775) for her *Poems, Dramatic and Miscellaneous.* Conscious that her letter might be perceived as the usual self-serving flattery, she seeks to defuse such criticism in her opening sentence: "Ambitious to avoid both the style and the sentiment of common dedication, more frequently the incense of adulation, than the result of truth, I only ask the illustrious Washington to permit a lady of his acquaintance, to introduce to the public, under his patronage, a small volume." She wants his "approbation," she says, and, "claiming the honour of private friendship, hopes for this indulgence." But once having tied herself in this way to the first president, she tries not to take too much: "it must be a bold adventurer in the paths of literature, who dreams of fame, in any degree commensurate with the duration of laurels reaped by an hero, who has led the armies of America to glory, victory and independence."[15]

Though modern readers have been tempted to see in such a letter a contradictory strategy of self-abasement coupled to self-aggrandizement, most of her correspondents did not respond as if that were so. Indeed, her letters often had the effect of eliciting protestations of humility or inadequacy from their recipients. Washington's response shows his characteristic stoical pose of self-erasure, coupled with a due sense of elevation for being attached to Mercy Warren: "Although I have ever wished to avoid being drawn into public view more than was essentially necessary for public purposes; yet, on the present occasion, duly sensible of the Merits of the respectable and amiable writer, I shall not hesitate to accept the intended honor" (4 June 1790, *WAL,* 2:318). Despite her strong views—for instance, she would be the only Revolutionary-era historian to criticize Washington—she seems to have had a way of disarming the men to whom she wrote. As one of the few women of her time who addressed public men as her equal, Warren claimed the attention of Washington and others not merely as the consort of General Warren but as someone whose pen fueled a cause for which they jointly struggled.

Another longtime friend and correspondent among this group was Elbridge Gerry, like the Warrens a Jefferson-leaning republican and at the end of his life vice-president under James Madison. As a Warren correspondent, Gerry has most often been identified with his role as peacemaker between Warren and John Adams in their dispute over Mercy's *History;* they were, however, exchanging letters three decades before, both firm believers in the idea of what a Gerry biographer has called the "virtuous patriot."[16] With Gerry, Warren is more playful than with Washington. One of her signature letter-writing characteristics is the extended—some might say overextended—image, allusion, or metaphor.

In a message to Gerry, written 22 January 1781, she spends four paragraphs expressing her desire to send him a poetical composition but regretting her inability to comply. The style in which she expresses this simple thought shows how completely she can give herself over to a strain somewhere between high-poetical and mock-heroic: "I could wish to Awaken the sleeping Muses, and call back the wandering Dieties. But Alas! Clio is Deaf, perhaps irrecoverably stuned till the Noise of War shall cease. The Harmony of Calliope suffers by the jaring of patriots. Melpomene is frighted by the Cry of the Miscerery, and the Fire of lost Urania quenched by the tears which flow for the loss of public and private Virtue."

Writing shortly before her move from Plymouth to Milton Hill, Warren describes how "their Ladyships," the Muses of history, epic poetry, tragedy, and astronomy, respectively, cannot remain amidst the current strife. And though she half-jests, she uses humor to show how seriously she wishes for their return, for should they "make a Temporary Visit to one almost secluded from society (which Brightens the Idea, or gives a polish to Expression)"—that is, the phrase serves as a euphemism for a lonely and perhaps depressed person—"an Exertion shall be made . . . to offer a Libation to the Image set up in Dura."[17] This last reference—to the golden icon set up by Nebuchadnezzar (Daniel 3)—she uses not only to emphasize how far she would prostrate herself to get the Muses back but also to lead into another extended allusion to Daniel's prophesies and their relation to the events of the present time. As Harvey Gardiner, the editor of the Warren-Gerry letters, remarks, "It would be difficult, in any other one short letter, to exceed this as a demonstration of MW's wide reading and ornate writing" (Gardiner, 153n3).

The reference to Daniel also suggests a cast to Warren's thinking that merits little attention in the usual discussion of her correspondence. Though her religious sympathies seem to follow a Christian-Stoic model, she was attracted to prophecy and millenialism. One of her correspondents was the liberal Unitarian James Freeman, but their letters are largely practical, having to do with the details of publishing the *History.* Another late-life correspondent, the Unitarian Joseph Tuckerman (who was married to a daughter of her friend Sarah Cary), later became famous as a "minister-at-large," working outside any religious institution and serving the poor; but their relationship developed only when Warren was considerably enfeebled by old age.[18]

For extended discussion on prophecy, she turned to the stepson of her friend Hannah Winthrop, James Winthrop, the librarian at Harvard. The author of *An Attempt to Translate the Prophetic Part of the Apocalypse of Saint John into Familiar Language* (Boston, 1794) and *A Systematic Arrangement of Several Scripture Prophecies Relating to Antichrist* (Boston, 1795), Winthrop tried to meld liberal politics with a rationalist millenialism, dating the end of the reign of the Antichrist first with the founding of Plymouth (*Attempt*), then with the French Revolution, of which he was an admirer (*Arrangement*).[19] Although Warren had known him for many years as the son of her friend John Winthrop and stepson of John's second wife Hannah, their active correspondence dates from 1787, when James was in his mid-30s. Almost all the surviving correspondence is from Winthrop, but one can surmise Warren's interests by the content of James's letters.

He was, it seems, a person she could rely on for fair-minded criticism of her own work; but more important over the years, he was an intellectual whose range of reading and perspicacity of comment she valued for being less tainted by politics than that of, say, John Adams.[20] In 1791, for instance, he sent her two volumes of Edward Gibbon's *Decline and*

Fall of the Roman Empire with the comment that protests from readers of earlier volumes "have not tamed him on the subject of Christianity." Warren, who shared Winthrop's beliefs on this matter, would have been gratified to have her views seconded, to wit, "that under our system [Christianity] every man almost has more virtue than the *saints of the infidels*" (3 August 1791, *WAL,* 2:327).

Yet it seems she was troubled by the whole scheme of prophecy, both wanting answers and finding the answers offered wanting. In responding to one of Winthrop's books, she seems to have objected, if with her "habitual politeness," to some of what he proposed (to provide a unified explanation of world religion through a reading of the Book of Revelation), for as he replies, "I will not teaze you with a long argument on this subject, for to be honest about the matter, we all of us have our own courses of reasoning, and I cannot expect those, who have been used to a different theory, at once to abandon it for the sake of supporting mine" (1 October 1808, *WAL,* 2:357–58). Still, he not only further explains his system but sends her books on Hindu mythology.

Though their intellectual exchange was broken briefly in 1808 with a necessary correspondence of grief and condolence for the death of James Warren, it resumed the following year. Mercy herself was not above teasing Winthrop for being the author of anonymous essays on prophesy in a newspaper, but in the one locatable letter to him, expresses her frustration with the whole matter of interpretation. "[I]t is painful to observe," she writes, that those who conjecture on prophecies, including Isaac Newton and George Stanley Faber, cannot agree "on all points"; "this is a proof that weak mortals minds wait until divine wisdom sees fit to disclose."[21] She wants to continue their long dialogue on this rarefied topic, she continues, but does so with this proviso: "I despair of seeing a clear solution of those things which infinite wisdom has seen fit to cover with a veil until his providential designs are fully ripened to display the glory of his power in bringing all the Kingdom of the Earth, in his own way, to become the Kingdom of our Lord and Saviour, Jesus Christ" (3 November 1810, BPL). Even so, she must never have lost interest in prophecy, for as late as 1813, Winthrop, responding to her letters, writes in detail about the connection among Daniel, Ezekiel, and modern political upheaval. That she encouraged such speculations from Winthrop in her eighty-fifth year tells much about the continued sharpness of her intelligence and curiosity.

However much she valued letters from Washington, Gerry, Winthrop, and other professional men, the one of that class who meant the most to her was John Adams. From 1773 until 1814, with some notable gaps, Warren and Adams maintained a lively, sometimes testy, and for a while angry correspondence that for all its variety really had only one topic: politics. They met as early as 1767, when Adams dined with the Warrens in Plymouth, although no startling impression was recorded on either side. After another dinner at the Warrens five years later, Adams pronounced the whole family "agreable."[22] Within a year or two, Adams and Warren had formed a mutual admiration society that remained fervent, even when admiration turned to sneers and gibes.

Part of the admiration each felt rested on belief in the literary abilities, whether as judge or writer, of the other, as will be seen in subsequent chapters. But beyond that, Adams was that active and patriotic political figure—and not her adoring husband—who valued and solicited her comments on current events. Even in a hastily inscribed note, she can rise to the occasion of writing to him with a declamatory period. Just days before Lexington and Concord, she asks of Adams (now a member of the Continental Congress), "Is there no hope that the Dread Calamity of Civil Convulsions may yet be Averted, or must the Blood of the Best Citizens be poured out to Glut the Vengeance of the most Worthless and Wicked men Ever Nursed in the Lap of America" (4 April 1775, *PJA,* 2:413).

Though the hope was dashed by the subsequent battles, Warren's rhetoric to Adams was not. In a longer letter written from Watertown, where her husband was serving as president of the Massachusetts Provincial Congress, she depicts the sufferings of Boston in the wake of the bloody conflict at Breed's Hill by excoriating British cruelty while questioning patriot resolve and the workings of providence. Why, she demands, was the "virtuous patriot" Joseph Warren killed before his time, while the British General Gage, "the Grey Headed Delinquent totters under the Weight of Accumulated Guilt And Counting up his scores is still Adding Crime to Crime till all Mankind Detest the Hoary Wretch" (5 July 1775, *PJA,* 3:58). To speak thus, she relies on what she assumes will be Adams's own sense of outrage at cruel deeds and perfidious men.

While Adams may have served as a sounding board for her fulminations against the forces that plunged the country into violence, he also was, for her, a respected political philosopher. In a cooler temper a few months later, she explains to Adams why she intrudes on his important government deliberations: "I cannot find myself willing to give up the pleasure of corresponding with a gentleman, I hold in high estimation, both as a defender of the rights of mankind, and as the faithful friend to a very worthy person who holds the first place in my heart. I think the last consideration gives me a claim to the indulgence of my scribbling humour, and frequently a letter in return."[23]

In this letter, Warren has much to say of a philosophic and a material nature. Writing with more care than in her earlier letter to Elbridge Gerry, Warren develops an extensive metaphor without lapsing into efflorescence. She worries about humanity at large and the way in which privilege corrupts the "primeval principles" of human goodness; with just a little power, "*man* in general . . . becomes so tenacious of *prerogative* that he is sore in every part that affects it, and shrinks at the approach of any thing that might injure the newborn bantling. He wishes to cherish the young embrio [*sic*] till it grows to a gigantic size, to a formidable monster, that endangers the choicest claims of society" (October 1775, *PJA,* 3:268).

Within the limits of her style, she can also be particular about persons. While at Watertown, she meets a number of worthies, including Benjamin Franklin, Washington, and two other generals, Charles Lee and Horatio Gates. The first demonstrates "affability and politeness"; the second is an "amiable and accomplished gentleman"; the fourth "a brave soldier, a high republican, a sensible companion, an honest man." The third, Lee, one of the most pungent figures in her *History,* she particularizes to this extent in the same letter to Adams: ugly, "careless, even to unpoliteness—his garb ordinary, his voice rough, his manners rather morose,—yet sensible, learned, judicious, and penetrating" (269). In short, Warren relies almost entirely on Adams's being able to translate her words into a picture of someone's soul; she assumes he is a literate republican for whom cadence and style give relish when abstracted character traits—a form of lofty shorthand—do not.

Despite the fervid and high-minded beginning to their correspondence, Adams's government travels to Europe and a sharpening of political differences changed the direction of their letters. In 1779, Adams records in his autobiography anger with the Warrens over apparent war profiteering by Winslow, blaming it on "Democratical Licentiousness"—his code phrase for what he saw as their overly liberal interpretation of republican principles (*DA,* 4:192). Three years later, Warren writes to Adams in Europe both to defend her husband from grumblings about his seeming lack of participation in postwar government affairs and to threaten Adams—prophetically, as it turned out—with the wrath of the historian if he does not send her more information on his negotiations with the Dutch government: "nor is any office so illustrious, or any character so sacred, but he must submit if he provokes the threatenings Even to the Menaces of a Woman" (24 October 1782, *WAL,* 2:180).

But the turning point came after Adams was elected vice-president. The reputation of the Warren family had suffered considerably during the late 1780s as a result of their imputed sympathies for the Shays rebels in western Massachusetts. After obligatory letters of congratulations on Adams's accession to high office, Mercy, in a following, "very free" letter gets more to the point. The attacks on her husband—in which Warren assumes Adams participates—"have endeavoured to wound in a still more tender part by levelling their envenomed shafts at the reputation of a son [James Jr.]." Now she resorts to what sounds like a threat, if not blackmail: "was there a propriety in calling your attention at this time to private objects, I could give you a curious detail of fact, relative to this matter. Yet I do not think it by any means necessary in order to secure your patronage" (7 May 1789, *WAL,* 2:310). Adams's response closed the door on anything more than restrained cordiality: "One thing is indubitable, that G[eneral] Warren did differ for a time from all his Friends and did countenance measures that appear to me . . . extremely pernicious." And as for patronage: "I have no patronage," he says; "neither your children nor my own would be sure of it if I had it."[24] The crises of the Adams presidency, which led to what the Warrens saw as their old friend claiming monarchical powers, further alienated the families. And of course the rift over Warren's treatment of Adams in her *History* led to a furious and voluminous correspondence that lapsed into a many-years silence.

Despite all that, letters to and from Adams remained signal documents in her life. After the restoration of family relations in 1813, correspondence resumed, with some pleasure evinced by Warren in the writing. In her next-to-last letter, written in the midst of the War of 1812, she rises to the news of his ill health to make clear what she has genuinely felt all along. He is, after all, one of the few surviving persons who experienced firsthand events in Revolutionary Massachusetts. In a sentence that more truly reflects her thinking and feeling on Adams than any in the *History,* she assures him, "I most sincerely hope that the life of a Gentleman who acted so great a part in a revolution that astonished the world and lived to set his seal to an honorable peace after a desolating war, may be spared to see peace again restored to the United States, notwithstanding the severe threats of our old inveterate enemy" (10 July 1814, *WAL,* 2:394).

Even though she did not live to see that peace, her wish for him, so characteristically and eloquently expressed, was granted. More important, between the accolades and denunciations each heaped on the other, the letters between Warren and Adams constitute an extended discussion of what is meant by republicanism and show how much close friends and political allies could differ on such a basic issue. At the same time, those philosophical differences mirror rival concepts of a woman's role as a speaker on public issues. Despite Adams's increased reluctance to consider Warren's or any other woman's political views, her success in resuming the correspondence shows that the former president was never immune to her words.[25]

Lettered Women

With women, Warren sought relationships that could be both intellectual and personal. Her writing could be expressive in ways that it could not be with men, but she could be formal, too, especially when giving advice. Warren wrote to a number of women initially because of politics—they were the wives of political men with whom her husband worked. In the cases of Sarah Brown Bowen and Dorothy Quincy Hancock, for instance, nothing much developed by way of a correspondence. With others, however, including Ann Thompson Gerry and especially Martha Custis Washington, she established more substantial relationships.

To some women she wrote out of an urgent sense of duty to provide solace for their grief; in one case, that of Janet Livingston Montgomery, she made a friend of many years' standing after the death of Janet's patriot husband Richard in 1775, gaining in the process yet another friend in Janet's sister, Catherine Livingston.[26]

With others the draw from the beginning was simple friendship (though the excuse for writing may have been a distant family connection), as with Sarah Walter Hesilrige, Hannah Fayerweather Winthrop, Hannah Quincy Lincoln, and Sarah Gray Cary. And some relationships that began formally ended in friendship, as with Catharine Sawbridge Macaulay and Abigail Smith Adams.

Although the tenor of her correspondence with men often depends on politics, with women Warren tends to rise above political difference. With Sarah Hesilrige (married to English baronet Robert Hesilrige), Warren had a family connection, but both women shared an intellectual bent, engaging in discourse on education and literature as well as consoling each other over a death or loss.[27] Before moving to England, Hesilrige lived in Boston, a place that in Warren's mind was the center of the American beau monde. Responding to an inquiry from her friend, Warren in one letter lets slip her consciousness of being in a cultural backwater yet tries to turn the simplicity of Plymouth into a virtue: "In this little village there are neither balls, concerts, or assemblies, there are no card parties, visiting, or routs. Yet be assured your friend has no right to wish to be happier in the present state" (1773, MWP1, 81).

Warren lets her friend know that her mind is ever active. Thanking Hesilrige for two books by two women authors, she proceeds to compare them. One is by "Mrs. C," who could be Hester Mulso Chapone, author of the book *Letters on the Improvement of the Mind* (1773); the other is by Phillis Wheatley, the African-American poet whose *Poems on Various Subjects, Religious and Moral* was published in London, also in 1773.[28] Without knowing anything about the authors, Warren says she would choose the English woman's as the better, that is, the more polished book; but when one factors in background—Mrs. C's advantages versus the rough transition from Africa to America by "the barbarian girl"—"I think the last must bear the palm of superior applause as best entitled to the claim of original genius."[29] This an unusual instance of an eighteenth-century female reader's—not a male reviewer's—response to Wheatley's ground-breaking book, and it demonstrates Warren's ability to understand the many factors that contribute to a writer's originality. At the same time, the comment shows how much Warren valued correspondence with well-read women as an outlet for her literary observations.

Another woman with whom Warren could share intellectual predilections was Catharine Macaulay, later married to William Graham. No woman served Warren better as a model than the English historian. An admirer of James Otis and a correspondent with John Adams, Macaulay naturally moved into a transatlantic relationship with the sister and friend of two Americans she much respected. Both women shared the Whig political philosophy; both desired to be known in a genre dominated by men, history; both were unafraid to criticize their respective governments when they disagreed with them on principle. Though Warren may have begun the correspondence out of admiration, she quickly moved to a stance of intellectual equality, showing her learning to be of the same caliber as Macaulay's.

In her first letter to Macaulay, written two years before the first military battles of the Revolution, Warren employs a device that fits the character of the receiver, the address to female qualities and virtues:

"Has the Genius of liberty which once pervaded the bosom of each British hero animating them to the worthiest deeds forsaken that devoted island; or, has she only concealed her lovely form untill some more happy period shall bid her lift her avenging hand to the terror of every arbitrary despot and to the confusion of their impious minions on each side of the Atlantic?" (7 June 1773, MWP1, 1). What is for the time a figure of speech—"Genius" (guardian spirit) as female entity—becomes an animating trope between two women who have claim to their own genius (creative intelligence) and their own principled and public interest in promoting liberty.

Another common figure of speech at this time—Britain as parent country—enlivens a second letter to Macaulay a year later. Again, the trope is made female, as per common pictorial practice in British and American newspapers and broadsides, but with a very different outcome from above: "Britain like an unnatural Parent is ready to plunge her dagger in the bosom of her affectionate offspring."[30] The cruelty and power in this image of femaleness contrasts with the prior personification of the genius of liberty; yet both dimensions feed Warren's view of women overall as capable in ways that the world is not always prepared to recognize. Further in the letter, she addresses the image of women in politics directly. Showing cognizance again of her recipient, Warren argues for a space on the political stage for women:

> You see madam I disregard the opinion that women make but indifferent politicians. It may be true in general, but the present age has given one example at least to the Contrary and pray how many perfecter theorists has the world exhibited among the masculine part of the human species either in ancient or modern times? When the observations are just and honorary to the heart and character, I think it very immaterial whether they flow from a female lip in the soft whispers of private friendship or whether thundered in the Senate in the bolden language of the other sex. (5)

With Macaulay as her example—and herself, perhaps, to follow—Warren gives to the image of woman both a metaphoric and a literal expansion; when liberty and history are at stake, women who speak on these matters, especially those who invoke female personae of power and virtue, release themselves from the shackles of imprisoning "opinion."

During the war, Warren risked the uncertainties of mail to Britain to keep the correspondence with Macaulay alive and expound on her favorite topic: political history. Several long letters to Macaulay in February 1777 describe wartime events in a detail and a tone that seem better suited to the history page than to the personal letter. Lines such as "Every species of rapine and outrage has marked the footsteps of the British army in the Jerseys" and "It is well known that from the beginning of the present contest the lamp of liberty has not burnt so bright in New York, New Jersey and Pennsylvania, as in other parts of America" make their way in somewhat different wording to the final text of her *History.*[31]

Well after the war, following Macaulay's visit to America (including a stay with the Warrens at Milton Hill), politics continues to play a part in their correspondence. Though Macaulay has given voice to concerns about the corruption of ideals that Warren herself wrote voluminously about during the 1780s, Warren defends America to her friend: "Yet not withstanding you acknowledge your disappointment and think our practice does not comport with the principles professed and inculcated in the day of our distress, I do not despair of America" (September [?] 1786, MWP1, 19). And as late as 1791 (the year of Macaulay's death), Warren was writing letters about Macaulay's new pamphlet in answer to Edmund Burke's attack on the French Revolution.

But in another postwar letter, Warren betrays to Macaulay an attitude that does not always emerge in her other writings: her stoical republican's unease with popular feeling. Having blasted the monarchical and aristocratic pretensions of Americans in the new ruling class, she explains her own ability, and that presumed to be Macaulay's as well, to resist temptation: "Thus from the instability of human character, I have learned to expect every thing, and to fear nothing beneath the Supreme Being. Why should we, if we feel a firmness of mind that renders us independent of popular opinion, of political changes, of the versatility of individuals in high office or the absurd enthusiasm that often spreads itself over the lower classes of life?" (July 1789, MWP1, 27). Aside from continuing the political discussion between the two historians that lasted the entire eighteen years of their relationship, Warren reveals another reason why she is attracted to Macaulay: class. Brought together by their associations, by gender, by mutual intellectual interests, and by political principles, Warren and Macaulay—at least in the former's view—belong to a class sufficiently monied and educated (if neither rich nor degreed) to rise above "enthusiasm." Though, like her Whig friend, she was more a radical republican than a conservative bluestocking, Warren in her letters to Macaulay reveals a need to be considered among the God-respecting intelligentsia—an attitude remarkably like that of the man she most consistently criticized at this time, John Adams.[32]

Indeed, it is Adams's wife Abigail who received the most varied letters from Mercy Warren. No correspondent outside the immediate Warren family ever embraced Mercy with as much delight as Abigail Adams; and no one, not even John, ever spoke as bitterly about her. More volatile than her friend, more given to concrete descriptions and less prone to polish, Adams has in our time had the far greater reputation as a letter writer. Nevertheless, Warren served as a model for the younger woman, someone with whom Adams could discuss matters from sewing to French drama and be assured of a respectful, intelligent reply.[33] For Warren, the correspondence not only strengthened her ties to John but also gave her the example of a woman like herself who was wife to a politician, a mother, and a literate, intellectually demanding person not content to limit herself to the dramatic confines of woman's traditional role.[34]

From the beginning, their correspondence seems extraordinary. An enclosure with Adams's first letter to Warren, a copy of Juliana Seymour's *On the Management and Education of Children: A Series of Letters Written to a Niece* (London, 1754), prompts a discussion of philosophy and practice of childhood education. Warren at first demurs on giving her opinion of the book or passing on any motherly advice, since she herself "is yet looking abroad for Every foreign aid to Enable her to the discharge of a duty that is of the utmost importance to society though for a number of years it is almost wholly left to our uninstructed sex" (25 July 1773, *AFC,* 1:86). Behind this stance of inadequacy are several ideas: that she would find it presumptuous to preach when execution frequently falls short of ideal; that few "foreign aids" exist; and that women are asked to perform "the mighty task of cultivating the minds and planting the seeds of Virtue in the infant Bosom" without being fully educated to the position. True, Warren's criticism in this letter only goes so far; educating children is "by providence devovled [devolved] on Every Mother" (86). So the best a woman can hope for "is the Conscious satisfaction of having Exerted our utmost Efforts to rear the tender plant" and, in a shift of metaphors, that "they may become useful in their several departments on the present theatre of action" (87).

Still, Warren feels enough tug of obligation to her new friend to leave her mark. Despite the earlier demurrals, she in fact has some criticism of Seymour's text, particularly that book's promotion of "Generosity of sentiment" as the first principle a child should learn. Is not this "too Comprehensive a term" and insufficiently affixed to "an invariable Attachment to truth"? For indeed, Warren uses this questioning to assert her first principle: that "a sacred regard to Veracity in the Bosom of Youth [is] the surest Gaurd [*sic*] to Virtue." Thus, Warren has very definite things to say about childhood education and, in fact, suggests one other reason why she feels drawn to both Adamses—their daughter Nabby (Abigail), "for whose instruction and improvment I wish for Every advantage to her preceptress" (87). As with other young women in the extended Warren and Otis families, Warren seems to have wished deeply to extend her ideas of educating youth to the unformed of her own sex. By writing of such matters to the senior Abigail, Warren seems to have wanted to impress on the Adamses her suitability to be another "preceptress" to Nabby.

By the next exchange of letters, Adams and Warren discuss, among other topics, the merits of the French comic playwright Molière. In his play *Le Bourgeois Gentilhomme* (*The Would-be Gentleman*), Adams discovers a hostility toward the objects of satire that she cannot condone: "he has not coppied from his own Heart."[35] Warren acknowledges her own preference for tragedy, with its emphasis on deep feelings, but nonetheless suggests that Molière the comic satirist serves the public good. Gently contesting Abigail's view that the French playwright has no usefulness for society, Warren argues that "when Vice is held up at once in a detestable and Ridiculous Light, and the Windings of the Human Heart which lead to self deciption [*sic*] unfolded it Certainly points us to the path of Reason and Rectitude. And if we do not Embrace the amiable image of Virtue we must Exculpate the Moniter and Attribute the Fault to the Wrong biass of our own Clamorous and ungovernd passions" (19 January 1774, *AFC,* 1:93). Warren's statement is significant for several reasons. Adams alludes in her earlier letter to Warren's play *The Adulateur,* printed in an expanded edition in 1773. Warren, as the author of a satiric though not especially comedic drama, would need to think on the matters of style and genre; if her work is to be consistent with her principles, especially the insistence on truth and the inculcation of virtue, then presentation matters a great deal. This letter is not the end of the question, as will be discussed in the chapter on Warren's drama, but it does show that for both women consistency of form and content was an issue of great importance.

Another favorite topic of Warren's, depicting character, emerges in the heady days just after the successful patriot siege of occupied Boston. She has spent time with the Washingtons and wants to satisfy Adams's curiosity. Martha is the ideal wife for George, with attributes that "Quallify her to soften the hours of private Life or to sweeten the Cares of the Hero" (17 April 1776, *AFC,* 1:386). Martha's daughter-in-law, Eleanor Calvert Custis, is "Engaging . . . , but of so Exstrem Delicate a Constitution that it deprives her as well as her Friends of part of the pleasure . . . from her Conversation" (385). Though Warren is not averse to depicting disagreeable characteristics, she sees in these women things to admire even when by the conventional measures an individual may fall short. This is especially apparent in another character sketch, that of Mary Hopkinson Morgan, wife of the chief army doctor, John Morgan: "She is what is Commonly Called a Very Good kind of woman And Commands Esteem without the Graces of politness, the Briliancy of wit, or the Merits of peculier understanding above the Rest of her sex Yet to be Valued for an Honest unornamented plain Friendliness, Discoverd in her Deportment at the first Acquaintance" (386).[36] Though both Warren and Adams were praised for many of the very qualities Mary Morgan lacks, the letter writer judges by standards other than the norms of urban society to evaluate these women.

Warren and Adams maintained an active correspondence until 1780. Thereafter, because she joined her husband in Europe, and with the political differences growing between the families, letters taper off and lose the freshness and intimacy of those from the 1770s. After a temporary break, caused by the flap in 1789 over government preferment for the Warren sons, letters resume when John Adams is elected president. Abigail, noting one such letter, writes to her sister, Mary Cranch, to tell her that Warren's most recent "Letter was that of an old Friend" (8 June 1798, Mitchell, 188). Correspondence continued without major interruption until 1807, the year of Warren's battle with John over her treatment of him in the *History.* Letters began again in late 1812. In one of the last letters available, Warren writes to Adams in thanks for a ring and a pin (each made from locks of the Adamses' hair) sent by Abigail and John as peace tokens, in exchange for one sent by her:

> when [Mrs. Adams] informs me she has placed the initials of my name on the faded lock I sent her, and means to wear it on her bosom as an eternal mark of her regard, it cannot but be pleasing to a mind who considers true friendship as one of the best cordials of human life, and wishes a reunion of those hereafter which have been formed, continued, and still exist in sincerity and truth. May ours be prepared and sublimated for an existence in endless peace! (26 January 1813, *CBAW,* 503)

Principles for Warren, though argued with vehemence, even satire, never fully replace affection as reasons to write or not. Sporting the ring and pin to her last days, Warren would hold her friendship with Abigail as something to be carried with her into the next life.

Though the friendship with Adams had claim as one of the longest among her female correspondents, another developed in the 1790s that proved to be more intimate. Through family ties to her brother Samuel and connections going back another generation, Warren had known Sarah Cary for many years.[37] Letters from Cary to others during the 1780s mention Mercy Warren more than once. The first letter available from Warren to Cary dates from 1793, and begins with a statement that declares one of the themes of their correspondence: "No my dear Mrs. Cary I have not forgotten you. I am not one of those who can forget their friends" (24 June 1793, CFP3, box 2). With Catharine Macaulay and Hannah Winthrop dead, Abigail Adams somewhat estranged, and others uninterested in writing, Warren found a receptive heart in the passionate, loyal Sarah Cary. By 1802, Warren needed her more desperately than she ever needed John or Abigail Adams: "You my dear Mrs. Cary are almost the only female friend I have left to whom I can without restraint pour out the flow of thoughts as they arise, amidst the chequered hue of my span of life" (7 February 1802, CFP3, box 2). Throughout the exchange, which lasted until 1814, declarations of fast and abiding friendship punctuate, even dominate, the letters.

Cary was a mother, albeit a younger one, and Warren saw in her someone who would understand loss (especially of children), illness, and the specter of death. The letters to Cary—begun in earnest when Warren was in her 60s—are often spiced with calls to the everlasting—"may we tread with composure dignity and rectitude our narrow path of duty untill the Curtain falls" (24 June 1793, CFP3, box 2)—or reminders of her friend-straitened state—"I have few—very few friends left whom I wish to see more." Thus Cary's significance grows: "I often think of and long to converse with one whose sentiments are so congenial to my own—with one who observes: who feels who thinks so much" (20 April 1797, CFP3, box 2). Having lost in her correspondence with Abigail Adams the connection to a woman whom she perceived almost as a soulmate, Warren seizes on the opportunity afforded by Cary's disarming and unassuming letters to reconstruct an almost life-sustaining bond with another woman.

To Cary she pours out in a more personal way than with almost any other female correspondent the sadnesses and pains of old age. In another letter, she begins, "I again resume the pen to speak to my dear friend once more on this side the Grave. I have stood in its marge." Her state, she says, only recently has been "emaciated languid & debilitated to a degree that I could scarcely speak to to friend from day to day" (8 June 1799, CFP3, box 2). And in yet another letter, she expresses her grief over the death of her youngest son: "I have expected your simpathizing tear over the tomb of my George.—whom had you have known you would have wept for as a sensible agreable acquaintance; as well as a most fillial amiable son of friends you love: and whom you doubtless pity when you recollect the lovely trio in the bloom of youth that they have consigned to the army of Death" (23 August 1800, CFP3, box 2). Indeed, so much does she dwell on this theme of loss and death that her son James, her personal secretary after 1800, begins to chide her about it: "Here my Amanuensis observes, I generally write in a rather gloomy stile to Mrs. Cary. Is it so, my dear friend? I always write from the heart, but am unwilling to think it is the influence of a gloomy mind" (15 June 1803, CFP3, box 3). Though we have observed in Warren's correspondence throughout a tendency to extend a metaphor or write in cascading periodic sentences, full of noble and stoical thoughts, we can see in these letters to Cary a less affected and more openly affectionate style than many of the published letters reveal.

This is not to say that she ignores other topics with Cary; politics, the philosophical fad known as Illuminatism, education, and, frequently, Warren's desire to have Sarah and her daughters down from Chelsea, Massachusetts, to visit all appear. But nothing supplants her nearly two-decades long meditation on death. Sometimes this recurring theme produces wry little passages. After a visit and beginning correspondence with Cary's son-in-law, the Reverend Joseph Tuckerman, Warren writes to Sarah: "I thank him for his frequent admonitions that my thread of time has almost run out, and doubt not I have his prayers that I may be ready when the last sands are exhausted from the warning glass that keeps poor mortals in continual dread of the extinction of the transient pleasures of life" (28 November 1813, CFP3, box 3).

Historical, political, philosophical, literary, and pedagogical though she may be in her other correspondence outside the family, in her letters to Cary—unguarded and unposed, yet true to her voice—Warren displays a side of herself that has received little attention in the literature about her. She is at the last a personal writer, too, one fully capable of self-deprecating humor at the same time she stares straight at death. That at age 85 she can still jest about the young minister's solemn reminders testifies to Warren's refusal to be undone by the specter of mortality.

But more often, there is a piquancy to her later letters to Cary—for whose visit Warren waited 21 years—that suggests her personal vulnerability. In the last letter to Cary, she again mentions a visit from the Tuckermans. The wryness is gone, but what remains is the voice of one poised on the "marge," passionate still in her attachments and hopes, and aware of the consequences of these all-too-brief visits made her so late in her life: "I think friends who meet so sudden should make a previous arrangement to protract the pleasure of meeting at least till the fatigue and the journey is a little over, before they bid adieu and hastily begin another, leaving the friend in the elbow chair to ruminate on the passing dream, adding to the innumerable sum which recollection presents to the scores she has counted up" (17 July 1814, CFP3, box 3). Less than three months later, she had at last a visit from Sarah—too short, no doubt—and a final letter from her friend, dated 9 October 1814. When she died 10 days later, Mercy Warren could finally seize that "passing dream," and if her faith did not deceive her, "ruminate" on it to the limit of her heart's often thwarted desire.

Passionate friend, advisor to young women, historian, political confidante, mother, wife, aunt, philosopher, providentialist, and always stylist, Mercy Warren wrote her letters in a variety of voices, all recognizable as hers. If she is not as concrete as some writers of her time or as personal as others, if her style seems to some ornate or showy, we should not be deterred from reading the letters now. In one of the most valuable correspondences of the late eighteenth and early nineteenth centuries, she offers to modern readers the example of a woman for whom provinciality and gender expectations could not suppress a keen mind and relentless devotion to duty from asserting themselves.

Chapter Three

Poetry

Of all the genres Warren worked in, poetry is second only to correspondence in the number of years she devoted to it—nearly 50. Her small but technically proficient body of work as represented in *Poems, Dramatic and Miscellaneous* (1790), gained admirers early on, not only from family and friends but from readers such as Sarah Wentworth Morton and Judith Sargent Murray. In the midnineteenth century, Warren's poems were anthologized in several well-known collections of verse by women.[1] Nevertheless, by the time Edmund Clarence Stedman's *An American Anthology, 1787–1900* was published in 1900, she had been omitted from the canon of verse writers then being established; thus, as a poet, she was for years nearly forgotten.[2] Fortunately, several publications released since 1980 have helped refocus interest on this dimension of her work.[3]

The causes of the neglect are several. One, of course, is the general devaluation of writing by women that occurred between 1860 and 1960, the end result of a process that began earlier with "the advancing doctrine of 'separate spheres,' the triumph of genteel poetry, and the ghettoization of women's writing."[4] Another is the nineteenth-century rejection of eighteenth-century verse styles favored by Warren and her contemporaries—notoriously, the rhymed couplet as used by Alexander Pope and his imitators. A third reason may for modern readers be the most difficult to overcome; that is, Warren's preference for philosophical themes over concrete scenes or situations. Although I will suggest a number of categories for her poems, one could justifiably say that almost all of Warren's poetry is philosophical, with tendencies toward abstraction and away from material images or richly developed figures of speech. Unless readers are willing to judge her on philosophical and technical grounds—in other words, on terms other than the twentieth-century predilections for free verse and concrete images—Warren's poems will likely be met with puzzlement or indifference. Without claiming greatness for her verse, I hope in this chapter to argue at least for a need to reevaluate her poems and the contemplative tradition in which she largely wrote.

There is currently no complete catalogue of Warren's poetry. Most of her extant poems have been published in two modern-day sources: Benjamin Franklin V's *The Plays and Poems of Mercy Otis Warren* and Edmund Hayes's "The Private Poems of Mercy Otis Warren." Still, many are available only in two manuscript collections—one each at the Houghton Library and the Massachusetts Historical Society—both primarily in the hand of Warren's son, James Warren, Jr.[5] In addition, uncollected Warren poems can be found in her letters. The total number of poems, discounting fragments, appears to be between 50 and 60, but a systematic combing of her correspondence might reveal more. Between her first datable poem (1759) and her last (1808), the average output is little more than one poem a year.

As a writer in forms other than letters, Warren must first have imagined herself as a poet. How seriously she took this role, at least at the outset, is somewhat difficult to tell. Many of her poems are occasional—New Year's Day, deaths of Otis or Warren family members or relatives of friends, political events—or responses to requests. Others—the personal meditative poems, primarily—seem to come from her own inner struggles or some crisis in her life. In other words, she probably wrote very few poems simply for the joy of writing or because, as a poet, she needed to be producing. Although in better economic circumstances than many women in colonial America, Warren, in common with other female (and most male) writers of the period, would have had little time to devote to poetry as a profession. She appears to have had a natural facility with language that, coupled with her intelligence, learning, and personal ambition, might in other circumstances have led to a considerable corpus of high-level work.

As it is, working with few female models and little cultural reward, she nevertheless produced a number of poems that are well worth new and continued critical attention. Indeed, later in her career she clearly took the writing of poetry quite seriously. The lead poem in the "Miscellaneous Poems" section of her collection *Poems, Dramatic and Miscellaneous,* "To Mrs. Montague [*sic*], Author of 'Observations on the Genius and Writings of Shakespeare,'" almost dares that female model—a British critic with alleged "anti-American" antipathies—to turn from Shakespeare to Warren and comment "with candour."[6] Since male British writers have failed to match the bard of Avon, perhaps "A sister's hand may wrest a female pen, / From the bold outrage of imperious men." If I get your praise, she tells Montagu, "I'll take my stand by fam'd Parnassus' side, / And for a moment feel a poet's pride" (*PDM/PP,*

182). By appealing to a female critic from England, Warren asks to be judged by the most stringent terms—but terms forged first in sisterhood and intellectual achievement, across national lines. Of all the people to whom she might have addressed her nondramatic poems, Montagu was a bold choice. Indeed, many of Warren's poems take risks—and if they sometimes founder, the earnest intellect behind them can still be perceived.

Political Poems

Although her first written responses to the crises that led to the Revolution were letters and plays, Mercy Warren wrote several poems during the period 1774–78 that satirized or reflected on the momentous events into which she and her husband James plunged themselves. At the request of her then fast and admiring friend John Adams, she penned an ambitious and amusing mock epic on the Boston Tea Party entitled "The Squabble of the Sea Nymphs; or the Sacrifice of the Tuscararoes" (1774).[7] Written in the style of Pope's "The Rape of the Lock"—a fact noticed by Adams—"The Squabble" pokes fun at the tempest stirred when men disguised as Indians ("Tuscararoes") dumped dutied tea into Boston Harbor in December 1773 (JA to JW, 9 April 1774, *PJA,* 2:82). Rich in classical allusions, Warren's relatively gentle satire is one of her most enjoyable poems.

"The Squabble" is a made-to-order production, initiated in the form of an elaborate suggestion from John Adams to James Warren in a discussion of the Tea Party and its aftermath. Indeed, Adams's paragraphs remain the best gloss on the allegory in the poem:

> Make my Compliments to Mrs Warren and tell her that I want a poetical Genius.—to describe a late Frolic among the Sea Nymphs and Goddesses. There being a scarcity of Nectar and Ambrosia, among the Celestials of the sea, Neptune has determined to substitute Hyson and Congo, and for some of the inferiour Divinities Bohea. Amphitrite, one of his Wives, vizt the Land, and Salacia, another of his Wives the Sea went to pulling Caps upon the occasion, but Salacia prevailed.
>
> The syrens should be introduced somehow. I cant tell how and Proteus, a son of Neptune, who could sometimes flow like Water, and sometimes burn like Fire bark like a Dog howl like Wolf, whine like an Ape, Cry like a Crokadile, or roar like a Lyon. But for want of this Same Poetical Genius I can do nothing. I wish to See a late glorious Event, cel-

> ebrated, by a certain poetical Pen, which has no equal that I know of in this Country. (*PJA,* 2:3)

Although flattered by the commission (and probably its manner) and agreeing to do it, Warren rather cleverly puts to Abigail the logical rejoinder: "I think a person who with two or three strokes of his pen has sketched out so fine a poetical plan need apply only to his own Genius for the Completion" (19 January 1774, *AFC,* 1:93). But she asks for further explanation from John, since there might be many who answer to Proteus.

No further suggestions arrived, leaving Warren on her own. The result, though, clearly pleased Adams, since he had it printed in the *Boston Gazette* and subsequently wrote to James Warren that the poem was "one of the incontestible Evidences of real Genius, which has yet been exhibited—for to take the Clumsy, indigested Conception of another and work it into so elegant, and classicall a Composition, requires Genius equall to [Pope's]" (9 April 1774, *PJA,* 2:82). Warren turns the Tea Party episode into one of her favorite themes, the discord introduced by those who rely on private luxury at the expense of public interest. The poem begins the night of the Tea Party, when the "heroes of the Tuscararo tribe" wait "To make an offering to the wat'ry god." Neptune, meanwhile, seeing that the gods have run out of nectar, calls a conference of the gods to decide what to do. The Titans[8] (the British) want "To travel round Columbia's coast" and despoil it, leaving nothing for the people, "Nor leave untouch'd the peasant's little store." In the matter of nectar, however, Neptune feels it right to consult all the gods, especially the females, "For females have their influence o'er kings, / Nor wives, nor mistresses, were useless things"—a sentiment fully in accord with the ideology of the Republican Mother, woman as virtuous advisor to man.

The "squabble," then, is a contest between two wives of Neptune. One is Amphitrite (representing Loyalists), whose companion is the shape-shifter Proteus and who wants to keep the tea in her sphere, on the land. The other is Salacia (representing patriots), who listens to the Nereids (children of the old sea god Nereus, associated with "truth and justice") and decides that tea will be just the thing for the aquatic deities.[9] The Tuscararoes agree "To aid the bright Salacia's care," and despite the contention created by the angry Amphitrite, they dump the tea. A last moment of tension is created when the syrens urge the patriots to "taste the sweet inebriating stream" created by the mixture of tea leaves and water, but the patriots resist. The deities then join in chorus to sing "fair Salacia's triumph" and "spread confusion" around Gov. Thomas Hutchinson at his residence in the "Neponsit hills"—Milton, Massachusetts.[10]

Although Warren in her 1790 version adds a note to distance herself from the political opinion expressed in the poem, she in fact works in one of her insistent messages: true patriotism requires sacrifice. Tea became a symbol of American dependence on British trade and a staple of the comfortable life; to reject it was to denounce more than a small tax. After the amusement of the warring goddesses, the poet clarifies the point. The Tuscararoes

> neither hold, nor even wish a place,
> While faction reigns, and tyranny presides,
> And base oppression o'er the virtues rides;
> While venal measures dance in silken sails,
> And avarice o'er earth and sea prevails;
> While luxury creates such mighty feuds,
> E'en in the bosoms of the demi gods. (*PDM/PP,* 204)

The Proteuses—those who ally with a side for money (hoping to pick it up "from Plutus,[11] or the naked strands") and thus stand ready to betray a cause—must be exposed to give meaning to sacrifice (*PDM/PP,* 203). Salacia becomes that voice who "bids defiance to the servile train, / The pimps and sycophants of George's reign" (*PDM/PP,* 205). In essence, Warren as poet takes on the role of Salacia, calling her readers to virtuous resistance to the Tory tools of British policy (Ostriker, 24, 214).

Further attacks on the Tories follow in poems probably written soon after "The Squabble." As Governor Hutchinson prepared to leave Massachusetts for England in April 1774, a number of groups sent "addresses," statements of loyalty to him and his policies. The signatories of these addresses were marked by Whigs as inimical to the true interests of the colony; indeed, some appeared to the public as Loyalists for the first time in these statements. In "A solemn debate of a certain bench of Justices to form an address to Governor Hutchinson, just before he left the chair" (1774), Warren mocks the efforts of three judges to determine whether it is in their interest to prepare such an address.[12] She is much more heavy-handed here about the quality of the opposition:

> For *Justices* of ev'ry size
> The weak, the wicked, dull, or wise

> No one who holds a King's commission
> Is quite devoid of some ambition,
> Although to rectitude or sense
> They seldom can make much pretence. (HL ms., 39)

Principle never enters their minds, only who is rising or falling. Because they cannot figure out what to do themselves, the judges hire a "barrister of skill / Learn'd in Coke and in quadrille" to help them out. Eventually they convey their address "To Massachusetts mimic King"—that is, Hutchinson. Rather than target them as enemies, Warren shows them to be fools, slaves to self-interest.

In another poem from the same period, "An extempore thought on some servile addresses from the long venerated seminary of Harvard College" (1774), Warren takes a historical view of her brother's and husband's alma mater.[13] The college was founded, she suggests, to counter the toadying support given to the Stuart kings by Oxford University ("Oxonia's sons"). For students at Harvard now to offer their "servile flatteries" to the current political administration is a blot on the record: "How are her annals now disgraced / How Harvard sons! alas! debased! / The genrous work's betray'd." Like her younger contemporary Phillis Wheatley, who in her poem "To the University of Cambridge, at New-England" (1773) chides Harvard students for wasting their privileges in vice, Warren as outsider addresses an institution she was smart enough to attend herself, had female attendance been allowed.[14] In each case, Wheatley and Warren know something the Harvard students do not—and they fear not to tell them.

Perhaps while she was writing these address poems, she received another informal commission, this time from her Cambridge friend John Winthrop, who "requested a poetical List of the Articles the Ladies" might consider as "Necessaries" in the suspension of trade with Britain in all nonessential goods. The result was a poem published in *Royal American Magazine* in June 1774, later simply called "To the Hon. J. Winthrop, Esq." in her 1790 collection.[15] Though in some ways both the idea and the poem bear strong similarities to "The Squabble," Warren turns a trivial suggestion into a more serious work. In fact, she only marginally replies to the originating idea; instead, she provides more commentary on female and male vices than a humorous list—what Winthrop seems to have wanted—and though parts of the poem do amuse in ways similar to "The Squabble," by the end, Warren has worked in a series of allusions that reinforce a political philosophy of stoicism.

Again, "The Rape of the Lock" provides inspiration, especially early, where the poem shows the dilemma of a fashionable woman, Clarissa:

> But what's the anguish of whole towns in tears,
> Or trembling cities groaning out their fears?
> The state may totter on proud ruin's brink,
> The sword be brandish'd, or the bark may sink;
> Yet shall Clarissa check her wanton pride,
> And lay her female ornaments aside? (*PDM/PP,* 209)

In lines before and after this section, however, Warren announces a larger and weightier theme than the pride of one vain individual. What women choose as "charms"—the "modest antiquated" ones of a Portia, or "gauze, and tassels well combined" of a lady of fashion—mirrors rival philosophical positions that argue "the best plan to save a sinking state" (*PDM/PP,* 209).

As with her earlier poem, the issue is determined in a debate among females—women now, not gods. Lamira, one of the "oratorial fair" and the author's voice in the poem, rises to put the demands on women in historical perspective. Not since "those ancient times / When Pharaoh, harden'd as a G[eorge] in crimes, / Plagu'd Israel's race," have women had to sacrifice as much; but like the Israelites who, once in thrall to Egypt, "Sigh'd for the leeks, and waters of the Nile, / [So] we for gewgaws from Britannia's isle" (*PDM/PP,* 209). As a consequence, the demand for luxury goods from abroad creates discord at home. With Prudentia describing further the ignominy the country must currently suffer, the women—"the good, the wise, the prudent, and the gay"—unite behind a single principle:

> Let us resolve on a small sacrifice,
> And in the pride of Roman matrons rise;
> Good as Cornelia, or a Pompey's wife,
> We'll quit the useless vanities of life. (*PDM/PP,* 210)

It is true, the poet suggests, that many women would find it hard to part with "feathers, furs, rich sattins, and ducapes"[16]; yet, in response to the request for such an "inventory," what about the men?

But while the sex round folly's vortex play,
Say, if their lords are wiser far than they;
Few manly bosoms feel a nobler flame,
Some cog the dye, and others win the game;
Trace their meanders to their tainted source,
What's the grand pole star that directs their course?
Perhaps revenge, or some less glaring vice,
Their bold ambition, or their avarice,
Or vanity unmeaning, throw the bowl. (*PDM/PP,* 212)

Despite the presence of men and women given to corrupt pastimes, there are still many "good Cornelias" and "gen'rous, worthy men" who will fight for freedom.

Warren's allusion to "Roman matrons" shows she writes for an audience with more knowledge and scope of interest than simply which bauble to lay aside. Three of the historical women she mentions—Portia, the politically engaged daughter of the republican suicide Cato, wife of republican regicide Brutus, and herself a suicide; Cornelia, who at the death of her husband Tiberius Sempronius Gracchus refused to marry again in order to devote herself to family and estate; and Arria Major, a Stoic who committed suicide in response to her husband's condemnation for conspiracy against the state—are notable examples of Roman sacrifice, even of life, for cause or some larger view than self-indulgence. Thus what she shows Winthrop, whom she calls Helvidius, after a first-century republican Stoic, is that American women have historical models for supreme self-denial in service to republican ideals. "Necessaries of life" turn from clothes to freedom and virtue, and sacrifice from giving up choice tea to yielding life itself. Rather than look to female vanity for humor, she argues, better to be moved by the examples of stoic men and women in this "vicious age" (212).

Warren's last prewar political poem is a dream vision, "A Political Reverie" (1775).[17] Having already shown predilection for the short mock epic, the poet here paints her broadest canvas yet. The poem begins with a 16-line introduction on dreaming itself; it is a contradictory piece, at once listing the "sportive dreams [that] infest all ranks of men," yet hinting that dream contains "visionary" truth (*PDM/PP,* 188). Once in the body of the main poem, Warren adopts a pose very much like that of Anne Bradstreet in her "Prologue" to the "Four Monarchies." In the way that the seventeenth-century poet excuses herself on the grounds that "To sing of wars, of captains, and of kings, / Of cities founded, commonwealths begun, / For my mean pen are too superior things" (Cowell, 33), so the eighteenth-century writer asks to be relieved from the burden of traditional epic:

> Let Grecian bards and Roman poets tell,
> How Hector fought, and how old Priam fell;
> Paint armies ravaging the 'Ilian coast,
> Shew fields of blood and mighty battles lost;
> . . . .
> To bolder pens I leave the tragic tale. (*PDM/PP*, 188–89)

Unlike Bradstreet, however, who demurs as part of a clever strategy of poetic self-abasement, Warren claims her limits to be based on morality: "No bold destroyers of mankind I sing; / These plunderers of men I'll greatly scorn, / And dream of nations, empires yet unborn" (*PDM/PP,* 189).

"A Political Reverie" is also a rising glory poem, one that prophetically views the development and triumph of a new America. It uses the theme of transplantation (*translatio*), as many such works do, to show how the good of Old World civilizations has been replanted in the soil of the New World. For Warren, it is not only *translatio studii* (arts and sciences) and *translatio imperii* (empire) but also transplantation of "virtue" that matters. One of many female entities in her political poems, Warren's figure of virtue departs the decaying civilizations of Africa, Asia, and Europe for "Columbia's distant fertile plains, / Where liberty, a happy goddess, reigns"; there virtue will "Her standard plant beneath these gladden'd skies" (*PDM/PP,* 189).

Much of the poem, however, is a lament for the Britain formerly revered by the colonists, now the enemy of liberty and virtue. Once the pride of all nations, Britain's hardiest people venture out into the world, to uncharted lands, "A race of heroes . . . Who pitch'd their tents beneath the dismal shade / Where wild woods roar'd, and savages betray'd" (*PDM/PP,* 190). Having received back great riches from the colonists, Britain, "ungrateful, . . . Broke the firm union whence her vigour grew, / Dissolv'd the bands, and cut the sinews through" (*PDM/PP,* 191). The poet, meeting a seraph, cries out, "'Has freedom's genius left Britannia's shore?'"

The seraph calms the poet's fears, and uses the language of transplantation to explain what has occurred: "Though far transferr'd from their lov'd native soil," the spirits of "patriots" who brought to America the political ideals of John Locke and Algernon Sidney have passed to present generations the fire of freedom (*PDM/PP,* 192). In the corruption that swallows up Britain, virtue and freedom have fled to the land most likely to nourish them. Hope exists in the vision of a "rising empire" that encourages "triumphant commerce"; but the poem ends where it begins, a fear of battle and discord of which the poet will not write: "let the muse forbear the solemn tale, / And lend once more, the '*Grecian painter's veil*'" (*PDM/PP,* 194).

Although "A Political Reverie" is sometimes slowed by wordiness or reiteration, it illustrates several dimensions of Warren's work. She captures the flavor of the epic well in heroic couplets, but demarks her own territory, one where the poet can on occasion "heave a sigh, and drop the tender tear" (*PDM/PP,* 193). Allusions to classical mythology—Homer's *Iliad,* Greek and Roman history, modern Euro-American politics—as well as to the writings of Locke and Sidney show Warren substantiating what might be dismissed as only a dream and magnifying the American cause to a rank suitable for epic treatment.[18] In short, she dignifies political disputes from the realm of "squabble" to a fearful vision of "faction's sword . . . brandish'd o'er the land" (*PDM/PP,* 194). This strategy of elevation and tasteful turning away from gore (the forbearing muse) marks much of Warren's future work, poetry and prose.

The tone of lament that ends "A Political Reverie" asserts itself during the war years as well. Once fighting began, Warren directed much of her political expression from poetry and plays to history. She could still be witty, as in the unpublished poem "[A new proclamation at the point of the sword],"[19] a satire written in late 1775 or 1776 that mocks the peace terms offered Americans by the British commanders, Adm. Lord Richard Howe and Gen. William Howe: "We'll bounce and bark—and cry *bow wow* / Till all detest the name of Howe" (HL ms., 43). Especially after James Warren's defeat in the 1778 election, however, she frequently attacked the intrusion of corrupt manners into wartime America. This is the topic of the last political poem she seems to have written, "The Genius of America weeping the absurd Follies of the Day.—October 10, 1778. 'O Tempora! O Mores!'" (1778).[20] So scathing is her indictment of her own country that she includes a footnote to explain the attack: "This piece was written when a most remarkable depravity of manners pervaded the cities of the United States, in consequence of a state of war; a relaxation of government; the sudden acquisition of fortune; a depreciating currency; and a new intercourse with foreign nations" (*PDM/PP,* 249). As in "A Political Reverie," she uses shades and spirits to help lend universality and historical significance to the phenomena she describes.

The poem begins with "Columbia's weeping Genius" mourning the betrayal of "freedom's cause by vice." Gone is the nobility of purpose celebrated in the earlier dream vision poem. Now, the Genius sighs: "Our country bleeds, and bleeds at every pore, / Yet gold's the deity whom all adore" (*PDM/PP,* 246). What had corrupted Britain now threatens to undo freedom's last bastion, America. While Columbia laments, the ghost of King George II visits his grandson, the present monarch George III. Disgusted by what he sees as a defilement of "the glories of my reign" (1727–60), the grandfather observes the carnage and the providential command to defeat—not support, as before—British policy. On his flight back to death, George II meets the goddess of virtue, who says she "urg'd the battle on" (*PDM/PP,* 247). And as long as the fight continued to be inspired by virtue, "Propitious heaven approv'd." Now, though, in strict cause and effect, war has brought an infusion of quick wealth and luxury. "So dissolute—yet so polite the town," that even the best satirists—Juvenal, William Hogarth, Jonathan Swift, and Charles Churchill—would find it difficult to lash the times as they deserved (*PDM/PP,* 248).

Though Warren overstates the case on one level, she has other objects in mind than merely expensive habits. To be sure, the noble sacrifices of earlier generations give way to "taste, high life, and pleasure's guilty joys," but what she sees writ large is "All public faith, and private justice dead, / And patriot zeal by patriots betray'd" (*PDM/PP,* 249). This leaves the door open to skepticism, one of Warren's chief bête noires. She derides the influence of Voltaire, Edmund Hoyle, Viscount Bolingbroke (Henry St. John), and Bernard Mandeville, skeptics all, who abuse reason by attacking religion: "Brought to the reas'ner's superficial test, / The Christian code becomes his wanton jest. / Scarce any decent principles remain" (*PDM/PP,* 251). Politics cannot be dissociated from metaphysics. To admit excess of fashion is to open the door to virtue-destroying doubt. The modish creed of carpe diem—seize the day—leads to crumbling of cause and loss of soul. Warren's decision to close her 1790 collection with this poem tells us much, both about her deep and abiding fear that America would be defeated internally before it lost on the battlefield and about her sincere belief in her own role as guardian of the nation's virtue.

Advice Poems

As guardian, Warren especially looked after the welfare of the rising generation—the youth so eager to pant after fashion. She imagined that they lacked a clear sense of both past and future, living in the present only, without regard for the principles of ancestors or the consequences of their actions. Four of her poems aim to right the wrong of aimlessness among youth.

"To a Young Lady, On shewing an excellent Piece of Painting, much faded," does not clearly identify time or person, and since many young women knew Warren, there is perhaps little point in pursuing the historical incident to which she refers.[21] One possibility, though, is that the woman in question was Abigail Adams, daughter of Abigail and John. She stayed with the Warrens from December 1778 until April 1779, and from the letters between Mercy and Abigail senior, one can readily see that Warren took to Nabby as if she were a daughter. Given, too, that the Warrens and Adamses felt comfortable through correspondence and other means to give assistance and advice to each other's children, this poem would be of a piece with that tradition. If this identification is correct, then the poem can be dated around 1779, about the time Warren gave up writing purely political poems.

Whereas in "The Genius of America" Warren attacks the philosophy of carpe diem, here she affirms it—with qualifications. As the poet and the young lady look at an old painting, the mature woman reminds her youthful counterpart that people are like fading pictures and thus must "seize the minutes as they pass." This does not mean grabbing what is nearest to hand, however; one should let the ticking clock "point you to pleasures more sublime; / And bid you shun the flow'ry path, / That cheats the millions into death" (*PDM/PP,* 206). Unlike the wartime youths who live without care for tomorrow, a true seizing of the day always has the next day firmly in mind:

> Snatch every moment time shall give,
> And uniformly virtuous live;
> . . . learn at wisdom's happy lore,
> Nature's great author to adore. (*PDM/PP,* 206–7)

Unthinking fun is unallowable; genuine pleasure rests on mutual recognition of death's inevitability and the certainty of divine order.

Another advice poem quite likely written for an Adams child is "To Torrismond. A young Gentleman educated in Europe, recommended to the Author's acquaintance, by a Friend of distinction."[22] Most likely the youth addressed is John Quincy Adams (1767–1848), who spent most of the 1778–88 period in Europe attending lessons while his father worked as a diplomat. The poem could have been written at any time; it is possible she wrote it during the early 1780s, at a time when young Adams was receiving admonitory letters from his family to keep to the right path. She might also have been thinking about her son Winslow, in Europe, too, during this time.[23]

In contrast to the simplicity of the previous poem, Warren ranges far, appealing to the well-educated young man with a vast survey of Western thought. She notes the movement over time from superstition to reason. In ancient Britain, when the druids command minds, people lack the tools to distill the truth from "monkish legends." Politicians seize on "weak credulity" and use "virtue as a state machine" to control behavior, not enlighten (*PDM/PP,* 183). Then at last, "from the dark impenetrable shade, / Reason appear'd, a bright, a heav'n born maid" (*PDM/PP,* 184). Genius reveals itself in Newton, Robert Boyle, and Locke. Unfortunately, though, some abuse the gift or do not understand the ramifications of reason: "Some visionary souls have lost their way" (*PDM/PP,* 185). But the worst that happens is the rise of skepticism; Voltaire, the Earl of Shaftesbury, David Hume, "modern metaphysic fools," lead youth astray. Thus her appeal:

> Ah! Torrismond! poor trembling, doubting youth,
> Pale with thy fears, and yet affronting truth;
> Come, my young friend, forsake the sceptic road,
> And tread the paths superiour genius trod. (*PDM/PP,* 186)

As with the young lady and the painting, Warren has her young man think on last things first; when his soul "quivers on the awful marge" between life and death, he will discover "the christian scheme / Is not the product of a brain sick dream" (*PDM/PP,* 187). Keep your common sense, she tells him, and "seek true happiness beyond the skies" (*PDM/PP,* 186). As in "A Political Reverie," where she attacks skeptics for failing to acknowledge the truth of dream, here too she seeks to restore to accepted religion its reasonableness.

One puzzling point in this poem is the name assigned to young Adams. Torrismond was an ancient Goth, son of the king, Theodoric, who in the fifth century was part of the combined Roman-Goth force that defeated the Hun chieftain, Attila, in Gaul. The reference may help to date the poem, since during the early 1780s Warren was busy reading in the history of the Fall of Rome for her play, *The Sack of Rome.* But further, Attila would have represented to the poet absolute barbarism, one whose success depended on the clouded minds of his followers. Torrismond, a prince who triumphs over the king of superstition but is part of a rising people, not a declining civilization like Rome, then becomes a symbol for a liberator of thought in the West.

While she may have had Winslow in mind while writing to John Quincy Adams, she did not neglect to address her son directly in other poems of advice. Living in Boston in early 1780, Winslow was the subject of rumors over war profiteering. His mother, hoping for a promised visit to Plymouth, wrote in a letter on 3 February of that year her concerns and included a poem for the son she imagined to be the most literary of her five. The first four lines tell all:

> The man who just and uniformly good
> Moves in a sphere beyond the servile croud,
> Who dauntless faced the storms of party rage
> Fears not the censures of a trivial age. (MWP1)

Since Mercy imagined the attacks on Winslow's character sprang from political criticism of her husband, she wanted to reassure her son that maliciousness cannot wound if one maintains his rectitude (Fritz 1972, 186–87).

Two years and a major misadventure later, Winslow, finally released from British custody, was living on the Continent. "To a Young Gentleman, residing in France," dated 1 January 1782, is a companion piece to the "Torrismond" poem, but with a different focus.[24] The handsome and worldly Winslow, to whom she had previously written the long letter condemning the philosophy of Lord Chesterfield, was more likely to be absorbed by pleasure than skepticism; her advice to him now is to avoid "folly, pride, or pleasure's guilty scenes," a line similar to one used in "Genius." Instead, "'Tis honest probity, with competence. / That calms the mind, and smooths the manly mein / And shews the world true happiness within" (*PDM/PP,* 222). She's a wise enough mother to anticipate a son's response: "'These old ideas are quite out of date,'" she imagines him saying. But if you look at the historical record, she replies, you will see the truth: the rise of "AV'RICE" and decline in America of "true public spirit" (*PDM/PP,* 224).

After a plunge into history of many lines, she returns to Winslow with a question: "Is thy young bosom warm'd with patriot zeal? / And ardent glow to serve the common weal? / Or does ambition lead thee to the field . . . ?" If the former, then return home: "Leave all the fopperies of a foreign court / *** [Winslow] come, with every virtue fraught, / By principle and precept, early taught" (*PDM/PP,* 225). Having just moved the previous summer to the former Hutchinson house at Milton Hill, she tries to make "home" seem as attractive as possible, including sights of "tufted flowers" and "the conic pine," as well as the pleasures of "A social board, with frugal plenty crown'd." In doing so, she abandons the stance of philosopher altogether for mother: "Return, my son, for nothing else we need, / To see thee happy, would be bliss indeed" (*PDM/PP,* 227). The stern visage of the stoic advice giver changes to the anxious, hopeful look of the worried parent. Still, she makes her point: the best life is one of virtue and "frugal plenty."

Poems to James Warren

The poet's attempt to evoke the image of the happy home to Winslow has its antecedents in a series of poems addressed to her husband. Written during the early part of her poetic career, these celebrate her love for James and the life they live together, commiserate in grief, and, as with the poem to Winslow, during absence express hope of reunion.

The earliest is "To J Warren Esq[r][:] An Invitation to retirement" (1766).[25] Composed at Clifford Farm, the Warrens' rural retreat just south of Plymouth, the poem seems to have been inspired by James's absence on public business. She was no doubt feeling vulnerable, with at least four children at home and possibly a fifth on the way (George was born in September), but rather than give in to expressions of melancholy, Warren turns the occasion to create a vision of a prelapsarian, pastoral world into which they might "retire." "Come leave the noisy smoky town / Where vice and folly reign," she calls to James; then, eight lines later, she reminds him that home is "Where innocence with cheerful health / With love and virtue reign." The contrast between the city, ruled by vice and folly, and rural home, governed by love and virtue, cannot in the poet's mind be resisted. After all, when together at Clifford, they live like Adam and Eve:

5. Like the first pair on Eden's banks
        Before the raging fiend
With bold illusive arts deceiv'd
        The mother of mankind;

6. We'll neither wish for wealth or fame
        Nor court the praise of men
Whose pride, in spite of conscious truth
        Expects applause again. (Hayes 1981, 206)

In one of her favorite metrical forms, numbered four-line stanzas in alternating lines of iambic tetrameter and trimeter, the poet carries the vision to death, anticipating then "Heaven's illuminating beams" (Hayes 1981, 207).

A poem to James from the following year, "On a New Years morning 1767 to a beloved Friend," has the usual hope that he will "True wisdom and virtue pursue," but the form is more playful, perhaps reflecting the happiness they felt personally and politically.[26] Although couplets or four-line stanzas are her norm, Warren in this case uses six-line stanzas with a scheme *aabccb* and a running rhythm of iambs and anapests. The *a* and *c* lines have only two beats, an iamb followed by an anapest (U′UU′), while the *b* lines have three beats, an iamb then two anapests. Thus in the expression of her final desire for James—that "when life must decay / And you've finish'd your day / May a seat be reserved for you!"—the first two words of the last line are elided and the *-ed* pronounced to meet the rhythm. Another example of this playfulness in form is the undated "An Acrostic," a poem probably from the same period, in which the first letters of the 11 lines spell out her husband's name (where, following eighteenth-century practice, *I* stands for *J*).[27]

As the brief period of calm after the repeal of the Stamp Act had turned and James took on increasingly important duties in the Revolutionary government, Warren forgoes playfulness for more somber poems to her husband. One, "To Fidelio, Long absent on the great public Cause, which agitated all America, in 1776" (1776), bears comparison to poems on a similar theme by Anne Bradstreet, specifically, "A Letter to her Husband, Absent upon Public Employment."[28] Where Bradstreet openly displays her desire for Simon's return and goes from mourning to joy in anticipation of their reunion, Warren struggles to accommodate herself to the sacrifice required by the times. She begins by assessing their good fortune to date—beauty, health, and rural retreat—but cannot help "brooding" in solitude that "'Tis social converse, animates the soul." Nonetheless, as a good stoic committed to a cause, she resists dwelling too long on her needs: "while the state, by fierce internal war, / Shook to the centre, asks his zealous care, / I must submit, and smile in solitude"; after all, "A patriot zeal must warm the female mind" (*PDM/PP,* 213).

While she, like Bradstreet, longs for her husband's restoration to domestic felicity, she grows somber again in recalling a woman whose sacrifice has already been larger than hers, Janet Montgomery.[29] The death of Gen. Richard Montgomery in Quebec in December 1775 had moved Warren to write to his widow in consolation, but in the poem she exposes her own fear that like "Janetta," she may be called on to give up even more than she has already. Torn between commitment to freeing the country "from despotic chains" and wanting the comforts of growing old together, the poet, while preparing herself for loss, can offer only a restrained hope that she and her husband will enter heaven at the same time.

Indeed, death had already interrupted their tranquility. Following the bloodletting at Breed's Hill, James had become the president of the provincial legislature. The person he replaced, slain on the battlefield, is the topic of her poem, "To the Honble James Warren Esqr President of the Congress of Massachusetts on the death of his friend Major General Warren, who fell in the Battle of Bunker Hill. June 17th 1775."[30] Few individual deaths moved patriots as much as that of Joseph Warren, the handsome young physician turned politician and general. Mercy's poem is but one of several artistic responses to the hero's gallant end, the most famous of which is John Trumbull's painting, *The Battle of Bunker's Hill* (1786). In her poem, though, one can see how difficult this death is for her to render. Not only must she justify the loss of this riveting figure at a time when conflict has only just begun, but she must balance this with her own hopes, ambitions, and fears for her husband (in time, by virtue of his militia rank, James would also be known as General Warren). Outwardly, she disguises her private feelings. Her strategy is first to compassionate James's loss of a friend, then to show events in cause and effect. The initiating cause, Gage's attack on and burning of Charlestown, forces the patriots to take the field; a bloody standoff ensues, until Joseph Warren steps forward: "He greatly fell, pierc'd by a thousand wounds / That seal his fame beyond time's narrow bounds" (Cowell, 80).

Rather than simply lament his death, however, Warren uses the opportunity to reiterate her stoic beliefs. According to the Stoic philosophers of ancient Rome, life was a divinely ordained drama in which each person had a part to play; an individual was judged, therefore, on how well he or she played the role that the gods had assigned. What Joseph Warren has done, the poet tells us, is simply to accept his destiny:

> Heaven . . .
> Had form'd his genius for the bold design,
> Early to tread the independent field,
> And plant the palm on fair Columbia's shield.
> Soft were his manners, gentle and serene,
> A manly courage mark'd his modest mein. (Cowell, 80)

He has done his part, and so must be praised accordingly; but in the last two lines quoted above, the poet suggests something of her ideal person, one who combines some portion each of what are often considered to be masculine and feminine traits. This might also apply to the other Warren in the poem, husband James—and another, just outside, the poet herself. After she anticipates how the burial spot of Joseph will become a symbol of freedom, complete with laurel and moss, Mercy conflates writer, mourner, and mourned. New heroes will arise who "dare to die, and mark the field of fame / As WARREN died, and leave a deathless name" (Cowell, 81). As the capitalization here and throughout the poem suggests, the one immortal name that readers will remember, whether it be Joseph, James, or Mercy, is WARREN.

Elegies

If war snatched the lives of many promising people, the common illnesses of the eighteenth-century took more. With one notable exception, all of Warren's remaining poems on death were inspired by losses caused by sickness rather than battle. In general, her way of coping is to acknowledge grief, then move toward some lesson or universal principle. She is not always successful; sometimes her poems do not convince us that the grieving is over by the time the balm of philosophy has been applied. Nevertheless, Warren bravely faces the many and often very close deaths she has to bear, including those of her sons, and writes documents of comfort if not elegies for the ages.

The 1760s may have been happy times for Mercy, James, and their young family, but the Otises had several deaths to confront. In 1763, Warren's 33-year-old sister, Mary Otis Gray, died, prompting the first known death poem by the author, "On hearing of the sudden death of a Sister, Mrs M———G."[31] This poem sets the pattern for many that follow. She begins with an exclamation that captures the immediacy of someone just "hearing" of a death of a beloved family member:

> Hah! Myra dead! the echoing vaults resound
> While my torn bosom bleeds beneath the wound.
> So keen the anguish of my aching heart,
> No language can describe the recent smart. (HL ms., 52)

Such loss defies words; the poem evokes the feeling of someone struggling to proffer more than the formulaic expressions she inevitably provides as a stopgap until better words emerge. But even then—and one sees this in many of Warren's elegies—death defeats the attempt of language to render the experience of loss and mourning.

The admittedly inarticulate poet then asks for help: "Oh! come some plaintive muse, assist my lyre / And weeping matrons aid the solemn choir." One of Warren's most frequent poetic images, the celestial choir, serves several functions: as chorus to celebrate or mourn; as many voices to give volume to the thin sound of a lone soul; and as emblem of some overarching universal principle, perhaps on the order of poet Sir John Davies's notion of the "music of the spheres." The poet asks the choir to "Attend the gloomy hearse with heart-felt sighs," but in doing so gains the strength to reject the feeling that in Mary's death "so much virtue dies": "*Die* did I say? No—virtue cannot die, / 'Tis but transplanted to the realms on high!" (HL ms., 53). Thus while the poet weeps, her sister's soul rushes onward and "outstrips the rolling spheres."

Three years after Mary's death, two younger Otis sisters joined her. "On the early death of two beautiful young ladies, Misses Eliza and Abigail Otis" and "On the death of two lovely Sisters" (both presumably composed in 1766) eulogize young women in their 20s who died one after the other.[32] In both poems, images of youth and spring are used to emphasize the shock of unexpected deaths. In the first poem, 20 numbered stanzas in alternating tetrameter-trimeter, Eliza dies first, "While every winning grace / . . . / Sat dimpling on her face." Abigail ("Abia"), at Eliza's burial, soon sickens herself and follows. Warren's best stanza describes the quickness, the evanescence of Abigail's death:

> Her cheerful tender frame dissolves
> A quick transition's made

> The sprightly form the smiling cheek
> Veils in the mirky [*sic*] grave. (Hayes 1981, 216)

There are lessons of course; to young women who think only of "bliss," the poet commands, "Come view a scene like this!"—an attitude reminiscent of the theme in Warren's "To a young Lady." And though the poet closes with a hope to meet the two women in heaven, earlier lines better express her emotions; there are no words, she tells us, for "The big swoll'n sorrows that invade / My too-too feeling heart" (Hayes 1981, 217). Perhaps that is the reason she feels obliged to write another poem on the same subject.

Many of Warren's death poems on nonfamily members read more like condolences than agonies of her own heart. "On the Death of Mrs. S——, who died within a few Days after her Marriage" turns the occasion into an exotic romance, in which the grieving Selim renounces "Wealth, pleasure, honour, airy fame" and goes out to battle in hopes of meeting death and the spirit of the late Orinda.[33] In "Alluding to the sudden death of a gentleman a few days after marriage," Warren calls her lovers Cyella and Almira, but undercuts the implied romanticism with lines that remind one of Edward Taylor: "Death! grizly pate, and ghastly shade."[34] Still, it ends in Gothicism rather than religious palliation, as Almira "faints and sinks in wild despair." More typical of her style is Warren's poem on the death of Rev. William Smith, Abigail Adams's father, in 1783.[35] "To an amiable Friend, Mourning the Death of an excellent Father" urges Abigail not to weep but to think of her father's death as an opportunity to escape all earthly temptation and limitation: "No private passion, nor a darling sin, / Can check his hope, when death's insatiate power / Stands hovering on the last decisive hour" (*PDM/PP*, 242).

Warren had more personal investment in writing about the death of a longtime friend and inspirer of an earlier poem. She puts herself at some remove from the subject of "On the Death of the Hon. John Winthrop, Esq. L.L.D. Hollisian Professor of Mathematicks and Natural Philosophy, at Harvard College, Cambridge" by addressing it "to his Lady," Hannah.[36] In the way that Phillis Wheatley often keeps the focus of elegies about men on the women they leave behind, so too Warren—in letters as well as poems—seeks to comfort the widow or daughter more than simply sing the praises of the deceased.[37] Her strategy in this poem is to give Winthrop some posthumous words to the world he departs. A scientist but not a skeptic, Warren's astronomer assures humankind that no truth surpasses revelation:

> The word on Sinai's mount reveal'd
> Has demonstrative proof,
> Nor less the condescending grace
> Of a redeemer's love. (*PDM/PP,* 237)

As he's whisked away by a cherub who will take him up to where his predecessor (and implied equal) Isaac Newton resides, those remaining on earth must ask the "great all perfect source" for someone of Winthrop's moral and intellectual stature who will serve as "A guide to Harvard's youth" (*PDM/PP,* 239). Thus the poet seeks to assure the widow that death has not robbed her late husband of voice or influence, for whoever follows him must inevitably strive to be like Professor Winthrop.

Whatever personal sadness lay behind the poem to her friend, it paled in comparison to that which inspired her last three elegiac poems—those to her sons. All reflect a mother's grief, often by emphasizing the transience of life; all use the metaphor of the stage to make their point. The very act of writing itself becomes its own theme: to write is both to confront and resolve and to hope and extend. The poems finally attempt to reconcile the pain of untimely loss with providential purpose.

Warren seems to have waited at least a year before trying to put the death of Charles into verse. The headnote to "Lines, Written on the anniversary of the death of Mr. C——— W———, an amiable and accomplished young gentleman, who died in St. Lucar, 1785," praises his "resignation, fortitude, and piety" as well as offers the statement that "reason justified to him the hope of the Christian."[38] But the point of the poem is as much to give voice to the parent's lament as to praise the youth's virtues. Life rarely delivers what it promises, the poet claims; it masks its true intent:

> Long have I trod o'er life's most brilliant stage,
> Read its deceptive, visionary page,
> Its richest hope in rapture lifted high,
> I now survey with retrospective eye. (*PDM/PP,* 240)

That I/eye sees that youth and promise, far from being allowed to grow to fruition, lie mouldering in the tomb. The question, of course, is why:

"Why was he lent—or why so soon expire?" The answer, also of course, cannot be discerned:

> Is it from life's best joys my heart to wean?
> Or are severer pangs behind the scene?—
> Let me now ask—but humbly bow my will,
> And own my God, the God of mercy still. (*PDM/PP,* 241)

Although she might be led to darkness, she chooses to remain faithful to the providential God; and if she bolsters her spirits in imagining her son's soul on high, she manifests her reconciliation in the play on words: "the God of [M]ercy still." Whatever wildness of grief she may have felt, she writes her way to reason, claiming to face even "the darkest providence . . . undismay'd" (*PDM/PP,* 241).

Six years later, she was called to the task again with the violent death of Winslow in St. Clair's defeat. She had had some time to prepare herself for Charles's death; he had been tubercular for a while, and his travels were desperate attempts to find a climate where he could bear his illness in some comfort. With the literary Winslow, death was sudden and, for his mother, unexpected. The poet of "Written in deep affliction," most likely composed in 1792, early tries to face up to the image of Winslow's wounded body on the battlefield, but abandons that task for a list of his virtues.[39] Warren cannot let the horror of his death slip away; she conjures now his corpse "beneath a distant oak" and mourns the loss of "My filial son—my faithful *friend*" (Hayes 1981, 221). Nevertheless, as with the previous poem, she yields to the punishment dealt out by the divine: "Let resignation to thy will / By thy correcting rod be taught!"

Warren preaches a tough message, one likely to puzzle readers in less stoic ages. Like Anne Bradstreet in her various poems of grief, the poet here adopts a contemplative mode. She feels compelled to move past loss to lesson and the gratification that religion provides:

> And when life's feeble taper sinks,
> And time has run his last career
> And clos'd the ebbing empty scenes
> On all the little actors here;
>
> Then my young hero may I meet
> Amidst a bright Angelic choir
> And with my youthful sons unite
> To tune my humble grateful lyre. (Hayes 1981, 221)

The brevity of life compared with the actor's spell on the stage and the contrasting performance image of the ever-singing celestial chorus are hallmarks of Warren's poems on death.

Eight years later, she was called yet again to write on the death of a son. "On the death of George Warren my amiable son, who expired Feby 15th 1800" is Warren's last known poem but one.[40] Like her other two sons in their decease, George died away from the Warren home, this time in Maine, "the Eastern coast." She has recourse to a familiar metaphor in addressing the divine: "Another *branch* by thine omniscient hand / Again is lopped, and left the stock to bend / To mourn." As with Charles, George is "the precious loan," not really hers after all. And since her son remained calm himself in the face of adversity, so should she, the mother emulating the child: "I'll learn my duty from his tranquil death / And check my grief e'en to my latest breath / And bow submissive o'er life's rugged stage" (Hayes 1981, 219). In that last line is writ much about Warren's elegies: they are appreciative reviews of the dramas on "life's rugged stage."

Philosophical Poems

The poems falling under the category of philosophical pursue—or arrive at—certain ideas through a largely public voice. They are to be distinguished from related, but more personal poems, the devotional works. Warren's philosophical poems fall into two basic subgroups: nature poems and addresses to individuals. Many explicate ideas already mentioned, but some use turns of phrase or modes of expression not always found in the categories above.

By modern standards, Warren's nature poetry is wretched. Overall, readers and writers today prefer responses to the particular snowfall of a certain day by a unique observer, not the generalized seasonal apostrophe of Warren's first datable poem, "On Winter" (1759).[41] The west wind is never that, it is almost always "Favonius"; winter has its special qualities, but in the end change of season is celebrated, not the wintriness of winter. Yet Warren, if not especially gifted in description of concrete images, has other ends in mind. To some extent, writing in a tradition later adapted by Ralph Waldo Emerson and Henry David Thoreau, Warren seeks the principle behind nature, not nature itself. "Admire great nature's charms," she says, "But only nature's God adore"; find pleasure in beauty, but never let that distract one from the deity "Who lends those charms to time!" (Hayes 1981, 205). With such a neoplatonic aesthetic, where the invisible god is preferred to the visible form, the poet has no interest in any more than the vaguest of sensory evocations.

Adoration of God, inspired by physical nature, is the lesson of several other nature poems, notably "From my Window in a very clear Star-light Evening," "Lines, Written after a very severe Tempest, which cleared up extremely pleasant," and "On a Survey of the Heavens."[42] All are fairly straightforward poems that move from observation of some phenomenon to praise for the orderer of nature. In the last, especially, the poet tries to have it both ways: nature can be divined by reason, but reason cannot discern fully the ways of the divine. Any attentive observer can detect "proofs of Deity" by looking in the heavens, but because God is also a moral force, pure physics, even that of Newton, falls short of full comprehension. In this tension between physics and morals, between thingness and no-thingness, Warren tries to negotiate a poetical path.

Her most interesting nature poem is one that imagines a literal travel and moves as haphazardly as many sojourners did in the uncertain modes of getting about in the eighteenth century. Addressing Hannah Winthrop in "To Honoria, on her Journey to Dover, 1777," Warren attempts to follow her friend to New Hampshire.[43] The opening of the poem, as in "A Political Reverie," denies that the poet will follow the martial muse, but she admits that she's struggling with this poem just "when most I wish to please" (*PDM/PP,* 216). In a moment of acute self-recognition, the poet laments that whatever eloquence she may strive for, Honoria can see firsthand and in more detail what the writer so vainly describes. Her strategy, as before, is to leap to other themes: *translatio studii;* John Winthrop's role in spreading "Harvard's fame throughout the world"; and a projected peace in which Joseph Warren's fame can be duly appreciated, since he bears "th' initials of her fav'rite name" (the husbands of poet and traveler). But she returns to her insecurity, imagining Helvidius (John Winthrop) criticizing the poem, and indeed ends up talking to the man, not the woman to whom she first addressed the poem. What she recognizes is that she cannot in fact turn nature itself into art; caught in her weakest moment, Warren fumbles through themes, showing at last that neoplatonic though she be, she wishes her poetry to resist the trend, to find a relation between word and thing that does not simply echo the echo of the muse. Structurally one of her worst poems, "To Honoria" nevertheless has a kind of personal honesty more likely to be found in Warren's letters than in her other nature poems.

More successful are Warren's philosophical poems that do not rely on nature as a stimulus. While "Extempore to a young Person beholding the motion of a Clock" jumps quickly to the expected lesson that life "is but a passing breath," a poem inspired by the beating her brother James received at the hands of John Robinson takes on a more challenging subject.[44] As she witnessed her brother's progressive mental deterioration, Warren had cause to reflect on what it meant for a person of genius—and finally any person at all—to be robbed of reason. "A Thought on the inestimable Blessing of Reason, occasioned by its privation to a friend of very superior talents and virtues. 1770" begins with a simple but clever conceit:[45]

> What is it moves within my soul,
> And as the needle to the pole
> Directs me to the final cause
> The central point of nature's laws? (Hayes 1981, 213)

The answer is that the "ray divine"—reason—gives direction to the human groping in the darkness; it is a light that distinguishes human from not.[46] Thus, should God ever eliminate reason, " 'Twould level proud imperious man / With the least worm in nature's plan" (Hayes 1981, 214). By extension, then, when Warren looks at her brother, she sees not only the tragedy of his fall from public acclaim to ridicule but also a fateful loss of all that defines him as human. Unable to write herself out of this subject, she begs never to have to sacrifice reason but to remain "calmly, mistress of my mind / A friend to virtue and mankind" (Hayes 1981, 214). To paraphrase Thoreau in his conclusion to *Walden,* Warren's claim on life might be rendered, Rather than love, than money, than fame, give me reason.

Some of the same issues are raised in a different context in "To Mr. Adams" (1773).[47] The question she entertains is whether all human action, "*good or evil, springs from the Principle of self Love, void of any real Benevolence, when traced up to its Source*" (*PDM/PP,* 195). Fascinated by the secret "springs" to human action, Warren clearly resists Adams's claim that self-interest motivates all behavior. Is it all "panting after fame," good or ill; is there "no permanent, no steady pole, / To point us on, and guide the wandering soul?" A platonic question follows this recourse to compass metaphor: "Is it all art, to gratify the sense?"—in short, a world of appearances only, or—in an implied metaphor—a theater like the

London stage and not the stoic *theatrum mundi*? If so, then the threat is severe:

> For if vice boasts her origin the same
> With social joy and patriotic flame,
> Then I must wish to bid the world farewel,
> Turn Anchoret, and choose some lonely cell. (*PDM/PP,* 197)

Rather than contradict Adams directly, Warren simply shows him the consequences of his philosophy: without any purpose higher than self-interest, better to become a hermit (anchorite) than imagine one's actions have meaning at all.

As the reference to Thoreau above suggests, Warren here and in another philosophical poem anticipates many of the themes the nineteenth-century writer would make famous. Though Warren never literally retreated to a cell, by living in Plymouth most of her life, she remained isolated from the urban political and literary communities that were her natural milieus. As a consequence, she never gave in, as she thought Adams had, to a doctrine of realpolitik; for her, poetry retained a certain purity as a form, appropriate for expressing ideas of the untainted life. Better to be reasonable than not; better to be alone than in the company of the self-interested; better to live in radical simplicity than even moderate luxury.

In her 1779 poem "Simplicity," Warren outlines the virtues of the simple life not only for individuals but for the country as a whole.[48] She imagines an "ideal golden age" in which the goddess Simplicity reigns, and a peasant couple live in health and innocence; inevitably, however, corruption enters when the "rich profusion that all Eden pours" turns out not to be enough for human demands (*PDM/PP,* 230, 231). As Warren pictures it in a tidy couplet, progress becomes measured in further deviations from original simplicity, "And each improvement on the author's plan, / Adds new inquietudes to restless man" (*PDM/PP,* 232). This anticipates Thoreau's attack on material progress, especially in his lines, "Simplicity, simplicity, simplicity!" and "Simplify, simplify" in the "Where I Lived, and What I Lived For" chapter of *Walden.*

The context for her poem is obviously Warren's late 1770s fear that pursuit of wealth was ruining the Revolutionary ideal, but philosophically she carries this past the politics of the time to an extended critique of Western culture. As Thoreau would castigate it later, Warren attacks the devil in the case, trade. In Rome, in Carthage, collapse follows demand for imported luxury goods: "What blotted out the Carthaginian fame, / And left no traces but an empty name?— / Commerce!" Neptune, whose appearance in this poem harks back to "The Squabble," has already abandoned Britain for America; will the sea god have to leave Columbia too? He will if simplicity is lost and ruthless pursuit of luxuries continues " 'Till virtue sinks, and in far distant times, / Dies in the vortex of European crimes" (*PDM/PP,* 234). What begins in play, ends in earnest; like the sayings of the Old Testament prophets, Warren's philosophical poems have a jeremiad-like streak, calling people to task with both the promise of glory and the threat of doom.

Devotional Poems

If her more public poems work out the consequences of philosophy for the country or for humankind as a whole, her personal religious poems focus largely on her concern for her own soul. In the main, she sustains the confidence that pervades the philosophical poems, but she also exposes more of her private insecurities. Like an earlier poet, Edward Taylor, Warren uses poetry as an exercise to work her way from crisis to calm, but her God bears more resemblance to the divine of Epictetus, the ancient Stoic, than to Taylor's Calvinist Jehovah. Still, we see in these poems more references to Christ than Warren normally allows herself, even though her reading of the Christian message remains problematical.

The basic pattern can be observed in several short poems. "A thought in sickness" recounts an illness that the poet feels took her close to death.[49] She desires "balmy sleep" in the hope that by dawn, she can "waft my early, grateful anthems on / To nature's God, before the morning Sun / Salutes the day." Although she's been confined to "the chambers of the dead," she has no fear as long as "the soft monitress of all mankind / The moral sense implanted in the mind" does not condemn her. In fact, true rest comes from knowledge that she is under the system of "free grace"; therefore, it does not matter whether she sleeps only an hour "Or wake no more, till the decisive day." In any case, she has peace.

In "[While life's encumber'd stage I tread]" (1770), the poet seems more restless, even though not threatened immediately with death.[50] Earth tempts the soul and strains it with demands. To put these demands in perspective, the human actor must keep in mind the notion of right acting always and find her place in the scene. In a collection of his sayings, Epictetus says this about conflict between will and the lot one has drawn in life: "Remember that you are an actor in a drama of such sort as the Author chooses—if short, then in a short one; if long then in a long one. . . . For this is your business—to act well the given part, but to choose it belongs to another."[51] This same concept becomes for Warren a doctrine of comfort in the soul's journey:

The all-pervading power who sees
  The proper place, the fittest part
For each performer on the stage,
  I trust will guide and guard my heart. (Hayes 1981, 210)

Grateful that she has survived both her youth and a decade of political upheaval and family mortality (the 1760s), she continues the *theatrum mundi* trope in asking for God's continued protection:

Oh! universal Lord of all
  Me still protect, of mine dispose,
As perfect wisdom judges best
  Till death at last, the drama close! (Hayes 1981, 210)

As with so many other poems, she ends with the image of perpetual song, the soul's utterance in gratitude for the direction given it while treading earth's cluttered stage. What succeeds the "drama" of the individual life, then, is a nondramatic performing state, where will and being are one and are directed only at praise for the divine.

Several shorter poems illustrate Warren's method of moving from outburst to resolution in her devotional works. "A Prayer," for example, is a "suppliant's cry" to God for faith.[52] As she warns others to beware, so she cautions herself about skepticism: "Let no erroneous faith betray / Or lead th' unwary heart astray" (Hayes 1981, 211). Indeed, one can imagine the reasoning engine of the poet's mind turning on received religion; even in her most devout poems, she rarely uses the conventional language of Christ and salvation and in fact almost never says God. Right thinking, like right acting, requires stoic submission:

Assist me Lord in each relation
To act that part in every station
Thy providence has me assign'd
With truth and purity of mind. (Hayes 1981, 211)

This fear of doubt can be seen in the successor to "A Prayer," titled "Another."[53] One of her favorite images in many poems is that of the impressed doctrine of God in the blank clay tablet of being: "thou stamp'st thine image on the mind / diffusing light to all mankind," she tells God. But she also recognizes the consequences of challenging that authority enstamped in consciousness. Using language like that reserved for her personal devil, Thomas Hutchinson, she declares of Satan, "I speak the dreadful truth with awe / The wretch rebell'd and broke the law. / Darkness succeeds, and clouds the mind" (Hayes 1981, 212). For Warren, doubt rushes to a logical and frightening conclusion—separation from the source. No wonder she dashes back and dons her robe, "Uniting with the Angelic choir!"

Two other poems of self-correction ask for aid in restoration of calm. In "A Sigh," a poem whose corruption theme mirrors concerns of the late 1770s and early 1780s, one can see Warren's devotional method at work.[54] It begins with an exasperated "Oh!" and a sigh for the gap between desire and reality. In the rhymes and regular rhythms that follow, some order is restored—in this case, to allow her to reject "pomp" and embrace peace. By the end, the "calm and tranquil mind" she seeks in the first line appears to be working in the last. The cry in almost all these poems is that of "Contemplation": "Call back my vain and wandering heart."[55]

Although Warren's literary allusions are drawn largely from the classics or English and Continental writings, she does occasionally meet the Bible head-on. Her poem "The Nineteenth Psalm" is an extended paraphrase of the Old Testament work.[56] As a number of other poems hint, she wrestles in this one with the problem of communication between eternal and temporal spheres—an issue in the psalm itself. Where the original begins, "The heavens are telling the glory of God," Warren starts, "His glorious works, no tongue nor speech can tell" (Hayes 1981, 207). That is, the messages of the eternal do not go out in ordinary speech; by the same token, the glories themselves exist beyond the abilities of speech to define them. The biblical text evokes what we have seen in Warren as a defining image: the unceasing celestial choir, whose music—not speech—becomes the form of transmission for heavenly magnificence. For her, then, attuning one's soul to that unheard but received music and hoping to be part of the choir at death become the means of resolving the conflict between the timeless and time-bound worlds.

This same theme of the inexpressibility of the divine through ordinary means is part of one of Warren's longest poems, "On reading the History of the sufferings of the Divine Redeemer."[57] Although undated, this work in its ambition seems a product of the poet's later years, possibly the 1790s, when after the deaths of Charles and Winslow she began writing frequently to James Winthrop about religious matters. Although her poems on the deaths of her sons always turn to some comforting thought, the loss of Winslow especially clearly preyed on Warren for many years. Thus one could certainly imagine, if the poem dates from the decade, the state of mind that led to her writing these opening lines:

> From the dead languor of a lukewarm frame
> Awake my soul, Almighty love proclaim!
> The sacred pages shall my muse inspire,
> Attune my harp, and animate my lyre.
> . . . .
> For what's my theme! Redeeming love I trace
> A theme too high for such a reptile race. (HL ms., 45)

The problem, of course, is expression. As in "The Nineteenth Psalm," where she tries to reconcile finite and infinite, here she imagines the "awful contrast" between the garden of Gethsemane—she rhymes it with "scene"—where the redeemer (never "Jesus") is betrayed, and the garden of Eden, "that water'd by *Hiddekel's* stream." What comes of the contrast is salvation out of suffering, a doctrine that "Exceeds the utmost stretch of human thought." All she can do is submit to its power: "Silent I bow, all language is too weak / The grateful homage of my soul to speak." To explain the system of God's love and redemption would only be futile, even frightening: "I seiz'd with terror drop the bold design, / Deep is the research—far beyond my line" (HL ms., 46). Other poets have pictured forth its consequences, especially at "the grand catastrophe." Her role is "submission," her task simply to be the yielding material on which the "great author of the human soul" can work his art (HL ms., 48). Rather than die a defiant individual, the poet's greatest wish is simply to be one of the choir. With this desire, Warren seems to have lived out her final years. The last poem that can be reasonably dated, "An address to the Supreme Being" (1808?), reflects on "fourscore years" of life; with "reason as my guide," the poet looks forward to seeing at last "the Saviour's face."[58] At this point, her poetry could go no further. Except for letters, Warren's last devotional poem obviated the need to write anything "literary" again.

Criticism of the Poems

In her own lifetime, Warren received some commendation for her poetry. In 1790, the publication year for *Poems, Dramatic and Miscellaneous,* she was a subject for half of the 12 issues of *Massachusetts Magazine.*[59] In April, while the subscription list was circulating to attract purchasers of the yet unpublished volume, Warren was made an excuse for the anonymous "Q" to discuss the under-recognition of both "female genius" and poets generally; then having "digressed" the space away, Q differentiates Warren from suffering genius by implying that she is of that "genius seated in the bark of independence, who leisurely sail with the stream, partaking the gale of prosperity."[60] The greatest praise Warren received came in July from fellow poet Sarah Wentworth Morton. In a poem called "Ode Inscribed to Mrs. M. Warren," Morton claims that no female American poet before her subject "Approach'd Pieria's spring" without "genius" hiding away.[61] Now, the country has a poet whom genius can call her own—Warren—someone to whom the ode writer bows as her superior. You write of both heart and mind, Morton (in her voice as Philenia Constantia) tells Mrs. Warren: "These are thy boast, and these shall grace thy name, / Beyond the glories of a deathless fame."[62]

In the September issue of *Massachusetts Magazine,* coinciding with actual publication, an anonymous writer began a three-part review of Warren's book.[63] The third section, in November, focused on the miscellaneous poems. Like Morton, the reviewer found much to praise; the nondramatic poems

> breathe a milder note than her Dramatic performances: yet the same enthusiastic love of her country is visibly predominant in every political piece: And all the domestic and social virtues shine forth in those Poems, which are inscribed to family or friends. The fervency of conjugal affection, the fondness of maternal love, the tender sympathy of friendship, a most sacred regard for the interests of religion, and a pure attachment to the weal of America, is amiably conspicuous in these pleasing, polished, animated and elegant pages. (692)

Although such encomium may have been written by a friend or champion of the poet, Warren must have been pleased that themes she had long asserted were recognized by someone else in a public forum.

Rather different praise came at the same time from Winslow Warren (to MW, 8 November 1790, MWP2). As he says, his mother had for some time been asking for his criticism of her work; receipt of the book gave him an opportunity to comply. He gives some general indication of his pleasure, but takes little time in finding lines to take apart. After citing some undignified lines in the tragedy *Ladies of Castile,* he starts with the poems. "To Mrs. Montague" has a bad third line if the name Corneille "is pronounced right"; "To Torrismond" has several awkward rhymes (for example, "Locke and Boyle" with "Britannia's isle"), but worse, it is filled with philosophical inconsistencies, especially urging knowledge through the book of Revelation but denying that God can be known; the "versification" of "A Political Reverie," Winslow tells her, "is not good." Far from the panegyric bestowed on her in public, the criticism extended through private letter is pointed and deflating. Surely, the poet must have cringed a bit when she read of one pair of lines, "Is this not tautaulogy join'd with the bathos? It certainly is redundant."[64]

Respect for the person but dislike for the poetry continued in the nineteenth century. Rufus Griswold says that her miscellaneous poems are "generally in a flowing verse, but frequently marked by bad taste and rarely evincing any real poetical power or feeling" (22). More generously, Caroline May claims, "She was a skilful and industrious writer . . . attempting and achieving great subjects, with a boldness and ease that prove her mind to have been of no ordinary stamp" (42). Elizabeth Ellet and Alice Brown remark on the poetry without significant praise, the latter noting that "it is only her abiding earnestness which succeeds in loosening the shackles of too elaborate artifice and lets her breathe and speak" (187).

For much of the twentieth century, these judgments have been reiterated. Maud Hutcheson, Katharine Anthony, and Jean Fritz mention poems, but offer little interpretive commentary. Benjamin Franklin calls Warren a "mediocre poet at best" (xxviii). Several recent critics, however, give Warren more credit as a poet. Emily Watts focuses on the religious and intellectual dimensions of the poems, seeing in the poetry an argument for "intellectual freedom" (39). Pattie Cowell recognizes the problems Warren's poetry creates for modern readers—"conventional imagery and diction and moralizing tone"—but also shows the poet's cognizance of gender issues and the "fresh look at revolutionary and early national themes" provided by the 1790 volume (74, 75). By reprinting her "private poems" with a substantial introduction, Edmund Hayes makes a case for the importance of Warren's nonpolitical verse. Cheryl Oreovicz delves more deeply than most critics into the importance of providential thought in the poetry and counters many of the early criticisms by rightly observing that Warren is "sensitive to language" (1987, 221). While no one yet argues that Warren is a great poet, these more recent comments take us back to her work for a more considered evaluation of the poems and the traditions in which she wrote.

Chapter 4
Political Plays and Verse Dramas

Were it not for her plays, Mercy Warren might have been largely lost to literary history. Mentions of her work by such literary historians as Moses Coit Tyler and Arthur Hobson Quinn have kept her name alive as one of America's first playwrights—indeed, she is probably the first American woman to write plays—even if critics have traditionally assigned little literary value to them. Typical of the commentary on her drama are the remarks by Benjamin Franklin V in his introduction to *The Plays and Poems of Mercy Otis Warren* (*PP*) that the political plays "lack character development, richness of plot, and adequate structure" and that the verse plays are "less obviously flawed but also less satisfying than her earlier, spirited plays" (*PP,* vii). With a little background knowledge, however, contemporary readers need not dismiss them simply as loosely structured dramas or relics of the past; on the contrary, her satiric political plays evidence a lively topicality while her historical verse dramas, far from being the "tedious" efforts they have been called by some critics, show Warren working out a number of issues related to politics and gender in the new republic.

Unfortunately, many problems, textual and otherwise, occur in talking about her earlier plays; in fact, determining Warren's corpus has yet to be done definitively. Five plays can be assigned to Warren with certainty: *The Adulateur* (those parts appearing in excerpt in 1772), *The Defeat* (1773), *The Group* (1775), *The Sack of Rome,* and *The Ladies of Castile* (both 1790). Three other plays are alleged to have been authored by her: *The Blockheads* (1776), *The Motley Assembly* (1779), and *Sans Souci* (1785). Unfortunately, none of these attributions can be made with certainty, though with *The Blockheads* and *The Motley Assembly* one might infer Warren's authorship. All of the plays will be discussed below, the last three with caveats.

Satiric Political Plays

Many of the earliest plays written in English-speaking America are political or historical in nature, and frequently satirical. A Virginian, Robert

Munford, wrote a play in 1770 or 1771 called *The Candidates, or the Humours of a Virginia Election* (not published until 1798 and not performed before the twentieth century) in which electioneering practices for the House of Burgesses are gently mocked in terms and characters of eighteenth-century British comedy.[1] An earlier play, *The Disappointment,* by Thomas Forrest (writing pseudonymously as Andrew Barton), was pulled from performance in Philadelphia in 1767 because its topical and local satire on groups and individuals in that city was thought likely to offend.[2] And before that, the first contemporary play printed in America, Robert Hunter's *Androboros* (1714), was a satire on the political enemies of its author, then royal governor of New York.[3] Aside from these plays, a few tragedies such as Thomas Godfrey's *The Prince of Parthia* (1765) and Robert Rogers's *Ponteach* (1766), and collegiate dialogues, there was little in the way of a homegrown tradition in dramatic writing for Warren to draw on.

At the same time, Warren probably never saw a play in her life, and most certainly could not have at the time she was writing them.[4] Laws in Massachusetts forbade the mounting of plays; the Harvard College code prohibited students from putting them on (though of course collegians could be resourceful)[5]; and during the war, legislation passed by the Continental Congress in 1778 made playacting a proscribed activity (Meserve, 61). Like many of her educated and literate contemporaries, Warren read plays: Shakespeare, Addison's *Cato,* Molière. But she also heard—and used—the metaphors of theater that abounded in late eighteenth-century literary and political culture (Richards, 201–44). Thus, while playgoing was a foreign experience, and playwriting an infrequent exercise among American writers, likening the world to a stage was so much a part of the public discourse of her time that Warren would not think it strange to write plays about politics.

Warren's first three plays have one basic subject: the evils of Tory administration in Massachusetts. In these plays, she sets out a stark, even dire contrast between the ambition of those loyal to invidious crown policies and the self-sacrifice of American patriots. This is often expressed in the theme of "freedom versus liberty."[6] Her particular antagonist is Thomas Hutchinson, toward whom she is ruthless in exposing as a Machiavel; as new grievances occur, however, she works in other American Tories, British officials, or Whig turncoats. At the same time, by using blank verse and asserting the virtue and honor of the Whigs, she enlarges what may seem to us now as picayune disputes into the tone, if not precisely the style, of tragedy. This "fashion" of characters speaking like "Greek and Roman patriots" may have struck Moses Coit Tyler and most readers of the last century or more as "grandiose," but for Warren and her fellow Whigs, the anathematizing of the Tories served a vital and justifiable propaganda purpose.[7]

The Adulateur

Warren's first play and most likely first publication appeared initially as extracts of a larger play in Isaiah Thomas's periodical *Massachusetts Spy* on 26 March and 23 April 1772.[8] Though her name is not attached to the published pieces, Warren left a partial manuscript, possibly prepared in the 1780s, in her writing (MWP2) and a copy of the same by her son James Warren, Jr. (now at the Houghton Library). A pamphlet version of the play appeared in 1773 with the title *The Adulateur. A Tragedy, As it is now acted in Upper Servia,* but with new material that Warren—disavowing involvement in its publication—called a "plagiary."[9] In addition, the pamphlet version has five acts; the extracted play is announced as having three, but the pamphlet numbers do not at all correspond to those we have for Warren's. Thus, there is no satisfactory version—only the out-of-sequence *Massachusetts Spy* fragments, manuscripts prepared after first publication and admittedly incomplete, and a pamphlet that Warren claims has only some of her writing in it. While we can offer a reconstruction of what Warren intended and reasonably assume what the "plagiary" in the pamphlet is, we do not know the identity of the other hand.[10]

Warren's portion of the play focuses on the political climate in 1772. Loyalist Thomas Hutchinson, the former lieutenant governor under Francis Bernard (the Brundo mentioned in the play), is now governor, and many in the inner circle of government are related to him by marriage or blood.[11] For Whigs like the Warrens, Hutchinson's appointment of staunch Tories to key government posts was more than just cronyism: it was a direct attack against the liberties of citizens and the independence of Massachusetts as a political entity. The governor in the play is called Rapatio, the rapacious one, and as the Houghton Library manuscript shows, his soliloquy ought to be read in act 1, scene 1. Rapatio, a satanically corrupt Miltonic villain, says in act 4, scene 2, of the pamphlet that he has "Suck'd the contagion from my mother's breast."[12] He feels some guilt for having undermined his native country, but relieves the pangs provoked by "phantom conscience" in the company of "fawning courtiers"—the flatterers indicated by the title word "adulator" (as we now spell it)—whom he has wed to his will.

Rapatio meets opposition in the figure of Brutus, Warren's brother James Otis, Jr., whose rhetoric inspires other patriots to resist the governor's intrigues.[13] In the manuscripts, Warren preserves the soliloquy printed in the 26 March version, intended for act 3 but reprinted in the pamphlet as 5.1, in which he weeps for his country and calls on divine power to "crush, crush these vipers" (*PP,* 29). The final scene in the 1773 version (5.3), originally printed in *Massachusetts Spy* for 23 April 1772 as intended for the first act but not included in the manuscripts, shows Brutus initiating a young patriot, Marcus, into the realities of struggle against Rapatio's evil. The play ends inconclusively, but with Brutus's expressed prophecy that some future good will emerge from the conflict.

In the pamphlet, however, the initiating events take place in 1770: the killing by customs officer Ebenezer Richardson ("E———r") of an 11-year-old boy, Christopher Seider (or Snider), on 22 February, and the street melee less than two weeks later that became known as the Boston Massacre. This new beginning was perhaps inspired by a despairing speech by Ebenezer in prison in the 26 March *Massachusetts Spy* extract, a piece that appears as 5.2 in the pamphlet, and the cynical spirit-rousing lines by Hazlerod in rejoinder. At the same time, the play charts the rise to power of Rapatio, from Bernard/Brundo's resignation to Hutchinson/Rapatio's consolidation of power with the help of Hazlerod[14] (Peter Oliver, 1713–91, Hutchinson's brother-in-law and chief justice of the superior court), Limpit[15] (Andrew Oliver, 1706–74, Hutchinson's wife's brother-in-law, secretary of the province and under Hutchinson's governorship the lieutenant governor), Meagre (Foster Hutchinson, 1724–99, Thomas's younger brother, Harvard classmate of James Otis, Jr., and a justice on the superior court), and Dupe (Thomas Flucker, 1719–83, a staunch Hutchinson man who succeeded Andrew Oliver as provincial secretary). Also helping out are British military officers Gripeall (Adm. John Montagu of the Royal Navy) and Bagshot (Capt. Thomas Preston of the Twenty-ninth Regiment, the commanding officer of the troops that fired during the Boston Massacre).[16] In opposition stand patriots Brutus, Cassius (names of conspirators against Julius Caesar), Junius, Portius, and Marcus (the latter two names from *Cato,* which play also provides the epigraph to the pamphlet).[17] Thus the material that is most probably Warren's (what she seems to have intended as acts 1–3) is moved to the end of the pamphlet play (acts 4 and 5), and the scenes concerning these prior events placed largely in acts 1–3.[18]

Not surprisingly, despite the unknown writer's attempt to keep *The Adulateur* moving forward in time, the play lacks unity; the patriots are much more hot-tempered in the Massacre portion of the play than later, though there is passion throughout; many scenes lack effective transitions or announce major venue changes before the scenes are technically over; and characters often appear at random or disappear without effective explanation. Still, the blank verse differs little in quality through the five acts, and much of it has an economy of presentation or sharpness of image that can, for the interested reader, sustain tension. In his soliloquy (Warren's manuscript 1.1, pamphlet 4.2), Rapatio describes how he brought Hazlerod to power:

> I from a fribbling, superficial dabler,
> A vain pretender to each learned science,
> A poet, preacher, conjurer and quack—
> Rear'd the obsequious trifler to my purpose,
> Rob'd him in scarlet, dignifi'd the man:
> An hecatomb of incense is my due. (*PP,* 26)

The key to appreciation lies in recognizing the historical-political background to which Warren and her plagiarist so concretely refer. As Gerald Weales rightly states, "The remarkable thing about the play at this date is its allusiveness, the way both Mercy Warren and her unknown collaborator understood that a line, a phrase, a single adjective could evoke a man, an event, a political attitude" (131). While a number of modern historians have quite justifiably tried to rescue Hutchinson from the bogey image that Warren so effectively fostered—patriot letter writers after *The Adulateur* appeared used "Rapatio" to refer to the governor—the fact remains that Whigs genuinely feared what seemed like a cabal, backed by the might of British military force.[19] Reading this play restores to us the fervency of feeling at the time.

Of considerable interest is Warren's postwar commentary (possibly in the mid-1780s) on this and her other two connected plays, *The Defeat* and *The Group.* Warren explains the political situation behind the plays and some of the personages, then justifies her inclusion of this information as being intended "to gratify the curiosity of her sons, with regard to any political tracts they may find in the cabinet of their mother; and if by accident they should fall into other hands, to apologize, not for the design, which was benevolent, but for the incomplete execution" (HL ms. 5–6). Thus it appears that she had posterity in mind, literally, when she came to arrange the "disconnected scraps" that nonetheless had the approbation of "the best judges." More important, she says she was playing a defensive role, writing "only to develope disguised characters, and parry the malignance of the busy incendiaries of the Crown" (she singled out Jonathan Sewall earlier). She concludes, "They [the political plays] were offered the public only as occasions arose, and the exigencies of the times required the vizard should be stripped from the face of intrigue, where flattery and illusion were hackneyed, as usual, by the minions of a Court" (HL ms., 6). Her apology is really none at all; bad people needed to be identified as such, she says. The rest, the "execution," finally matters less.

The Defeat

Like *The Adulateur,* to which this play is a sequel of sorts, *The Defeat* does not exist as a satisfactorily complete text. It appeared in the *Boston Gazette* in two installments (24 May and 19 July 1773), again as excerpts, and as with its predecessor, the order of publication is at odds with manuscript evidence. Before discussing the specifics of the play, however, I will say something about the historical background, especially since some statements about the origin of the play, including Warren's own, may not be fully accurate.[20]

The inciting episodes are several. In the Houghton Library manuscript, Warren claims that she wrote *The Defeat* in response to the "plagiary" that turned her *Adulateur* into an unauthorized pamphlet about the Boston Massacre; that is, she wanted to reclaim her original territory, the attack on Hutchinson's aggrandizement of power. Events unfolding after mid-1772, however, provided her with other reasons to continue her dramatic politics, even if we assume that the pamphlet version of the *Adulateur* appeared in early 1773. For one thing, Hutchinson, who makes a return appearance as Rapatio, was able to secure from the crown responsibility for his salary, hitherto the obligation of the province. This aroused a great deal of protest from residents of Massachusetts who wished to use their control over salary as a check on the governor's power, but in itself the argument would not have created a major rift between Assembly and administration. But then Bostonians learned that the salaries of the superior court justices, most of them Hutchinson allies, would also be paid directly by the crown. This development led to a Boston town meeting in November 1772 and the publication of an incendiary pamphlet authored by Samuel Adams, *Votes and Proceedings of the Freeholders . . . of . . . Boston,* that directly challenged the authority of the government to rule. This radical step was welcomed by

James Warren—and presumably by Mercy as well—who called for a meeting in Plymouth to second Boston (JW to SA, 8 and 17 November 1772, *WAL,* 2:399–400). One result of the contest between Boston (with other towns in support) and the governor was a protracted debate in early 1773 that involved Hutchinson and the General Assembly over the rights of provincial citizens versus the authority of the crown-appointed government. Mercy Warren refers to this debate in a manuscript note.[21]

Another development arising from this debate concerned a former Otis family ally, William Brattle (1706–76). The militia general, along with James Otis, Sr., and James, Jr., had opposed the Stamp Act, even participating in a street protest that forced Andrew Oliver to step down as stamp master for Massachusetts. Perhaps because Brattle was wealthy and tended to move in the same social circles as the high Tories, he changed colors; in a Cambridge town meeting that occurred shortly after Boston's, Brattle revealed that he supported the crown salaries for judges.[22] The vituperative private and public reaction of John Adams, who by this time had become a close friend of the Warrens, suggests how startled and angry the Whigs were when one of their own, or so they thought, turned coat.[23] In Warren's play, Brattle is called Proteus, after the Greek sea god who could change shape.[24]

A third event—the timing of which is important—also plays a part. In March 1773 Thomas Cushing, then Speaker of the Massachusetts House, received from Benjamin Franklin letters written by Thomas Hutchinson and Andrew Oliver to Thomas Whately, a former Treasury secretary in Britain and an architect of the Stamp Act. These letters, sent during the 1760s, contained phrasing that Whigs saw as threatening to American rights, including one famous line by Hutchinson arguing that in the colonies there must be "an abridgment of what are called English liberties" (quoted in Bailyn 1974, 243). In public debate, however, the existence of the letters was officially made known on 2 June and they were published 16 June, against the original conditions set by Franklin for their circulation in Massachusetts.[25] In the months between arrival and printing, the Warrens might have had some opportunity to see or learn about the letters.

In the Houghton Library manuscript, a footnote to a sentence that introduces the play declares, "Written on the discovery of Hutchinson's and Oliver's letters." Given that Proteus is a main character and that nothing in the May installment alludes directly to the letters, however, this statement seems not quite correct. It seems more plausible that

Warren began the play sometime in March or April 1773, that is, after John Adams had stopped writing his letters to Brattle in the *Boston Gazette* (22 February) and Hutchinson had given his last speech to the Assembly in their debate (6 March), but before Warren had firsthand knowledge of the Whately correspondence. After the first excerpts of *The Defeat* were accepted by the *Gazette,* she then learned of the letters, or had time to read them in the press, and wrote the July excerpts in that light. One episode that refers to the physical existence of the letters occurs only in manuscript, however—a dialogue between two of the "virtuous senators," Honestus and Hortensius. Therefore, allowing for errors of chronology in Warren's hindsight, we have to see *The Defeat* as being about several issues, not all of them intended at the beginning of composition.

As with *The Adulateur,* some amount of reconstruction is necessary to understand *The Defeat.* In the version published in the *Gazette,* the play has for the 24 May scenes the following: Rapatio's soliloquy in 1.1, where he promises to buy loyalty; a scene presumably from act 2, in which Proteus defends Rapatio to Honestus (James Bowdoin, active Whig and later governor of Massachusetts) and Hortensius (John Adams), who has only one speech; an unsequenced scene between the previous one, which is labeled "End of the second Act," and the next, clearly labeled as such, in which Proteus proclaims his changeability to match whoever has power; 3.1, described only as a "battle" that leads to the defeat of Rapatio and company; and the "concluding Scene of the 4th Act," when Rapatio soliloquizes his doom. A single long scene, in which Rapatio and Limpit (Andrew Oliver) discuss the letters, is all that was published for the 19 July installment. The gaps and irregular act and scene numbering attest to the rapid unfolding of events and Warren's shift in direction from the crown salary issue to that of the Whately correspondence.

The manuscript presents the scheme for a more ordered play, however, a fact that suggests Warren might have tried even near to the time of original composition to develop some kind of dramatic wholeness from her disparate materials. This version offers the following: 1.1 has Rapatio's soliloquy, as above; 1.2 Proteus and Honestus, without the single speech by Hortensius, then Honestus and Hortensius alone, noting that the incriminating letters are that moment being carried by "good Rusticus" (James Warren); 1.3 Proteus solus, another version of the unsequenced scene in the pamphlet; 2.1 the lengthy dialogue between Rapatio and Limpit that is labeled 3.2 in the 19 July printing; 2.3–4, which Warren says she is "passing over" to get to 3.1, the battle scene; other scenes, "striking and very affecting to every human heart," also "passed over" to get to the concluding scene, unnumbered, but apparently one that would end act 3; and in the manuscripts an epilogue in which the author expresses compassion for the criminals, though contingent on their admitting their wrongs. The wording suggests that this was written some time after the events, but possibly before Hutchinson's death in 1780. As a dramatic composition, the manuscript version is more unified than the scattered scenes that appeared in the *Boston Gazette.*

Unlike *The Adulateur,* in which the patriot Brutus serves as a counterweight to the villain Rapatio, *The Defeat* focuses almost entirely on the wicked "bashaw of Servia" and his toadies. As Edmund Hayes notes, Rapatio is more a Vice figure—a static villain whose evil is undercut by his clownishness—from medieval drama than a slowly developing character; he is a hypocrite and tells us directly all of his devilish machinations (Hayes 1976, 443). As he sinks to his infernal doom in the last soliloquy, however, Rapatio resembles more dynamic evildoers, like Milton's Satan or, as Hayes also remarks, Faust (441). That Warren turned Hutchinson into such a figure tells us something about her and her times. She lived in a period when the rhetorical conversion of events was a standard strategy for depicting reality. Clearly, she and her fellow Whigs imagined that Hutchinson's actions had implications far beyond local politics—and while her play portrays characters in stark, unbelievable contrasts, subsequent events proved that her reading of the seriousness of the dispute was correct. Like the Puritan writers of the previous century, Warren makes social or political antagonisms fit familiar paradigms of good and evil, nobility and cowardice. Three generations after Cotton Mather's *The Wonders of the Invisible World* (1693), in which the Puritan minister turned the witchcraft trials into a battle between the devil and God's people for control of America, Warren transforms people isolated by popular opinion into Satan and his minions.[26]

On the other hand, as in all her political plays, she seeks a high ground by stressing those virtues required by a society to survive as a free people. This issue becomes a theme in her *History* as well. In *The Defeat,* the dramatis personae as listed in the manuscript include figures from Warren's personal pantheon, several of whom never enter as speaking characters: Cassius (Sam Adams) and Brutus (James Otis, Jr.) from *The Adulateur,* Helvidius (Harvard professor John Winthrop) and Rusticus, new here. They and others appear through the medium of Rapatio's condemnations. The scheming bashaw wants to keep the Senate free from virtue's influence and identifies persons he will prevent from taking any official seat. For instance, Rapatio tells Limpit, "The hated Cassius['s] soft pathetic Tongue / Pleads Virtues Cause, which calls for my Destruction" (Hayes 1976, 454). But some he will have a hard time denying; Helvidius, for example—whose "deep Researches into Nature's Laws, / Not more his Duty than his Chief Delight, / Have kept him ever from the Mazey Path, / Of busy Courtiers and their publick Wiles"—gives Rapatio "no Pretext" to deny the astronomer his House seat.[27]

One other issue emerges in the exchange between Limpit and Rapatio—the paper war between Whig and Tory. Jonathan Sewall (1728–96), the P[hilanthro]p of *The Adulateur,* is mentioned here in his several pseudonyms, most notably as Philalethes, the defender of Hutchinson in the Whately letter affair.[28] Limpit calls him "the dangerous Foe / Of Liberty, of Truth, and of Mankind, / Who undermines their happiness below, / Then knocks away the Props of future Peace" (Hayes 1976, 457). Contrasted with the Sewall character are Lucius (William Phillips, one of three Council members negatived by Hutchinson after the May elections and author of a scathing attack on the governor in the 21 and 28 June issues of the *Boston Gazette*) and Hortensius.[29] As early as 1766, John Adams had been responding in public to the printed barbs of his Harvard classmate Sewall[30]; most recently, he had rejected Brattle's defense of the crown salary issue. Like Phillips, Adams had been negatived by Hutchinson in May. In the play, Rapatio remarks of Hortensius,

> He talks,—he Writes,—Regardless of my Wrath:
> From pale Fac'd Perjury, he strips the Veil,
> Declaims aloud, and points him to the World
> . . . .
> A Crime for which he n'er shall by forgiven.(455)

Although the battle that brings Rapatio's defeat is not pictured, Warren makes clear that virtue, honesty, incorruptibility—expressed in large measure through the pen—are the real weapons available to Whigs to resist the transparent motives of Rapatio and his followers.

The Group

The third and probably last play in this series, *The Group* is Warren's best-known and most acclaimed satiric political drama. As with the first two plays, there are textual problems, but *The Group* is unique for existing in a satisfactory printed text. It first appeared in partial form in the *Boston Gazette,* 23 January 1775, and in *Massachusetts Spy,* 26 January (act 1, scene 1, and act 2, scene 1). Pamphlet editions were printed in Philadelphia and New York, but without some last scenes. An alleged Jamaican edition has never been recovered. This leaves the Boston pamphlet version, published by Edes and Gill in 1775, as the most complete and authoritative text, virtually identical to surviving manuscripts.[31]

Many things had happened in Massachusetts since Warren wrote *The Defeat.* The tea consignment to Boston was tossed overboard by Whigs dressed as Indians in December 1773. Many Whig sympathizers turned Tory as events took a more militant turn. Under increased pressure to step down, Warren's archenemy Hutchinson departed for England, leaving a military man, Thomas Gage, in the governor's chair. And Parliament passed several restrictive measures—the so-called Intolerable Acts—aimed at curbing Massachusetts radicalism, including the Boston Port Act (virtually closing that city to shipping), the Impartial Administration of Justice Act, and, most notorious of all, the Massachusetts Regulatory Act, or the Massachusetts Government Act (Middlekauff, 230).

It was at this latter measure and its results that Warren took aim in *The Group.* The act allowed for continued popular representation in the House but stripped locals of the ability to select members of the Council, the upper chamber. These persons, the ones closest to the governor, were to be appointed under a writ of mandamus, a legal term derived from the Latin word that means "we command." In other words, the king (through advice from the governor and his London ministers) would name the council directly, with no say from voters or the House. The mandamus councillors, as they were called, were to accept their appointments by oath in August 1774, some four months after the departure of Hutchinson. The former governor, in London by this time and visiting British government ministers almost daily, had a large hand in the choice of people to serve.

To Warren and other Whigs, this last step by Britain was an outrage, further evidence—if any was needed—of the existence of a conspiracy to deprive Massachusetts of its rights under previous charters. So widespread was the protest that of the 36 councillors named by the crown, only about 10 actually took the oath of office. Many had to renounce their appointment or flee from the towns they represented to Boston—in many cases, never to return home. Seizing on the antipatriotic implications of accepting mandamus appointments, Warren crafted a play that focused almost exclusively on tensions and attitudes among the mandamus councillors themselves.

Beyond the immediate party politics, Warren's play reflects two other concerns for her as a writer: the role of a woman who writes satire and the continued turning of politics into familial themes. Both issues resolve themselves back into the text of the play.

The scenes printed in the *Gazette* (1.1 and 2.1) were sent to John Adams in manuscript by James Warren, probably in the hand of James Warren, Jr. (*PJA,* 2:214nn2–3). The scenes, James Sr. wrote, were "[c]omposed at my perticuler desire. They go to you . . . without pointing or marking. If you think it worth while to make any Other use of them, than a reading you will prepare them in that way and give them such Other Corrections and Amendments as your good Judgement shall Suggest" (15 January 1775, *PJA,* 2:214). At the time he received the letter, Adams was engaged in writing his propatriot Novanglus essays, the responses to Massachusettensis, now known to be Daniel Leonard, a lawyer figured in the play as Beau Trumps. After the scenes appeared in the Boston newspapers, Mercy Warren herself wrote to Adams, both to thank him for the praise he had lavished on her in a previous letter and to ask him for his opinion on the tone of her play: "Personal Reflections and sarcastic Reproaches have Generally been Decry'd by the Wise And the Worthy both in thier [*sic*] Conversation and Writing, and though A Man may be greatly Criminal in his Conduct towards the society in which he Lives, how far sir, do you think it justifiable for any individual to hold him up the Object of public Derision" (30 January 1775, *PJA,* 2:389).

With rectitude always near to consciousness, Warren worries that sarcasm will reflect badly on any writer; yet she recognizes that satire, as understood in the eighteenth century, was justified as a corrective literature, a mode that served the public good by holding public officials to account. At the same time, however, she fears that satire may not be an appropriate form of expression for her sex: "But though from the perticuler Circumstances of our unhappy times A Little personal Acrimony Might be justifiable in your sex, Must not the Female Character suffer. (And will she not be suspected as Deficient in the most Amiable part therof that Candour and Charity which Ensures her both Affection and Esteem.) if she indulges her pen to paint in the Darkest shades Even Those whom Vice and Venality have Rendered Contemptable." By her very act of writing the play—and, of course, this is not her first effort at satire—Warren has largely answered the question for herself. Still, she wants Adams's approval, hoping he will see her work as "Beneficial to society" (390).

Adams's response must have gratified Warren considerably; indeed, his letter of 15 March 1775 marks perhaps the high point of their mutual admiration. For Adams, satire develops from "natural" gifts in some to provoke in all people that fear of scorn that keeps them on the path of virtuous behavior. For many persons, legal judgments have less effect than the stain on reputation produced by a satirist—and in some ways, jails or stocks may be said to be forms of satire. "But classical Satyr, such as flows so naturally and easily from the Pen of my excellent Friend had all the Efficacy, and more, in Support of Virtue and in Discountenancing of Vice, without any of the Coarseness and Indelicacy of those other Species of Satyr, the civil and political ones" (*PJA,* 2:407). Thus Adams finds in satire a tool essential for ensuring public behavior—but he never fully answers Warren's question as to sex of satirist. Instead, he concludes his letter with extravagant praise for Warren's talents, an answer Warren may have taken, with other comments elsewhere by Adams, as outwardly confirming her right to satirize:

> Of all the Genius's which have yet arisen in America, there has been none, Superiour, to one, which now shines, in this happy, this exquisite Faculty. Indeed, altho there are many which have received more industrious Cultivation I know of none, ancient or modern, which has reached the tender, the pathetic, the keen and severe, and at the same time the soft, the Sweet, the amiable, and the pure, in greater Perfection. (*PJA,* 2:408)

Yet Adams's choice of words suggests, in fact, that a woman's satire will be different from a man's; no male satirist in the eighteenth century would wish to be praised for "the soft, the Sweet, the amiable" qualities Adams extols in Warren.[32] Although the playwright did not take offense—indeed, her letter begs this response—in other circumstances she would likely recognize in Adams's commentary a hidden diminution of female abilities that later becomes overt in the aftermath of their great debate on her *History.*[33]

If satire may be made useful as an instrument of public correction, who is Warren trying to help? Gone now is Rapatio (Thomas Hutchinson), though he lives on in spirit. Hazlerod (Peter Oliver) and Dupe (Thomas Flucker), in their roles as councillors, remain from earlier plays. Accompanying the latter two are several other of the mandamus councillors, many now quite obscure; the new governor, here called

Sylla; and an unnamed woman, a wife perhaps to one of the councillors, who speaks the concluding lines. Why Warren chose some and not others cannot be completely determined, although she does include 8 of the 10 who actually took the oath. Because many of the councillors had longstanding connections either to the Warren-Otis family or to John Adams, Warren no doubt had personal reasons for excoriating the real-life figures behind the characters of *The Group.*[34]

Most of the play is a discussion among the councillors about their anomalous situation as Americans who are yet betraying their native land.[35] The first scene takes place in a "little dark parlour"; Simple Sapling and Crusty Crowbar begin to lament the decisions they have made to grasp at "honours purchas'd at the price of peace." They are typical of a class who, with little thought or concern for principle, "blindly swore obedience" to the will of Rapatio (*PP,* 3). Simple is Nathaniel Ray Thomas (1731–87) of Marshfield in Plymouth County, a Harvard graduate (1751) and wealthy farmer; he once had a skinned ox returned to him by the Sons of Liberty into which was stuffed the fellow to whom the Loyalist Thomas had sold the beast.[36] Crusty is Josiah Edson, another Plymouth County resident and Harvard graduate (1730), a friend to Timothy Ruggles, the Brigadier Hateall of the play (Shipton, 9:214). In the small world of Plymouth politics and society, the Warrens would certainly have known both Edson and Thomas. The doubts the Loyalists express in the play manifested themselves in real life, since both Thomas and Edson refused to take the oath of office for the council.

In the play, however, they are overwhelmed in argument by Hazlerod, their superior in sophistry. Hazlerod, who as Peter Oliver was in Hutchinson's absence one of the most influential of the Boston Loyalists, claims that once he too "Obscurely trod the lower walks of life, / In hopes by honesty my bread to gain" (*PP,* 4); but once he "banish'd conscience," he found it easy to rise in preferment, especially after being swayed by the writings of Philalethes (Jonathan Sewall). Yet neither Hazlerod nor another speaker, Hector Mushroom (Col. John Murray of Rutland), can match the dominant character in the scene, Hateall, for vitriol.[37]

In the fashion of Whig sentimental style, Hateall sweeps away all qualms on his side in language sure to stir readers to an opposite position:

> How I could glut my vengeful eyes to see
> The weeping maid thrown helpless on the world,
> Her sire cut off.—Her orphan brothers stand

While the big tear ro[l]ls down the manly cheek.
Robb'd of maternal care by grief's keen shaft,
The sorrowing mother mourns her starving babes
Her murder'd lord torn guiltless from her side. (*PP*, 6)

The monster who delivers this speech is Warren's version of Timothy Ruggles (1711–95), a profane and irreverent Plymouth County lawyer who later moved to Hardwick. Ruggles was something of a judicial rival to Warren's father, James Otis, and the butt of a famous joke. Otis told a tavern woman to expect that Otis's "servant"—the unsuspecting Ruggles—would arrive shortly and that he would be easily identified as a "tall, ugly, ill bred, swearing fellow" (quoted in Shipton, 9:200). Later, after the Stamp Act crisis, Ruggles was reported by John Rowe to have had "[s]ome disputes and hard Language" with James Otis, Jr. (quoted in Shipton, 9:211). Thus, Warren probably added to the public reputation of Ruggles as a difficult, rough character the many little family stories that had circulated among the Otises for years. Not surprisingly, then, Hateall concludes act 1 by declaring that had he the power, he would send the patriots "murm'ring to the shades of hell" (*PP,* 6).

In act 2, "the scene changes to a large dining room," furnished with drinking vessels, cards, and a book cabinet. In the latter, we find the Tory's ideal reading list: Hobbes's *Leviathan* (arguing for strong central control by the state); Thomas Hutchinson's *History of Massachusetts-Bay,* a book whose value as history was overshadowed in Whig eyes by what seemed to be a justification for Hutchinson's views; Bernard Mandeville's *Fable of the Bees* (1714), a work that asserts that all human action is motivated by self-interest; the self-referential "Philalethes on Philanthrop, with an appendix by Massachusettensis," all of which Warren assumes to be by Sewall; and several other works, including "Sipthrop's Sermons" and "Wedderburn's speeches." The former alludes to sermons of "passive obedience and non-resistance" by Robert Sibthorpe, a seventeenth-century British clergyman[38]; the latter refers to the vicious speech delivered by Alexander Wedderburn (1733–1805), British solicitor general, in the "Cockpit," the meeting place of the Privy Council's Committee on Plantation Affairs. In response to a petition from Massachusetts that requested the removal of Hutchinson and Andrew Oliver from the governor's chairs, Wedderburn used the opportunity not only to defend the royal governor and lieutenant governor but also to attack Benjamin Franklin for his role in the Whately affair.[39] This speech was published in Boston in April 1774 and answered in a letter to Wedderburn by John Adams (*PJA,* 2:85–87 and 87n1). In short, such reading would reinforce the intolerance of the mandamus councillors for liberty and American patriotism.

The most interesting dimension of scene 1 is the presence of an eloquent but troubled council member, Beau Trumps. Because of conflicting identifications for this figure in contemporary copies of *The Group,* some scholars have seen this character as Warren's version of either John or William Vassall (W. Brown, 170; Shipton, 9:355–56). But the Houghton Library manuscript quite clearly identifies this character as Daniel Leonard (1740–1829). A wealthy Harvard graduate (1760) with a master's from Yale (1766), Leonard was a lawyer, king's attorney for Bristol County, Massachusetts, member of the House from Taunton, and close friend of John Adams. Until the Boston Tea Party, Leonard was generally Whiggish in political sentiment, but by spring 1774 was signatory to the address to governor Hutchinson (a benchmark for Tory sympathies). Leonard was a stylish man who, unique among his colleagues at the bar, rode to Boston in a chariot; his defection to the Loyalists was seen less as betrayal than a real loss. It is possible that John Adams, to whom Leonard communicated some of his shift in thinking, conveyed his internal debate to Mercy Warren. Unbeknownst to John Adams, who was writing as Novanglus, it was his old friend Leonard, not his other old friend Sewall, who was writing the Massachusettensis essays.[40]

In Warren's play, Beau Trumps converses with Monsieur de Francois (James Boutineau), Scriblerius Fribble (Harrison Gray), Collateralis (William Browne), Hum Humbug (John Erving, Jr.), and others who are present but silent.[41] Monsieur sets the tone by lamenting the disparity between his current actions and those of his emigrant Huguenot father, who came to Boston for freedom. This is picked up later in the scene by Beau Trumps, a man who has once been the "sworn friend" of Rusticus (James Warren). Using theatrical metaphor, the Leonard character charts his history from Whig to Tory:

> When first I enter'd on the public stage
> My country groan'd beneath base Brundo's hand,
> Virtue look'd fair and beckon'd to her lure,
> Thro' truth's bright mirror I beheld her charms
> And wish'd to tread the patriotic path,
> And wear the Laurels that adorn his fame;
> I walk'd a while and tasted solid peace
> With Cassius, Rusticus and good Hortensius,
> And many more, whose names will be rever'd. (*PP,* 8)

Unfortunately, the combined association with Sam Adams, Warren, and John Adams are not enough to offset his desire for profit and the conniving power of the governor:

> I saw Rapatio's arts had struck so deep
> And giv'n his country such a fatal wound
> None but its foes promotion could expect;
> I trim'd, and pimp'd, and veer'd, and wav'ring stood
> But half resolv'd to show myself a knave,
> Till the Arch Traitor prowling round for aid
> Saw my suspense and bid me doubt no more;— (*PP,* 9)

As with the two previous plays, all evil is laid at the feet of Rapatio, who, though no longer present in either play or colony, still exerts his devilish influence on American affairs. Beau Trumps, onetime friend to fast patriots, has in his weakness fallen prey to the wily arts of the seducer.

Through Beau's speeches, however, Warren implicates another designing fiend, "false Philanthrop" (*PP,* 9). Jonathan Sewall has been mentioned before in *The Adulateur* and *The Defeat,* but here Warren reveals a special antagonism to this highly skilled Tory propagandist. In some ways, Warren may have seen herself as Sewall's opposite number; indeed, it is possible to some extent that the reverse is also true. Sewall early on entered Warren's life as antagonist by siding with Bernard in his appointment of Hutchinson over her father for a superior court judgeship and his defense of executive powers in his J and Philanthrop essays.[42] As attorney general for Massachusetts and advocate general for the customs commission, Sewall made a ready target for Whigs who painted him as the governor's sycophant; but he further sullied himself in Otis-Warren eyes by engaging in negotiations with John Robinson, after the latter left the country in the aftermath of the Otis beating and lawsuit, for a possible exchange of government positions. The last straw for Warren was his Philalethes letters, Sewall's defense of Hutchinson in the Whately affair. Thus, as one whom she had personal reason to dislike—and one who used the pen in defense of what Warren thought were indefensible principles—Sewall earned a special measure of enmity.

There is one more factor that demonstrates the closeness, finally, of Sewall and Warren. Like many of the councillors, Sewall was forced to leave his home (Cambridge) for occupied Boston. While in the city, he wrote a play, *A Cure for the Spleen, or Amusement for a Winter's Evening,* in which he satirized Whig attitudes.[43] In essence, he was doing what Warren had been doing—using dramatic form to attack rival positions.

While Sewall's play was probably published after *The Group* first appeared, the recursive dimension of the hostility should not be ignored.

Philanthrop's treachery is more subtle than Rapatio's, and perhaps more dangerous. All while courting his country's enemies abroad, says Beau, he keeps his "social ties" at home intact "with a phiz [face] of Crocodilian stamp." But his is only a "feign'd pity" for his country's woes. Even so, Philanthrop has helped bring Beau Trumps into the camp: "I know his guilt,—I ever knew the man, / Thy father knew him e're we trod the stage," Beau tells Humbug; "But as for interest, I betray'd my own / With the same views" (*PP,* 10).[44] By the end of his last speech, then, Beau Trumps shows himself to be fully Rapatio's and Philanthrop's man. Alluding to Leonard's chariot, Warren has Beau hope that

> by my abilities and fame,
> I might attain a splendid glitt'ring car,
> And mount aloft, and sail in liquid air,
> Like Phaeton, I'd then out-strip the wind,
> And leave my low competitors behind. (*PP,* 11)

Self-interest, coupled with the seductions of Machiavels, ever undoes the work of virtue, unless that self-interest be constantly scrutinized and converted into desire to secure the common good.

After a brief scene between Collateralis and Dick the Publican (Richard Lechmere, 1727–1814),[45] in which their situation is contrasted with the united virtue of the Whigs, the play reaches its climax in scene 3. The remnants of the council have dragged themselves into conference with Sylla, the new governor (Gen. Thomas Gage). Meagre, Dupe, and Hazlerod, holdovers from *The Adulateur,* are present, along with Simple Sapling, Dick the Publican, Hateall, and Collateralis. Unlike his predecessor, Sylla has some principle. Frustrated at being cooped up in Boston and disgusted by the sycophants who swarm about him, Sylla seeks honor, but in the old-fashioned way:

> I only wish to serve my Sov'reign well,
> And bring new glory to my master's crown,
> Which can't be done by spreading ruin round
> This loyal country. (*PP,* 16)

Calling on the memory of such British military and intellectual heroes as Hampden, Wolfe, Marlborough, Sidney, Harrington, and Locke, Sylla recognizes the nobility of the American patriots' cause and sees that the empire's fate hangs in the balance.[46]

One other item of note here concerns the incorporation in act 2, scene 3, of material related to women. Sapling has asked Sylla if his house could be used to barracks British troops—as in fact the house of Nathaniel Ray Thomas was employed in the winter of 1774–75 (*AFC,* 1:251n3). The governor, horrified, wonders in return,

> Hast thou no sons or blooming daughters there,
> . . . .
> Hast thou no wife who asks thy tender care,
> To guard her from Belona's hardy sons? (*PP,* 14)

Sapling callously replies, "Silvia's good natur'd, and no doubt will yield / And take the brawny vet'rans to her board" (*PP,* 15), suggesting that she'll do more than feed the soldiers to keep them happy. And when Dick the Publican says, "I pity Sylvia," Hateall waves off his concerns with "what's a woman's tears, / Or all the whinings of that trifling sex," offering his wife, "nut brown Kate," as an example of one reduced to submission by extortion, "crabbed words," "surly looks," and beatings.[47] Yet after all the dramatis personae have left the stage, an unnamed "Lady nearly connected with one of the principal actors in the group" speaks the valedictory: a patriotic mourning for America (*PP,* 21). As Warren will later develop the motif in her *History,* the playwright here figures suffering and justice as female—and thus further decries the American Tories (but not yet the British) for their abuse of women and thus the country. Men who with glee expose their wives to pain support no good cause.

Attributed Plays

The Blockheads

Published anonymously in early 1776, *The Blockheads: or, The Affrighted Officers. A Farce,* is a satiric drama in prose about Boston in the days of Washington's blockade, just before the British evacuation to Halifax.[48] The instigating episode in the play is Gen. John Thomas's brilliant occupation of Dorchester Heights. By quickly constructing formidable redoubts and mounting artillery that threatened British warships, the historical Thomas—a Warren correspondent—made further occupation of Boston by the British untenable. In the play, the military and their

Tory supporters show all the signs of confined rats, complaining and turning on each other. As Shallow (Maj. Gen. James Grant of the British army) remarks of their situation, "Curs'd alternative, either to be murder'd without, or starv'd within—These *yankey dogs* treat us like a parcel of poltroons" (*PP,* 3). Throughout the play, low humor and scatological imagery mark the Loyalists and British as fools—in other words, blockheads. At the end, the playwright makes merry with both the frivolousness of General Burgoyne's writing satirical plays and the title of one—*The Blockade of Boston,* an anti-Whig farce—when he and the other officers have done nothing militarily to counter the siege.

Much ink has been spilled in an attempt to make this play fit the Warren canon. Early champions of her authorship include Paul Leicester Ford and Moses Coit Tyler; Arthur Hobson Quinn, Katherine Anthony, Norman Philbrick, John Teunissen, and Walter Meserve have all assumed the play to be hers.[49] More recently, Benjamin Franklin V, Jean Kern, and Krystan Douglas have offered a number of reasons why the play could or should be assigned to Warren.[50] But ever since the theory was broached, some have had their doubts; these include Worthington C. Ford, Maud Hutcheson, and Jean Fritz.[51] Unfortunately, neither those arguing for nor those against have clinched the case.

Almost all of the evidence for her authorship is circumstantial. As a Whig satire about British officers and their toadies, the American Loyalists, in Boston, the play bears a surface resemblance to Warren's earlier work. Franklin and Douglas list other parallels, including self-incriminating characters, derogatory comments about women from the villains, and a depiction of "Tory suffering and remorse" that inspire patriot sympathies (Douglas, 90). One standard objection to the work's being Warren's—the presence of words like "shit"—Douglas and Kern dismiss as a prudish criticism of a woman who grew up on and continued to reside at a farm.

While scholars are certainly right to force us away from the image of Warren as an overly proper drawing-room lady, no argument in support of Warren's authorship is convincing enough for us to accept the play as certainly that writer's. For one thing, no manuscript evidence survives, not even a letter to or from Warren that even hints the play might be hers. Since in the case of five other plays (the three satires previously discussed and the two verse dramas from the 1780s), clear manuscript or named publication information exists to support her authorship, the absence of evidence among the carefully maintained Warren papers should be noted. Another—and to me more telling—fact is the degree of inconsistency between *The Blockheads* and the three earlier plays. Some of the character names are the same, indicating the author's familiarity with Warren's previous efforts—but in a major departure from the other three, the names do not match Warren's original attributions.[52] Meagre, who is Foster Hutchinson in *The Adulateur,* is here Harrison Gray (the Scriblerius Fribble from *The Group*); Simple, a name given to Nathaniel Ray Thomas in *The Group,* is transferred to Josiah Edson, previously called Crusty Crowbar; Timothy Ruggles (Hateall) is assigned the name Surly; John Murray (Hector Mushroom) has become Bonny; and William Brattle, the Proteus from *The Defeat,* is now called Brigadier Paunch.[53] Since it is clear that Warren took pains to create continuities among her first plays, such changes by an author make no sense. With *The Adulateur,* some other hand eagerly stepped in to "swell" Warren's original play with a "plagiary." One of the many Whig propagandists three years later might have done something similar here—create a Warren-like play, but in a more rollicking, lowbrow style, without concern over artistic connection to her earlier work.

No doubt, some readers want to see this as Warren's work. Some of it is quite funny, and in the laudable attempt to humanize a writer who has been too narrowly judged by history, sympathizers might wish to expand Warren's concept of humor to include farm jokes. A logical case can be made that this play could have been written by a woman. Nevertheless, *The Blockheads,* written in colloquial prose rather than the blank verse that marks the previous Warren plays, has a juvenile humor more like an early effort by a young adult than the later work of a mature person. For example, when Simple uses the phrase "come out, and perhaps at both ends," his wife, Jemima, entranced by British manners and hoping to engage daughter Tabitha to an officer, replies, "I like no such coarse phrazes; if I had *fifty ends,* my modesty should forbid any thing from coming out of either" (*PP,* 17). Women have more lines here than in Warren's first plays, and Jemima is lampooned; Warren's plays are generally sympathetic to the plight of women, even those married to Loyalists. Granting that she would have been *capable* of the satire and some of the off-color humor found in *The Blockheads,* but possessing not a single shred of external evidence to support her authorship, we can best categorize this play as inspired, but not written, by Mercy Warren.

The Motley Assembly

Published in Boston in 1779, *The Motley Assembly, a Farce. Published for the Entertainment of the Curious,* centers on the fashionable set in Boston and satirizes those longing for a return of the "genteel" British to that city.[54] P. L. Ford and M. C. Tyler both suggest the play is Warren's (though Tyler lukewarmly calls the attribution "not improbable"); more recent commentators generally accept Warren's authorship.[55] As with the previous play, however, no external evidence exists that leads to Warren's door; in addition, internal evidence is quite weak, there being no echoes of any of the other four plays discussed above in *The Motley Assembly.*

The play itself, a revealing document into the social tensions of postevacuation Boston, has little of the urgency of Warren's earlier plays. Mrs. Flourish and Mrs. Taxall, fashionable ladies with socially active daughters, both complain that Whig government has meant an end to the kind of elegant entertainments once put on by the British officers. Social assemblies are now "motley," leading Mrs. Flourish to forbid Miss Flourish from attending. Mr. Runt, manager of the assembly, counters by citing the example of Mr. Turncoat, a Tory who has been able to give the appearance of a switch in political allegiance to the Whig side and thus allow his daughters to attend. But Captain Aid, a Continental officer with an eye for the ladies, finds he cannot pursue women who do not also support the Revolutionary cause. At the end of the play, he and Careless, "an honest young sea captain," commiserate that however pretty a woman might be, "honour and patriotism forbid" one "to take a little damn'd paracidical viper to his bosom" (*PP,* 15). They then criticize Whigs for not being wary of falling under the influence of attractive but "dangerous" Tories.

Some of the themes of the play echo Warren's interests. In her poem "To the Hon. J. Winthrop, Esq." (1774) she criticizes certain women for desiring the latest bauble from Britain rather than "freedom." Thus, one might see the satire on socialites to be in the same vein. The playwright here also engages in a little gender warfare. In the first scene, Mrs. Flourish laments to Mr. Runt, "O why has Heaven permitted our passive sex to be so long deceived and misled by the idle and groundless opinion of the superior wisdom of the male sex!" (*PP,* 5). Since Warren's letters to women argue for the independent cultivation of the female mind, one could also see this as linking *The Motley Assembly* to her interests.

Still, these are tenuous connections. Indeed, the matter of gender conflict as expressed above more closely resembles the writings of Judith Sargent Murray than anything Warren says elsewhere. Among other problems of attribution are an "Advertisement" that identifies the writer as male[56]; a lack of correspondence between characters and persons previously satirized[57]; an absence of verse, except a crudely written poem that serves as epilogue; and a similarity in the play to modern comedies of manners rather than to tragedy, Warren's preferred model, even for satire. In addition, Warren, still living in Plymouth in 1779, would not be as familiar with the Boston social scene as someone resident in the city—a more likely candidate for authorship. While Franklin asserts that the play can "be included in Warren's canon with some confidence" (*PP,* xxiii), I must express my distinct lack of confidence, without further and more conclusive evidence, that *The Motley Assembly* is Warren's.

Sans Souci

When an irregular little comedy appeared in Boston in early 1785 satirizing members of a newly formed Tea Assembly, one reader was quick to stitch the play to Mercy Warren's cloak. *Sans Souci, alias Free and Easy: or, an Evening's Peep into a polite Circle. An Intire New Entertainment in Three Acts,* took to task those wealthy or social-climbing republicans who sought to emulate their British counterparts in operating a club whereby men and women together could play cards, dance, and the like.[58] *Sans Souci* has little plot, but it was notorious in its time, quickly selling out and instigating threats against the publisher.[59] The idea of the Tea Assembly was anathema to certain staunch patriots, and a vigorous exchange of letters in the public press between Samuel Adams, who was against it, and Warren's nephew Harrison Gray Otis, who was for it, exposed the cultural rift between a generation raised on stoical sacrifice and one glad the privations of war were finished.[60] Not surprisingly, "Guess Who," writing in the 14 February 1785 *Boston Gazette,* targets Mercy Warren as the author of this and other "illiberal abuse of newspaper essays" she allegedly has penned. His advice: stop the satire and "let the features of your sex be traced in the compositions of your pen; and thus shall you receive the applause which is due to real genius" (quoted in C. Warren 1926–27, 342).

It is highly unlikely that Mercy Warren would have bothered to write a play like this in 1785. She was busy with her historical verse dramas and her history of the Revolution; the time for little satires was past. As she writes to George on 7 March 1785, after the play's appearance, "I hope I shall never write anything I should be so much ashamed to avow as that little indigested farrago" (7 March 1785; quoted in C. Warren 1926–27, 343). Moreover, she is a character in the play. As "Mrs. W——n," she appears in one scene with her recent visitor, "Republican Heroine" Catharine Macaulay Graham. The latter opines to Mrs. W—

——n that "ladies of established character" in America should speak up against the rising tide of "dissipation" (*SS,* 12, 11). The Warren character agrees, but does not imagine the Tea Assembly will last, once the "respectable characters among them"—including Perez and Sarah Wentworth Morton—"consider the dangerous tendency of this assembly" and end it (*SS,* 12).[61] This sanguine view does not match other Warren pronouncements about the bad state of the country at this time; and anyway, she would never put herself so baldly in a play at the same time she is inscribing herself more subtly in the heroic dramas. Thus, as with the previous two attributed plays, the evidence lies against Warren's authorship; but the *Sans Souci* episode does illustrate how much of a public figure she was presumed to be in mid-1780s New England and how much some people feared the power of her pen.

Historical Verse Dramas

Prompted at least in part by a request from her son Winslow, Warren wrote two plays during her residency at Milton Hill that deserve to be considered as her major imaginative writings.[62] As the title of her 1790 *Poems, Dramatic and Miscellaneous,* indicates, she considered the plays included in that volume to be dramatic poems. Without the press of topicality or the threat of military conflict nearby, Warren used her postwar leisure to construct plays that rely more on traditional dramaturgy than on satiric wit for their effects. As a result, she seems to have written more consciously with the stage in mind, and overall she shows knowledge of the techniques used by English and French playwrights in the eras of Shakespeare and Racine.

The introduction to the first-written historical drama, *The Ladies of Castile,* is in the form of a letter, "To a Young Gentleman in Europe, at whose Request a regular Dramatick Work was first attempted" (*PDM/PP,* 99). Dated 20 February 1784, the letter explains that Warren has written this play only at the repeated behest of her "very dear friend," that is, Winslow. In the usual manner, she proclaims that the result "may not afford equal entertainment with the compositions of a Corneille, a Racine, or a Crebillon," but perhaps the recipient will still enjoy it "in your closet" even if it is not "*encored* on the stage" (*PDM/PP,* 99). Again, as with many of her poems and the early plays, she writes to meet the demand of a family member or friend but then uses the opportunity to expand her range and reflect seriously on her art and its place.

From Warren's perspective, these historical verse dramas first earn their place as texts to be read; then, if valued in the closet, as plays to be acted.

Thus it appears that as Boston and other American cities debated the presence of theater in their jurisdictions, Warren the closet dramatist had come to accept that the stage had its place in republican society. In an introductory essay for *The Sack of Rome,* "To the Public," Warren shows the change in thinking from Puritan times to the present: "Theatrical amusements may, sometimes, have been prostituted to the purposes of vice; yet, in an age of taste and refinement, lessons of morality, and the consequences of deviation may perhaps, be as successfully enforced from the stage, as by modes of instruction, less censured by the severe; while, at the same time, the exhibition of great historical events, opens a field of contemplation to the reflecting and philosophic mind" (*PDM/PP,* 11). She aligns herself with the view that the stage can be justified only if it is instructive; but then proceeds to claim that the stage is as good a school as any. Her "first wish," she says, "is to throw a mite into the scale of virtue"; her "highest ambition to meet the approbation of the judicious and worthy"—that is, "the determinations of the candid public" (*PDM/PP,* 12).

The seriousness of her determination to see her plays performed can be found in at least two places (Anthony, 150–51). She sent a copy of *The Sack of Rome,* with a dedication, to John Adams in London and requested that he try to get it staged. He dutifully showed it around to "several good Judges" as well as to two playwrights, Arthur Murphy and Richard Cumberland. But he said that regardless of quality, a play can only make it to the stage through "interest and Intrigue"; and unless the play is acted, there is no market for a printed one. Besides, added Adams, "nothing American sells here" (25 December 1787, *WAL,* 2:301). In the version published in 1790, the dedication to Adams has been removed. There is, however, an epilogue asking readers who approve of the play to request that it be staged (*PDM/PP,* 96). No record of the staging of either play can be found.

The Ladies of Castile

Given the comments in her introduction to the play and its date—20 February 1784—*The Ladies of Castile* was probably the first historical verse drama Warren wrote, although it appears second in *Poems, Dramatic and Miscellaneous.* While it lacks some of the immediacy and satiric humor of *The Group,* this new drama displays the author's skills in structure and language to better effect than any of her earlier plays. Political issues still emerge, but not in the form of a thinly veiled allegory about contemporary events; *The Ladies of Castile* strives for a more universal perspective. Winslow had defined the limits under which she must operate: nothing American, and probably nothing British (*PDM/PP,* 100). This the author laments, given the recent extraordinary events in America; but she deliberately seeks an analogue, in this case a moment in Spanish history, in its "last struggles for liberty, previous to the complete establishment of despotism by the family of Ferdinand" (*PDM/PP,* 100).

The time of the play, at least as it parallels history, is 1521–22, and most of the action occurs in the Duero River region of north-central Spain.[63] Then the Castilian king was Charles (1500–1558), whose accession to the Spanish throne in 1516 (as Charles I) was followed by his selection as emperor of the Holy Roman Empire in 1519. In that latter capacity, as Charles V, he established his imperial government in what is now Belgium, leaving his Spanish dominions to be run by regents.[64] Meanwhile, discontent among the Spanish peasantry and some nobles about Flemish influence and Charles's protracted absence led members of the Cortes, the Castilian assembly, to demand greater freedom. Eventually, the rebels formed an army, led first by Pedro de Giron and then, after he retired, by Juan de Padilla. Royalist forces defeated and captured Padilla; his wife, Maria, continued the rebellion but finally had to escape to Portugal; and the aspirations for something like democracy in Spain were crushed.

Warren focuses on the rebels and selected opponents, leaving monarchs offstage. Thus Charles himself never enters the scene, but his supporters do. This strategy is to some extent a continuation of Warren's policy in the early plays; in *The Group,* the Tories are seen as dupes not just of Hutchinson but of the unseen yet potent crown. Warren is also able to simplify an otherwise highly complex political situation. For instance, in 1521, Charles was entering into the first of several protracted conflicts with an imperial rival, King Francis I of France, and the historical Maria sought assistance from the French invaders; in the play, Warren has Don Juan refer to the defeat of Francis in Navarre (3.3) but keeps the actual battle out of sight.

Other historical figures are sometimes referred to but kept from clogging the action. These include Adrian of Utrecht, Charles's regent in Spain; his predecessor, Francisco Ximenes de Cisneros, one-time confessor to Queen Isabella, grand inquisitor, and church legalist; Ferdinand, king at various times of Castile and Leon, Aragon, Sicily, and Naples and grandfather of Charles; Joanna, daughter of Isabella and Ferdinand, wife to the short-lived Philip I (son of Emperor Maximilian I and Mary of Burgundy), mother to Charles, and technically the queen. Indeed, one has to understand the rebels' cause in the context of their assumption of authority from Joanna, whose mental illness led first her father, then her son to govern in her stead.

Sometimes Warren refers to historical figures who have no immediate relevance to the plot but whose importance is assumed by characters as they lay out the European political situation. "Calabria's injured noble prince" refers to an attempt by members of the Holy Junta, the ruling body of the rebels, to marry the widowed Joanna to the Spanish prince who ruled over southern Italy (*PDM/PP,* 112). "Solyman the great" is the Ottoman emperor Sulayman I (1494–1566), whose enthrallment to his Russian slave mistress Roxalana led him to kill his son by another slave, Mustapha (138).[65] But all the references to historical figures serve to ground Warren's drama firmly in the period; whatever the analogy of the struggle for liberty to the American one, the playwright wants no one to suspect she has not been (relatively) faithful to the actual history of Spain.

A likely source for her play is William Robertson's *The History of the Reign of the Emperor Charles V,* originally published in London in 1769, but available in American editions as early as 1770. An enormously popular work at the time and for many years thereafter, Robertson's history was already in a fourth London edition by 1782.[66] Most of the action in Warren's play can be traced in the early pages of Robertson's book 3, with background references tied to material in book 1.[67] Because Robertson at the outset of his work sets the context of his history with the Fall of Rome, it is also possible that Warren conceived the idea for *The Sack of Rome* while writing *The Ladies of Castile.* As in her other historical verse drama, in *Ladies* Warren draws her own emphases and conclusions, especially with female characters.

At the outset of the play, two nobles, Don Juan de Padilla and Don Francis (Maldonada), discourse on liberty and will. Don Juan speaks from ideological purity, a spokesman for freedom in the high Whig style; he chides his friend for growing soft over love for Louisa, the sister (in the play) of their Royalist opponent, Conde de Haro: "When virtue arms, and liberty's the prize, / No cloud should set on brave Don Francis' brow" (*PDM/PP,* 104).[68] Thus Warren links a love plot to a liberty theme and shows how the two frequently enter into conflict.

In contrast, Don (Inigo de) Velasco, the high constable of Castile and historically a regent appointed by Charles to aid the foreigner Adrian, speaks of his desire "to crush this rebel race"; his son, Conde de Haro, adopts a more liberal view, recognizing the appeal of the "great ideas of liberty and law" with which the rebels have inspired themselves (*PDM/PP,* 107). Warren's Velasco is a descendant of her Rapatio, although not comic in the least, but single-minded in his determination to "chase these miscreants from the land— / Cut down their line, and blast their idle hopes, / And extirpate the bold seditious race" (*PDM/PP,* 108). A second theme, then, is might versus right, Machiavellian power contrasted with high virtue and idealized justice. Within both camps, however, are internal conflicts: father against son, warrior against panting lover.

The Ladies of Castile shows a marked advance from Warren's earlier political plays in complexity of character and motive; Conde de Haro, for instance, is largely a right-thinking man trapped by circumstances and filial duty on the wrong side. Whereas characters in *The Group,* for instance, sometimes express their doubts about being Tories but eventually fall into line with their models of wickedness, here de Haro never entirely forfeits his dignity despite being the agent for the patriot de Padilla's defeat. At the same time, the rebels have their own traitor, Don Pedro de Ghiron (Warren's spelling). Although historically it is unclear entirely what de Giron's motives were for first getting command of the rebel army, then blundering away advantages and allowing the army to lose key territory, and finally retiring to his citadel, Warren shows that being a member of the right cause cannot make up for deficiencies of character; she leaves no doubt that de Ghiron is a villain, while de Haro, despite his opposition to the rebels, earns some respect.

Warren's most dynamic character is Donna Maria (Pacheco), wife of Don Juan and, in the play, sister of Don Francis. A fierce republican, Donna Maria will go to great lengths to secure victory for the rebel side. One famous episode from history was Maria's disguised looting of the cathedral at Toledo in order to help finance the army. In the play, Maria puts her action into the context of modern thinking and justice:

> To make atonement for the guilt of men,
> Altars are dress'd, and saintly relics shine:—
> Instead of real sanctity of heart
> They churches decorate with costly gifts:—
> But reason, bursting from a sable cloud,

On a bright throne erects her regal stand,
And gives new sanctions from the voice of God,
To free the mind from superstition's reign.
No fables, legends, dreams, or monkish tales,
Shake my firm purpose, or disarm my mind,
When duty calls to make my country free.
The churches' treasures were our last resort. (*PDM/PP,* 113)

In Robertson, Maria is presented as having "a boldness superior to those superstitious fears which often influence her sex" (168)—an attitude that Warren confronts. When Don Francis speaks of her plan to strip the church of its wealth, he remarks,

Thy soul was form'd to animate the arm
Of some illustrious, bold, heroic chief,
And not to waste its glorious fire away,
Beneath the weakness of a female form. (*PDM/PP,* 114).

This stereotyping elicits a blistering response from Maria:

Men rail at weaknesses themselves create,
And boldly stigmatize the female mind,
As though kind nature's just impartial hand
Had form'd its features in a baser mould:
But nice distinctions in the human soul,
Adopted follies, or inherent vice,
May be discuss'd in calmer times than these:—
We'll reason then—if possible regain
Whatever nature, or its author gave. (*PDM/PP,* 114)

For Warren, Donna Maria represents the woman of unimpeachable motives. Her actions all speak for liberty and sacrifice yet at the same time demonstrate the capabilities of the sex. Maria shares Warren's own view that in times of national crisis, gender conflict serves only to debilitate the cause; Maria also, however, speaks to the author's belief that there is no distinction in nature between male and female intellect. If anything, *The Ladies of Castile* most fully represents the Warren brand of feminism: Women prove by doing, not by pining, but men must own up to the distortions in their old beliefs and, out of the nobility of their souls (if they possess it), grant to women equal opportunity for rational, patriotic, and noble behavior.

In a scene that deviates from history, Warren takes this issue of woman's perceived "weakness" even further. After de Padilla's defeat, capture, and death sentence, de Haro arranges for a disguised furlough to allow Don Juan to meet his wife one last time. Their meeting produces the expected joy and anguish, and when her husband departs to go back to prison and certain death, Maria must face up to both the feelings in her heart and the predicted response of a distraught woman. Her struggle represents thinking that is vintage Warren:

> But shall Maria shroud herself in grief,
> And sink beneath life's disappointed hopes,
> A feeble victim to her own despair?—
> A soul, inspir'd by freedom's genial warmth,
> Expands—grows firm—and by resistance, strong:
> The most successful prince that offers life,
> And bids me live upon ignoble terms,
> Shall learn from me that virtue seldom fears. (*PDM/PP,* 162)

Maria's continued leadership and defiance mark the dramatic interest of the last part of the play, but even so, Warren sometimes plays a more traditional card. When Conde de Haro comes to her after her husband's death to profess his love for her, she imagines he only wants to enslave her and calls on "heavens and earth" to "Revenge this outrage on my feeble sex!" (*PDM/PP,* 166). Coming so late in the drama, long after Maria has stated and shown otherwise, her defense of her "feeble sex" makes little sense. Indeed, when de Haro finally arranges for her and her son to escape, the play collapses. In its evocation of Romanized dramas like Addison's *Cato* and fated-lover plays like Shakespeare's *Romeo and Juliet,* the double suicide of Louisa and Don Francis in the last scene adds gore, but it detracts from the play's powerful treatment of a united defiance of tyranny by a man and woman of strong character. Don Juan and Donna Maria—no doubt reflecting James and Mercy Warren—convert scenes with the potential for melodramatic expressions of love into displays of stoical patriotic duty. This heroic pair show the other characters, who still pursue each other with foolish and self-destructive passions, to be weak, however shrill their death-rattle rhetoric.

Except for the responses of some of Warren's contemporaries, reaction to this play and to *The Sack of Rome* has rarely been favorable. The *Massachusetts Magazine* reviewer sees a parallel between *The Ladies of Castile* and the American Revolutionary situation in 1775 (628). For her part, Judith Sargent Murray, writing in the *Gleaner,* admires Donna Maria and calls Warren "the *Roland* of America" (764). Nevertheless, beginning with her son George, to whom she first showed the historical dramas, critics have found her alleged faults to define their response (Fritz 1972, 234). Elizabeth Ellet thinks both *Sack* and *Ladies* to be "more remarkable for patriotic sentiment than dramatic merit"; despite the poetic qualities of Warren's writing, she finds the language "often wanting in the simplicity essential to true pathos" (103–4). Alice Brown—herself a playwright—dismisses the plays as "long and very dull" (183), while Walter Meserve (74) and Benjamin Franklin V (*PP,* xxiv) stress their conventionality. Gerald Weales remarks what many seem to think: the verse dramas are "static affairs full of high moralizing, reminiscent of the kind of ponderous English play best exemplified by Joseph Addison's *Cato*" (Weales, 891).

Of the two historical plays, *The Ladies of Castile* has in recent years garnered more attention than *The Sack of Rome.* Katherine Anthony calls it "by far the most powerful writing that Mercy had ever done" (149). But, more important, critics have discovered in Donna Maria a character of power who may stand for an expanded view of female abilities. Franklin refers to her as "the most convincing character in Warren's last two plays" (*PP,* xxv). Beyond that, as Emily Watts claims, Maria is a mother and a hero, wiser than any male character (41–42). The most influential recent commentary is that of Linda Kerber, who sees in *Ladies* not only a strong female figure (Maria) contrasted with a weak one (Louisa) but also the whole American Revolution and its aftermath encoded within.[69] In the most complete critical discussion, Cheryl Oreovicz, while recognizing aesthetic flaws in the play, most fully describes the "salutary" heroism of Maria for other characters.[70] The purport of these last critics is that *The Ladies of Castile* should not be dismissed as a dilettante's parlor drama; in its reflection of the Revolution and the tensions within 1780s American culture, the play deserves more and better attention than it has received.

The Sack of Rome

Printed as the first item in Warren's *Poems, Dramatic and Miscellaneous,* the blank verse play *The Sack of Rome. A Tragedy in Five Acts,* demonstrates her continued interest in finding parallels in world history to the American Revolution.[71] Like *The Ladies of Castile,* however, *The Sack of Rome* takes on a theme larger than local politics—the fall of empire through corruption—and establishes the action firmly in the historical past.

The period dramatized is A.D. 453–455, when Rome—the major city but no longer the capital of the Western empire—is once again threatened by barbarian invasion.[72] The first sack of Rome by Alaric and the Visigoths in 410 was memorialized by St. Augustine in *City of God,* and Warren may have felt that it had achieved sufficient notoriety without her efforts. The particular plundering of Rome she writes of was in fact a more fatal blow to the empire, but as she says in her introduction, "the author of a piece, now offered the public, does not recollect to have seen the weakness and cruelty of *Valentinian*—the character of *Petronius Maximus*—the resentment, indiscretion and revenge of *Edoxia*—(the more immediate causes of the invasion of the imperial city, by the Vandals)—chosen for the subject of theatrical instruction" (*PDM/PP,* 9). In consonance with her idea that the stage should be didactic, she feels the world has need for such a work.

Roman history during the middle of the fifth century is a swirl of tribes, battles, kings, and emperors. Hardly a simple story of internal corruption by effete politicians and external invasion by unwashed German hordes—though from Warren's view that polarity figures prominently—the politics of the period involve peoples from several regions in Europe and Asia as well as Roman individuals of good and bad character. The emperor of whom Warren writes was Valentinian III (419–455), son of Constantius III (emperor for seven months in 421) and Galla Placidia, sister to the emperor in the West, Honorius (384–423), and regent for the first years of her child's reign (425–c.432). During Valentinian's rule, a number of notable invasions of the empire took place. In the north, the Huns, sometime allies of the Romans, turned against both the Eastern government at Constantinople and the Western one at Ravenna and stretched their hegemony from Asia to Western Europe. Under the fierce Attila (406[?]–53), who at the start of Warren's play is spoken of as still alive, the Huns suffered their single defeat at the hands of a combined force of Visigoths under Theodoric and Romans under Aetius. From Gaul, however, the Huns moved southeast to Italy and encamped outside Rome; only the pope, Leo I, was able to dissuade Attila from sacking the city.[73]

Meanwhile, in North Africa, another band, the Germanic Vandals, had left their power base in Spain and crossed at Gibraltar to aid the Roman count, a general named Boniface, in his rebellion against the government at Ravenna. The Vandal king, Genseric (or Gaiseric), not content with helping Boniface, ended up taking control himself, defeating Boniface—a rival of Aetius—and occupying Carthage in 439. Despite new treaties with Ravenna that gave him enormous power in Africa, Genseric eventually used his navy to cross over into Italy. Warren chooses to begin her play at the moment when Rome is threatened by the Huns to the north and the Vandals to the south.

Yet these threats, certainly real enough in 453 to figures like Aetius who had few military resources to combat them, were not seen by Warren as the cause of Rome's collapse and were not the basis of her interest in this period. In keeping with her belief that the stage should be moral, she explains that at this moment in history, "the character of man was sunk to the lowest stage of depravity." That is, corruption—"the habits of every species of luxury"—coupled with superstition and ignorance, is what sinks empire (*PDM/PP,* 9). Given Warren's own attacks on the iniquities of imperial British manners and her fears that enervating dissipation was threatening the republican virtue of postwar America, her assertion that Rome furnishes matter for both moralist and philosopher matches her desire to play those roles in the infant republic (*PDM/PP,* 10). Nevertheless, to the author's credit, the play offers no ready nostrums or overly melodramatic depiction of vice and virtue.

At the beginning of the play, the general Aetius and his son Gaudentius appear as noble Romans of the old stripe. Aetius especially sees little will from emperor or citizens to fight the threatening "boors" that gather outside Rome, but Gaudentius voices the hope that

> If party rage and luxury should cease,
> And peace give time to make a just reform
> Through each corrupted channel of the law;
> Or if simplicity again returns,
> And government more energy assumes,
> Her ancient codes restor'd on equal terms,
> She yet might reign from Danube to the Po. (*PDM/PP,* 16)

Unfortunately, their friend and one of Rome's leading citizens, Petronius Maximus, grows increasingly distracted over the death of his wife, Ardelia. She has been raped by the emperor, and thus his concerns center on his grief and quandary over the implications of seeking revenge—not on fighting the Huns. Momentary good news arrives in Rome when Bishop Leo announces the death of Attila.

Meanwhile, Valentinian, fearing both Petronius Maximus and Aetius, who have reason to be angry with him, is goaded by his eunuch Heraclius into attempting to kill both men, but succeeds only in murdering Aetius (who historically had been the effective ruler of Rome during Valentinian's majority). Gaudentius, promised in marriage to one of the emperor's daughters, Eudocia, finds his love for her complicated first by his accusation that her father has killed his; then by the assassination of Valentinian (as well as Heraclius) by Maximus and the barbarian warrior, Traulista; and finally by her charge that Gaudentius has sanctioned the counterkilling. In the confusion following Valentinian's death, Maximus becomes emperor and claims Valentinian's wife, Edoxia, as his own.

At this point, the action picks up speed. Edoxia resists becoming the wife of her husband's murderer and calls Genseric to her aid. Maximus flees; Genseric plunders Rome; Hunneric, Genseric's son, claims Eudocia as his and plots with Traulista to kill Gaudentius; surprised by the assassins, Gaudentius kills Traulista; Hunneric in turn kills Gaudentius; and before the Vandals take Edoxia and her daughters back to Carthage, Eudocia avoids ravishment and dies of grief on the corpse of her now-redeemed lover and defender, Gaudentius.

Whatever other sources she might have used—she had probably studied Roman history with her brothers at Reverend Russell's—Warren quite likely referred to the early volumes of Edward Gibbon's *Decline and Fall of the Roman Empire.*[74] Most of the action can be found in chapters 35 and 36 of Gibbon's history (569–73), but other turns of phrase and little tidbits of information can be found over the course of several chapters. Warren does more, however, than merely put Gibbon's narrative into acts and scenes; she rewrites the narrative to match what she perceives as theatrical demands for a love plot. Overall, she is relatively faithful to her source, but some details, particularly those involving the women characters, she enlarges or alters for the purposes of the drama.

In fact, Warren converts the entire episode into one in which either the way men treat women or the words and actions of the women themselves define the characters. The wife of Petronius Maximus, Ardelia, while she never appears in her own right, is spoken of as "the good—the chaste Ardelia— / The first and fairest matron left in Rome!" (*PDM/PP,* 19).[75] Thus her violation, coming at a time when Maximus has attained popular favor, is seen as especially execrable. The rape sets in motion the series of events that lead to Valentinian's murder, the corrupted demand by the new emperor that Edoxia submit to his desires, and Edoxia's invitation to Genseric to enter Rome. Edoxia's daughters, Placidia and particularly Eudocia, are in some ways the stock virgins of so much of late eighteenth-century literature, torn by the entreaties of lovers, filial duty, and the fear of seduction or forced sex.[76] As such, Eudocia makes clear that Gaudentius cannot be worthy of her until he repudiates the assassination of her father—regardless of his vile deeds—and adopts a higher moral course. At the end, Eudocia's choosing to die marks Hunneric as an inconceivable lover for a woman of such lofty motives and spotless reputation.[77]

The most complex of the female characters is Edoxia. In the play, she makes much of her "Horatian" blood line, claiming descent from Valerius Poplicola, a perhaps mythical figure said to be an originator of the consul system in Rome in 509 B.C.[78] This claim of antiquity gives her the strength to be decisive and a cause for her husband's fear. After Valentinian has raped Ardelia and ordered the death of Aetius, Edoxia enters, prompting this from the emperor:

> But hah!—here comes my torment—
> My other conscience—to kill me with a look—
> The fair—the excellent—the wrong'd Edoxia;
> Her presence freezes all my powers of speech;
> I dare not lift my eye to meet her frown—
> I'm all confusion—guilt—perdition—death. (*PDM/PP,* 28)

Yet far from dwelling on her wrongs, she urges practical action based on the principle expressed in the lines, "Forgive my lord, my soft officious care / To guard thy peace from each domestick foe" (*PDM/PP,* 29). Preserving her husband and daughters from harm, decrying the turmoil of the times, resisting Petronius's advances, Edoxia has much in common with Warren's model of the republican heroine. But she makes one mistake: inviting Genseric. By not making the final sacrifice, foregoing revenge, she brings, as Gaudentius tells her,

> Those savage, hostile guests to riot there,
> To subjugate the state—subvert thy house,
> To extirpate thy name, and rudely reign
> And triumph o'er the West. (*PDM/PP,* 75)

As with Petronius Maximus of the wealthy Anician house, who, seduced by luxury, carries his revenge too far, Edoxia forfeits some of the moral power she seeks to exert.[79]

In the end, the Fall of Rome, figured in the deaths of the young and virtuous Gaudentius and Eudocia, registers as a tragedy. No one character in Warren's play reaches tragic proportions, however, although either

Petronius Maximus or Edoxia might have been targeted for these ends. Rather, the loss of leading citizens to the corruptions of wealth, the betrayals of confederates, and the lusts of emperors, along with the promised decimation of high culture by the barbarians, make the collective empire the hero who rises, then falls by pride.

In the world of the play, however, two lessons emerge: one is that blind revenge always leads to disaster, regardless of the justice of cause; the other is that good treatment of women and good behavior by women preserve the essential virtue of a culture. When the barbarian Traulista chides Gaudentius for his softness in worrying about whether Eudocia will approve of him—thus advocating an amoral, antifeminine cult of war—we see in his death at the hands of Eudocia's defender Warren's commentary on the origin of true masculine strength. To Americans reading the play, Warren is saying, Remember the principles of the Revolution. Don't be swayed by the material corruptions of (the British) empire; don't become obsessed by revenge against those thought to be traitors. Keep to the path of republican rectitude, as imaged by the moral and filial virgin, and rise above party divisions and internal squabbling that might expose the country to external destruction. The strength of the play is that Warren does not make the message obvious.

In her own lifetime, Warren was praised by *Massachusetts Magazine,* which reported that *The Sack of Rome* "preserves a confidence of character, and energy of language, not often excelled" (*PDM* review, 560). Her most noteworthy champion for this play as well as for *The Ladies of Castile* was Judith Sargent Murray. In essay 96 of the *Gleaner,* Murray cites Warren as an example of a good playwright whose works yet go unproduced in America. Using a male persona, Murray at first claims that her counterpart's fame is already well trumpeted, but "he is constrained to say, that her excellent tragedies abound with the pathetic, the beautiful, and the sublime, and that they apparently possess sufficient scenic merit and variety of situation to bestow those *artificial advantages* which are necessary to insure their *stage effect*" (763–64). The value of Murray's commentary is that it is geared toward possible stage production. She can easily imagine her favorite actress, Mrs. S. Powell, in the roles of Edoxia or Eudocia[80]; the characters of Gaudentius and Maximus as they mourn their losses she finds especially moving. Her point, though, goes beyond Warren to the state of drama reception in America: "If compositions of this description find no place on the American stage, what can the more humble adventurer expect?" (764)

Modern criticism of *The Sack of Rome* follows largely along the lines of *The Ladies of Castile.* Emily Watts asserts that both plays "are better than most of the bombast created by her contemporaries. . . . the plays feature noble women acting decisively in times of national crisis" (40–41). Watts is nearly unique in believing *The Sack of Rome* to be Warren's better historical verse drama (41–42). Following up on the *Cato* connection suggested by Gerald Weales, Cheryl Oreovicz offers the most incisive criticism of the play: "One problem Warren fails to solve in *The Sack* is the proper balance between the twin concerns of the heroic play, the conventional conflict between honor and love or between virtue and passion as they impinge on human values and the actions these values inspire" (Oreovicz 1992, 198). While Aetius rightly should be the moral center, his early death leaves the mantle to Gaudentius; but that youth, Oreovicz argues, "is too dull or blinded by love to see Rome for what it is" (199). Thus with only an "antihero" as the object of grief, the play lacks the moral force Warren may have helped to convey.

Despite that criticism, *The Sack of Rome,* even more than *The Ladies of Castile,* needs reevaluation. Warren's careful attention to historical antecedents suggests that the ideal republican drama can teach lessons to an educated populace of both men and women without the author's having to create cardboard characters or one-dimensional plots of virtue and vice. If the playwright has not found "balance," she has managed to work in a theme of great complexity—that of sorting out true republicanism from its shallower, baser shadow.

Chapter Five

Political Essays and History of the Revolution

During the 1780s, while she lived in the former Thomas Hutchinson house at Milton, Warren essentially completed her career as a belletrist. With no more plays to write after *The Sack of Rome* and only a very few occasional poems, Warren devoted her last decades to correspondence and to prose writings of a political-historical nature. The major work was her three-volume history of the Revolution, but some years prior to its appearance, she published an essay and an introduction to a work by Catharine Macaulay that give some insight into her political thought.

Political Essays

In the fall of 1787, as the draft of the Constitution was being sent to the state conventions for ratification, Mercy and James Warren declared their vehement opposition to the document. They, Elbridge Gerry, Richard Henry Lee, and a few other prominent patriots complained that the proposed government was another version of the despotism they had freed themselves from only a few years before. With no guarantees of individual liberties, great power vested in the chief executive, and new limitations attached to the rights of states, the Constitution seemed completely antithetical to the kind of pure republicanism imagined by the Warrens. As part of the local Anti-Federalist opposition to ratification, James wrote a series of essays under the pen names Helvidius Priscus and A Republican Federalist.[1] Other letters and articles by Warren acquaintances Elbridge Gerry and James Winthrop (writing as Agrippa) stirred up the wrath of the proconstitutional Federalists. With an issue of such moment before the American people and with her husband and friends joining the fray, Mercy Warren could hardly keep silent.

Her essay, *Observations on the new Constitution, and on the Federal and State Conventions. By a Columbian Patriot,* appeared as a pamphlet in February 1788. Long thought to be the work of other writers (Elbridge

Gerry was often assigned authorship), *Observations* was written with the intention of swaying those states that had yet to vote for ratification. Massachusetts was one, but despite having the majority at the beginning of its convention, the Anti-Federalists had already been defeated and the Constitution ratified by the time Warren's essay was in print.[2] Many copies were then shipped to New York, but the local Anti-Federalist Committee in Albany thought the piece written "in a style too sublime and florid for the common people in this part of the country" (quoted in C. Warren 1930–32, 144). Despite expressing what in her own state was a majority voice, Warren discovered that her essay, like those of other Anti-Federalists, could not stop the Federalist juggernaut from securing ratification.

Regardless of the problem of style—the Albany committeeman had a point—and the essay's consequent lack of influence at the time, *Observations* is notable for several reasons: it is the only significant Anti-Federalist publication by a woman; it contains a vigorous defense of radical republicanism; and it displays many influences on Warren's thought.[3]

Early in her essay, the author establishes what she sees as essential "political axioms," namely,

> that man is born free and possessed of certain unalienable rights—that government is instituted for the protection, safety, and happiness of the people, and not for the profit, honour, or private interest of any man, family, or class of men—That the origin of all power is in the people, and that they have an incontestable right to check the creatures of their own creation, vested with certain powers to guard the life, liberty and property of the community: And . . . the people have an undoubted right to reject their decisions, to call for a revision of their conduct, to depute others in their room, or . . . to demand further time for deliberation on matters of the greatest moment.[4]

The Constitution, in her view, gave public officials too much security in their posts. In the way of the old Massachusetts colonial elections, she argues for one-year terms as well as an undefined right to recall officials or by some popular mandate to reject their decisions. In short, Warren's views are dangerously close to democracy, a form of governance rejected by many of the people we style the Founding Fathers.

Warren is clearly influenced by a strain of English Whig thought that goes back at least to Algernon Sidney (1622–83). That English political theorist, accused of conspiracy and executed, argued for the continued right of the people to overturn governments that separated themselves from a free people.[5] Her demand that "trial by jury in civil causes" be retained she derives from William Blackstone, *Commentaries on the Laws of England* (*Observations,* 7). She even quotes Cervantes's *Don Quixote* in a dark joke about American liberties being sent to "the *Federal City*" (1).

Perhaps the most interesting set of influences on *Observations* are those of French writers. For the most part, when Warren mentions figures from the French Enlightenment, she does so critically; Voltaire, for instance, is a favorite whipping boy, largely for his denigration of religion. In her attack on the Constitution, however, she mentions two with favor: Gabriel Bonnot de Mably (1709–85) and Claude Adrien Helvétius (1722–71). Abbé Mably's *Observations sur le gouvernement et les loix des Etats-Unis d'Amérique,* addressed to John Adams, whom Mably knew personally, had appeared in English translation the year of its first publication in French, 1784.[6] In that work, titled in English as *Remarks concerning the Government and the Laws of the United States of America,* Mably surveys the various state constitutions and comments on the features of American political thought he admires and those he finds to be cause for concern (including the freedoms of religion and the press). Before that time, however, Mably had written several books on classical civilization, and it is likely that Warren knew his *Observations on the Romans* (English translation, 1751). What she culls from a writer who had a reputation as a radical thinker—but whose *Remarks* show a deep suspicion of democracy—are comments that justify extreme measures to root out incipient despotism in government.[7]

The case of Helvétius is more complex. Even among the philosophers, the author of *De l'Esprit* (1758) and the posthumously published *De l'Homme* (1772) was thought to be a dangerous thinker. Arguing from the premise that all human beings have equal abilities, Helvétius urged, as did Locke, that environment and education determine differences. This accords with a philosophy of radical democracy, but Helvétius was also a hedonist, further maintaining that government should defer to the pleasures of the people. Again, Warren is selective, quoting a passage to the effect that despotism is the worst "'enemy to publick welfare'" (*Observations,* 2). Willing to consider the ideas of French writers who were thought to be extreme in their time, Warren nonetheless reads them to support a philosophy of traditional English liberties minus a monarchy and landed or legal aristocracy.[8]

This issue would come up again in a brief unsigned introduction written by Warren for Catharine Macaulay's *Observations on the Reflections of the*

Right Hon. Edmund Burke.[9] Possibly at the prompting of James Winthrop, Warren sent the London imprint of her friend's rebuttal to Burke to her publishers in Boston, Thomas and Andrews, who republished it in late 1791.[10] For Burke, one-time supporter of American liberties, the French Revolution was all wrong in its excesses and its constitution. By contrast, Macaulay affirmed popular sovereignty, announcing instead that the French Revolution was a case unique "in that *perfect* unanimity in the people" and the display of "a *sudden spread of an enlightened spirit*" (Macaulay 1791, 10). Warren shares Macaulay's views, claiming that "Whatever convulsions [may] yet be occasioned by the revolution in France, it will doubtless be favourable to general liberty, and Mr. Burke may undesignedly be an instrument of its promotion, by agitating questions which have for a time lain dormant in England, and have been almost forgotten, or *artfully disguised,* in America" (Macaulay 1791, 2).

Warren's support for Macaulay against Burke put her once again among the more radical Whigs in America, not out of any special love for France but out of conviction that any government that limits popular authority is a bad one. Although the death of Winslow quieted her public voice until the appearance of her *History,* Warren would hold onto a faith in republicanism that would survive even the dark days of the French Revolution.

History of the Revolution

When precisely Mercy Warren began her book on the Revolution is not clear, but she was well into gathering materials from the earliest days of armed conflict. On or near 5 November 1775, in response to a short note from her Plymouth friend, Abigail Adams tells Warren, "I hope the Historick page will increase to a volume. Tis this hope that has kept me from complaining of my friends Laconick Epistles" (*AFC,* 1:322). Five months later, on 17 April 1776, Warren writes to Abigail from Watertown that after entertaining the family of George Washington, "I kept house a week amusing myself with my Book, my work and sometimes a Letter to an absent Friend" (*AFC,* 1:386). And more than a year later, on 14 August 1777, Adams complains that "a certain person who once put their Hand to the pen" has stopped writing her history at a time when "many memorable Events which ought to be handed down to posterity will be buried in oblivion" (*AFC,* 2:313).

Start and stop that history Warren did for three decades. She was probably finished with most of it by 1791, but the death of Winslow in that year caused her to put it and nearly all writing but letters aside. As she tells her readers in her prefatory remarks, the "several years [that] have elapsed" since the book had taken its present form were the result of many factors: "Local circumstances, the decline of health, temporary deprivations of sight, the death of the most amiable of children, 'the shaft flew thrice, and thrice my peace was slain,' have sometimes prompted to throw by the pen in despair" (*H,* 1:v). If she did throw by her pen, she never forgot where it lay.

Even in grief or physical pain, she did not lose her interest in events; and some time during the 1790s, perhaps after Washington's retirement from public life in 1797 but before his death two years later, she began again, eventually bringing the book as far as the end of John Adams's administration in 1801. By the early 1800s, however, Warren's eyesight had deteriorated to the point where she could do little writing herself. With the help of her son James, who wrote out the last drafts, and the Reverend James Freeman, who helped with publishing details, Warren prepared the work that occupied nearly half of her life. After frustrating delays by the printer, volume one of *The History of the Rise, Progress and Termination of the American Revolution. Interspersed with Biographical, Political and Moral Observations* by "Mrs. Mercy Warren" came off the press in late 1805, with copies of the complete three-volume set not reaching booksellers and subscribers until 1806 and 1807.[11]

In Warren's day, books were often sold by subscription; that is, in advance of publication, friends, family, and selected public figures were solicited to commit to purchasing one or more books—or in this case, sets—to help defray costs and give the publisher some reasonable assurance that his investment would be recouped.[12] For the *History,* Warren turned to some who had helped her with her first book; one of those, the recently reelected president Thomas Jefferson, subscribed himself and, as he told her in letter, managed to encourage all the "heads of departments" in Washington not already on a list to subscribe as well (8 February 1805, *WAL,* 2:345). To her nephew, the Federalist Harrison Gray Otis, Warren had to make a special subscription appeal, assuring him that her history was not a "party" work, and therefore he should not be afraid to encourage sales of his republican aunt's books (4 February 1805, HGOP3).

Yet as one of the people assisting her made clear, Warren fought an uphill battle. Two histories of the Revolution had appeared within a few years of the 1783 peace treaty: the Englishman William Gordon's *The History of the Rise, Progress, and Establishment of the Independence of the United States of America* (1788) and the American David Ramsay's *The History of the American Revolution* (1789). As her solicitor and longtime champion Judith Sargent Murray made clear, however, a more recent work cut directly into Warren's subscriptions: John Marshall's *The Life of George Washington* (1804–1807). Instead of names on a list, she tells Warren in a letter, Murray for her efforts only received "apologies"; Marshall's work, her acquaintances said, "forestals, if not wholly precludes, the utility of this history." Murray lists other obstacles: "the political principles attributed to the otherwise admired writer" composed one obstacle (in other words, the septuagenarian Warren was thought a radical by conservative Bostonians); the fact that "in this Commercial Country, a taste for Literature has not yet obtained the ascendency" was another (*WAL,* 2:346). But one reason she does not give must have certainly been on her mind. As Murray, in her capacity as champion of female authorship, well knew, Mercy Warren's history was the only contemporary study of the Revolution by a woman. That fact alone was enough to prevent its popularity then—though it is certainly one reason to look at it now.

Nevertheless, despite the obstacles and apologies she faced, the *History* was an impressive work; in three volumes (with appendixes, more than 1,300 pages total), the book covers 40 years (1761–1801) of the most extraordinary period of American history to that time. Written by someone who knew many of the principals personally, who had at her disposal not only official documents but also letters addressed to her and her husband as well as others lent by friends, and who was aware early on that the events she describes were worthy of a history, Warren's work has value for us now both for what it includes and what it—sometimes by design—omits.

Volume 1 begins with what is essentially Warren's last piece of public expository prose, "An Address to the Inhabitants of the United States," dated March 1805; in it she outlines her reasons for writing, the difficulties she faced in completing the project, and her hopes for the country and for the treatment of her book. In chapter 1 she provides a brief history of America from the early settlers to the 1760s. The remaining nine chapters cover events from the Stamp Act protests of 1765 and the stormy governorships of Francis Bernard, Thomas Hutchinson, and Thomas Gage to the beginning battles, the debates in Parliament, the Declaration of Independence, and the campaigns in the middle states in 1776 and 1777. Volume 2 (chapters 11–20) describes the northern campaigns, including the battle of Saratoga, political debates on both sides of the Atlantic, and the southern campaigns, ending with Cornwallis's army entering Virginia in summer 1781. Volume 3 (chapters 21–31) examines the final battles, including the great American victory at Yorktown; the various treaty negotiations with European countries; the recriminations in England with the failure of British military policy in the now-former colonies; and, in a last chapter of nearly 100 pages, the events in the first 12 years of the new republic. Each volume has additional material in the back, often long passages from other works, which serve as supplements to Warren's narrative or observations.

The *History* differs considerably from historical works of the present era. Like many even now, Warren's book has a narrative thread; she chooses to style that narrative, however, as a somewhat progressive moral story, with examples chosen from events and people as much for their moral value as political or military importance. She also reflects frequently on philosophical issues: the elements constituting human nature, the relative merits of republican and other forms of government, and public morality being three of the most important. Finally, she digresses on many occasions to offer observations on various aspects of America: on its history, national character, relations with American Indians and foreign powers, the meaning of the Revolution, and the country's future.

According to historian Michael Kammen, Warren's book, along with the other histories written at that time, has "an antique quality . . . and a rather tedious tone."[13] To be sure, the *History* employs a historiographic method that is out of fashion now; but a response that dismisses the work as "tedious" fails to account for Warren's narrative strategies. For Warren, as evidenced in her letters and her history, a woman writing means a teacher teaching. Without the stuff that comprises what Kammen identifies as its "antique quality," history, in her view, would hardly be worth the writing. Even more, the *History* brings together Warren's literary, historical, philosophical, religious, and interpersonal thinking and feeling in a more comprehensive way than does any other of her works.

Warren sees history as purposeful chronology, an inexhaustible source of moral lessons, and a genre whose importance demands an attention to style and posterity. Above all, one must draw from it a code of behavior that can stand as a model for future generations. As Lester H. Cohen remarks, she writes "self-consciously . . . in [the] tradition of exemplary history."[14] In Warren's version of that tradition, the example reigns in place of comprehensiveness; as she says at one point, the "primary object" of her book "is not a dry narrative of military havoc" (*H,* 1:386n). In the first two paragraphs of chapter 1, she identifies explicitly what she has in mind by her use of the key title word:

> History, the deposite of crimes, and the record of every thing disgraceful or honorary to mankind, requires a just knowledge of character, to investigate the sources of action; a clear comprehension, to review the combination of causes; and precision of language, to detail the events that have produced the most remarkable revolutions.
>
> To analyze the secret springs that have effected the progressive changes in society; to trace the origin of the various modes of government, the consequent improvements in science, in morality, or the national tincture that marks the manners of the people under despotic or more liberal forms, is a bold and adventurous work. (1–2)

Warren begins the story part of her book with the "forefathers," the word her generation used to refer to the early English settlers in America. These were a people fleeing religious persecution, but their "indiscreet zeal" often displayed a spirit of "illiberality" that was at odds with their sufferings. Many of these "errors" can be blamed on "the fashion of the times," but such an instance of persecution as that of the Quakers by the Puritans "can never be justified either by the principles of policy or humanity." Thus what we see here becomes the narrative model for the rest: noble instigating motivations in a people with "persevering and self-denying virtues"; struggles by those people with forces from without (British government, Quakers, and the like); errors, even inexcusable ones, or other failures by persons who should know better; and the eventual triumph of the people of principle whose story this is (*H,* 1:13).

Although Warren is remarkably evenhanded in her approach to the Pilgrims and Puritans, avoiding unquestioning worship, she does borrow her narrative method from the latter. Her history is in essence an extended jeremiad. The *jeremiad* is a sermonic form that has several functions: to remind people of their sturdy founders; to review for them the originating ideals; to call people to account for their failures in keeping the first principles alive; to prophesy their doom for continued inaction or misfeasance; to picture the glory that awaits them for timely restoration of the founding virtues. This design appears not only in sermons or in sermon-style poems—for example, Michael Wigglesworth's "God's Controversy with New-England" (1662)—but also in such Puritan histories as Cotton Mather's *Magnalia Christi Americana* (1702). And as Sacvan Bercovitch points out, the jeremiad survives not only the Puritan era but Mercy Warren's as well, in one form or another.[15]

But there are differences between Puritan jeremiads and Mercy Warren's history, mostly occasioned by the premises and predicted conclusions. The Puritans begin with the first generation, the sturdy emigrating founders whose faith was unshakable and unimpeachable. Warren also begins essentially with the same people, but sees them as flawed, awaiting correction by a later age for whom reason exerts a strong influence. For the Puritans, the end aimed at was the establishment of a commonwealth of religious believers whose faith would glorify God. Although most adherents would be able to identify that sociopolitical conclusion, they usually would see that end as nearly unreachable in the present time; in other words, there is always more work to do. For Warren, the end is the creation of a politically independent republic of virtuous citizens whose secular glories would be commensurate with their basic faith in the workings of providence and in the maintenance of their essential virtue. As for the Puritans, however, that end only becomes visible later. In the beginning of the struggle that leads to revolution, that is, during the later years of the Bernard governorship (1760–70), few wish to see that far: "INDEPENDENCE was a plant of later growth. Though the soil might be congenial, and the boundaries of nature pointed out the event, yet every one chose to view it at a distance, rather than wished to witness the convulsions that such a dismemberment of the empire must necessarily occasion" (*H,* 1:54).

That inability at the time, however, does not prevent the historian from finding those moments when independence is pushed inexorably forward. After the "convulsions" of the Stamp Act riots, the resistance to the Townshend duties, the increased tyrannies (as she sees them) of Hutchinson, the presence in Boston of a standing army, and the Boston Massacre, Warren's people of principle—the radicals of the "middling classes" most opposed to British policy in the colonies—gather (at Warren's fireside, as it turns out) to chart out a plan of resistance. "Perhaps no single step contributed so much to cement the union of the colonies, and the final acquisition of independence, as the establishment of committees of correspondence" (*H,* 1:109), she says of the plan devised by James Warren and Samuel Adams.[16] Indeed, her description of the committees is both lucid and "concise" (a word she repeats to remind readers of her method), and at the same time she outlines her own principles for determining the course of the narrative:

> The plan . . . proposed that a public meeting should be called in every town; that a number of persons should be selected by a plurality of voices; that they should be men of respectable characters, whose attachment to the great cause of America had been uniform; that they should be vested by a majority of suffrages with power to take cognizance of the state of commerce, of the intrigues of *toryism,* of litigious ruptures that might create disturbances, and every thing else that might be thought to militate with the rights of the people, and to promote every thing that tended to general utility. (*H,* 1:110)

Respectable persons, great cause of America, Tory intrigues, rights of the people, general utility, independence—these become the social and political terms by which the progressive narrative is shaped.

Thus everything else becomes read in these lights, to which must be added the workings of providence, whose "secret hand" uses people as "occasional instruments for the completion of the grand system" (*H,* 1:127).[17] The historian herself must then, as far as humanly possible, make her narrative follow the providential wheel. As late as 1774, during the military governorship of General Gage, "few on either side comprehended the magnitude of the contest," yet that does not diminish the significance of what is to follow: "one of the most remarkable revolutions recorded in the page of history, a revolution which Great Britain precipitated by her indiscretion, and which the hardiest sons of America viewed in the beginning of opposition as a work reserved for the enterprising hand of posterity" (*H,* 1:128). For Warren, providence supplies the narrative frame; she need only follow its signs.[18]

These reminders of the end toward which all things move are sprinkled throughout the *History;* in other words, progress is read in prophecy. Warren sees the formation of the Continental Congress in autumn 1774 "as a *prelude* to a *revolution* which appeared pregnant with events, that might affect not only the political systems, but the character and manners of a considerable part of the habitable globe" (*H,* 1:140). The armed resistance to a detachment of British soldiers who attempted to seize cannon from Salem in February 1775 shows that the people "stood charged for a resistance, that might smite the sceptred hand, whenever it should be stretched forth to arrest by force the inheritance purchased by the blood of ancestors, whose self-denying virtues had rivalled the admired heroes of antiquity" (*H,* 1:169). In ways perhaps not so different from Puritan historiography, in which small events become the emblems of spiritual-historical truths, Warren catalogues those moments that predict if not the outcome then the manner in which the conflict will play itself out.[19]

In contrast with New England, the situation in the South favors the British. Southerners, in Warren's view, are neither accustomed to self-sacrifice nor interested in maintaining the rectitude of first principles—in other words, they are not Massachusetts yeomen. In South Carolina, especially, "The opulence of the planters there, the want of discipline in their militia, the distance and difficulty of reinforcing them, and the sickly state of the inhabitants, promised an easy conquest and a rich harvest to the invaders" (*H,* 2:187). In North Carolina, a state that Warren imagines to be filled with ruffians of a low stripe, "The inhabitants of the country were indeed divided in opinion; bitter, rancorous, and cruel, and many of them without any fixed political principles"; they allied themselves as easily with the British as with supporters of "American independence" (*H,* 2:308).[20] Yet the wheel of providence keeps turning. The British general who nearly conquered the South, Cornwallis, finds at Yorktown "the catastrophe of the fatal day, which reduced . . . an officer of highest military fame and pride, to the condition of a prisoner" (*H,* 2:387). At last, with military victory comes recognition of independence, establishment of a republic, and a future in which the country "exhibits the happiest prospects" (*H,* 3:434). Proud past, principled struggle, attacks from without, dissension and wavering within, hope, gloom, reversal, and glory are the jeremiadical tensions by which Mercy Warren sustains her story.

As some of the passages above indicate, Warren placed great value on character, not simply as solidity of person but more the set of individualizing traits that marks someone for greatness or infamy. James Otis, Jr., Thomas Hutchinson, Samuel Adams, John Adams, Richard Montgomery, Benedict Arnold, Banastre Tarleton, Lord Cornwallis, John André, and others become subjects of Warren's assessment. In Warren's day, the delineating of character was thought to be something of a scientific art; if one observes carefully, takes the whole view, and applies reason to the judgment, one should be able to draw out a character—akin to what we today call personality, though the older word has more substance—that will stand the test of time. Thus despite the providential rhetoric that runs through her text, Warren's emphasis on character affirms the value of the individual: "in human life the most important events sometimes depend on the character of a single actor" (*H,* 3:198).

Early in her work on the *History,* Warren made a deal with John Adams in which he agreed to send her written portraits of the persons he met when traveling on official business.[21] And though over the years Warren reminded her correspondent of his obligation, Adams only occasionally complied. He seems to have felt inadequate to the task (though he could certainly do it with bite and wit) and begged off when Warren reminded him of his duty. But she never gave over the idea that history is made by (or operates through) character.

In the *History,* Warren often portrays characters by means of contrast, one of the most important techniques that Warren uses in her narrative strategy. In volume 1, consistent with her decades-long detestation of him, she describes Gov. Thomas Hutchinson as "dark, intriguing, insinuating, haughty and ambitious," with "abilities . . . little elevated above the line of mediocrity"; he was a man who had "diligently studied the intricacies of *Machiavelian* [*sic*] policy, and never failed to recommend the Italian master as a model to his adherents" (*H,* 1:79).[22] A few pages later, she picks up the character of her brother, James Otis, Jr., Hutchinson's chief public opponent; while she does not say so directly, the contrast is obvious: "This gentleman . . . possessed an easy fortune, independent principles, a comprehensive genius, strong mind, retentive memory, and great penetration," as well as "that extensive professional knowledge, which at once forms the character of the complete civilian and the able statesman" (*H,* 1:85).

Sometimes the contrasts can be seen among members of a single party or side. Two of the American negotiators to France, Arthur Lee and Benjamin Franklin, are honorable men but have quite different leanings. Lee "was a man of a clear understanding, great probity, plain manners, and strong passions" whose "predilection in favor of Britain" led him to be skeptical of a French alliance (*H,* 2:132). In contrast with "his jealous and more frigid colleague, Mr. Lee," Franklin, a man of "great abilities, profound knowledge, and unshaken patriotism," was "intoxicated by the warm caresses and unbounded applauses of all ranks" in France, making him "little less a Gallican than an American" (*H,* 2:133, 131, 132, 133).

Few of Warren's characters, on either side of the Revolutionary conflict, escape some censure (James Otis and James Warren being two of those); by the same token, few leave the scene without some praise. At her worst, she gives vent to strong attachments or antagonisms under the guise of character, though even in the case of the much-hated Hutchinson, she finds some good to say (he was consistent) (*H,* 1:125–26). At her best, Warren strives to outline the complexities of character, "the secret springs" that give some of the Revolution's most notable figures their color. With the rise of modern psychology, this kind of character assessment has gone out of style; yet even within the limitations of its terms and lack of substantiation for some of her remarks, the balanced sentences and judgments rendered still make compelling reading. When she says of the ruthless British officer Tarleton that he told a "lady of respectability" in England "that he had killed more men, and ravished more women, than any man in America," we know by his boast and the context for it that we have his measure (*H,* 2:197).

One of the most interesting characters she outlines is Gen. Charles Lee, an experienced and cosmopolitan officer who, because he coveted Washington's job as commander in chief, is constantly thrown into comparison with that frequently praised hero. The character of Lee becomes a test case for patriotism. He had many admirable qualities, she remarks, including a "bold genius and an unconquerable spirit," but his fighting in the American cause came more from "resentment" at king and ministers in England and "a predilection in favor of freedom, more than from a just sense of the rights of mankind" (*H,* 1:292). Thus it is not enough that one enlist on the patriot side; motives must also be scrutinized. And whatever Lee's value as a soldier, his motives would, of necessity, lead him astray: "Without religion or country, principle, or attachment, gold was his deity, and liberty the idol of his fancy: he hoarded the former without taste for its enjoyment, and worshipped the latter as the patroness of licentiousness, rather than the protectress of virtue. . . . Ambitious of fame without the dignity to support it, he emulated the heroes of antiquity in the field, while in private life he sunk into the vulgarity of the clown" (*H,* 1:292). Lee, like the Cornwallis in volumes 2 and 3, is a figure whose immense talent can never compensate for his failure to align himself with the workings of providence; that is, she criticizes him for not making himself into the figure of the virtuous republican Warren so often touts in her text.

The passage on Lee is also instructive for understanding Warren's method of composition. Very often in writing her history she began with letters, those of someone like John Adams who was involved intimately in key affairs, or her own. One set of letters that she used heavily was a pair written to Warren's model of the female historian, Catharine Macaulay. As recorded in the so-called "Letterbook," the drafts purport to acquaint Macaulay with events in wartime America, but the formal style shows that Warren is already thinking ahead to some future use. In the case of Lee, Warren wrote a preliminary assessment in a 15 February

1777 letter to Macaulay that was somewhat more flattering than her final judgment: "he appears to me sensible, learned, judicious, and at times agreeable; he is allowed to be firm, penetrating, sagacious and brave;—he is a man of an unconquerable spirit, a warm, indefatigable friend of America, but I think more from an unshaken love of freedom and an impartial regard to the inherent rights of man, than from any attachment to particular persons or countries" (MWP1, 16). Thus the *History* reflects not only observations made at the time of events but years of reflection. The character of Lee is informed by more than just an interesting bit of gossip or even psychologizing; rather, Warren's final portrait of the general is indicative of a larger principle, the conflict between freedom, as a license to exercise self-interest, and liberty, a cause to which one sacrifices the self to higher purpose. What was in her letter to Macaulay a minor flaw in a man abused by his enemies becomes by the time the *History* came to be finished the root cause of Lee's unhappy career and his demise as an American hero.

Almost all the character studies focus on men. Warren does not ignore women, but uses a different method to incorporate them into the narrative: the example story. Employing what Kenneth Silverman calls "Whig sentimentalism," Warren emphasizes suffering and injustice in general by examining how events affect women in particular (82). Not every woman mentioned is a victim. Catharine Macaulay enters as writer; women serve the patriot cause by making saltpeter, a key ingredient in gunpowder (*H,* 1:43, 237). Nevertheless, Warren seems to get the most mileage from the image of woman in suffering. These pictures of female victims tend to be even more generalized than those of the political and military actors to whom she devotes character passages, but such was Warren's belief—that all women have within them some fundamental goodness—that almost any one woman can stand for the whole.

In one example, she describes how Loyalist women in New Jersey are abused by British and Hessian troops, the very people who should be protecting them. Warren doubles the emotional value by showing not only the women's suffering (albeit in outline) but also the spectators to that suffering: "The elegant houses of some of their own most devoted partisans were burnt: their wives and daughters pursued and ravished in the woods to which they had fled for shelter. Many unfortunate fathers, in the stupor of grief, beheld the misery of their female connexions without being able to relieve them, and heard the shrieks of infant innocence, subjected to the brutal lust of British grenadiers, or *Hessian Yaugers*" (*H,*

1:350–51). In this situation, women represent all the values of hearth and home; the British and Hessian troops not only violate both women and home, they do it in the sight of those most concerned for the women's welfare. The invaders are full of Tarletons; there is no safety, as the narrative goes, in hiding behind redcoats.

This use of the female victim, of which there are many other examples, reinforces the visual icon of Columbia or Liberty in suffering that was prevalent during the Revolutionary period. As one can infer from the various cartoons and prints reproduced by Linda K. Kerber and Lester Olsen in their very different studies of Revolutionary emblems, the pictorial representation of the country or of the ideal for which people struggled as a victimized female created a cultural sign that not only links women to sexual or eroticized suffering but also identifies relief of their plight with resistance to British oppression.[23] Nina Baym asserts that Warren's incorporation of the female-centered example story makes her history a "gendered melodrama," a didactic, pathos-inducing narrative that serves the idea that women and men operate in separate spheres. Whether Warren's treatment of these episodes has only one "gendered" result, to link women in public with the threat or execution of rape, is an arguable point, but Baym correctly identifies the importance of the female example story to the shape of Warren's text.[24]

As with the New Jersey episode, the lesson about the violence of British perfidy can be drawn from the story of the "principal ladies of Fairfield." Those Loyalist women, despite passes from the British governor Tryon, are brutalized by an expeditionary force of Tory, British, and German troops and later found wandering in the swamps, "half-distracted" (*H,* 2:147). Only in this situation, Warren adds another element: female education. Women find themselves subject to depredation and abuse not because of innate weakness but "from their little knowledge of the world, of the usages of armies, or the general conduct of men" (*H,* 2:147). The British are brutal, and the forced taking or killing of women proves it. Women, however, if they read history or observe politics more closely or study and speak on those subjects thought to be "out of the road of female attention," can begin to protect themselves and avoid situations in which their ignorance of the world's ways makes them the easy dupes of unprincipled men. In other words, Warren suggests that women cannot simply rely on the good offices of men in political power to protect their virtue. She implicitly rejects the kind of lament found in Royall Tyler's Maria and the heroines of later stage "melodrama": that the only place a woman of virtue can find protection—aside from total seclusion—is in the arms of a man of honor.[25] Yet at the same time, her images of women suffering rather than women fighting—she never, for instance, mentions her fellow Plymouth resident and war veteran Deborah Sampson Gannett—reinforce the idea that women will be made victims of men of dishonor.

For all the group examples, Warren knows that nothing grips like the individual story. Widows—such as Janet Montgomery—whose husbands fall in the cause or wives—such as Mrs. Walker—whose husbands suffer indignities, make their entrance with some frequency (*H,* 1:67, 252). The episode of the New Jersey minister's wife, Mrs. Caldwell, removes all doubt that of all combatants, the British troops deserve the most opprobrium for their conduct. "This lady was sitting in her own house, with her little domestic circle around her, and her infant in her arms; unapprehensive of danger, shrouded by the consciousness of her own innocence and virtue; when a British barbarian pointed his musquet into the window of her room, and instantly shot her through the lungs" (*H,* 2:203). When Mr. Caldwell returns to find his house burned and his wife murdered and hastily buried, he publishes the event, but in two years time is killed himself "by some ruffian hands" (205). This latter addendum not only multiplies the horrors of the event but also reminds readers of the inability of an essentially good man to protect his essentially passive wife by his own actions. Thus even those ideals of the late eighteenth and early nineteenth centuries, innocence and virtue, fail to protect people who, though ardent patriots, had never harmed anyone. Warren herself does not argue that innocence should be eliminated; only that in war it cannot serve alone to protect one from harm.[26]

Both character depiction and the example story serve to enhance the narrative of a people struggling for independence. At some further remove from the immediate persons and events of the period are other topics that fall under Warren's rubric of "observations." These are the political or philosophical ruminations, occasioned by the details of the historical narrative, that Warren as teacher and advice-giver feels compelled to dispense. For modern readers, these observations are what give the book its "antique" quality, to use Michael Kammen's word. In some ways, however, they are the most interesting part of Warren's book, for they reveal how she thinks about issues. In addition to comments on individuals or on specific events associated with the Revolution, the topics of these observations include reflections on human nature and public morality; comparisons of political systems, with a special attention to republicanism; and digressions on various aspects of American or world history and society.

Unlike many of the "ladies" of whom she writes, Warren did not think herself a starry-eyed innocent in evaluating human nature. Still, she was opposed to religious skepticism, and affirmed some basic value in humankind. For Warren, human nature and politics go hand in hand. Essentially, her principles can be boiled down as follows: (1) all persons have an inborn "noble principle" and a desire for freedom; (2) all persons are also susceptible to the tug of self-interest; (3) individual behavior is influenced by society; and (4) reason is salutary in balancing the needs of individuals and society (*H,* 1:1–26).[27]

Unfortunately, the noble principle—that is, the desire to do good for its own sake and not merely personal gain—can easily be overwhelmed.[28] Commenting on the behavior of arch-Tory Andrew Oliver, Warren notes how successful he was in getting American patriots to drop their agreement not to import British goods: "A regard to private interest ever operates more forcibly on the bulk of mankind than the ties of honor, or the principles of patriotism; and when the latter are incompatible with the former, the balance seldom hangs long in equilibrio. Thus it is not uncommon to see virtue, liberty, love of country, and regard to character, sacrificed at the shrine of wealth" (*H,* 1:70). As this passage suggests, Warren clearly sees that without some forceful direction, human nature will assert itself in the negative over those principles she and humankind in general value most.

On the surface, this seems a Hobbesian view, though one can quickly surmise that Warren would never allow herself to see human nature in such unrelievedly negative terms. Indeed, in many ways, social controls do not have the effect of protecting human beings from themselves, as Hobbes argues in *Leviathan,* but have the opposite result. In her first chapter, Warren outlines the causes of political distress: (1) when secrecy replaces openness; (2) when people are excluded from choosing their leaders; and (3) when "illiberality," excessive control, reigns. In other words, while most people may give over to "private interest" in a battle with honor, the effects of repressive government are worse, producing in people wickedness or, when the repressions are suddenly lifted, the kind of freedom that becomes license or reintroduces repression in the name of punishing the formerly offending class. Thus her chief argument in the *History* is that the Revolution was necessary to remove those conditions that denied the inherent need for freedom its rightful expression.

Warren does not, however, subscribe to a philosophy that elevates the state of nature. In a sense, Warren's view is contradictory; that is, like Rousseau, she sees society (or at least one dimension of it) as destructive to the first principles of human goodness; but like Hobbes, and unlike Rousseau, she denies human beings in the savage state any intrinsic worth. In fact, as one passage makes quite apparent, Warren believes that "civilization" is what saves human beings from their most barbaric impulses. After describing the attack by John Robinson on her brother James Otis, Jr., she notes how the attacker fled for protection to the ships of the Royal Navy:

> In a state of nature, the savage may throw his poisoned arrow at the man, whose soul exhibits a transcript of benevolence that upbraids his own ferocity, and may boast his bloodthirsty deed among the hordes of the forest without disgrace; but in a high stage of civilization, where humanity is cherished, and politeness is become a science, for the dark assassin then to level his blow at superior merit, and screen himself in the arms of power, reflects an odium on the government that permits it, and puts human nature to the blush. (*H,* 1:87)

The key word, then, is humanity. In other words, civilization at its best introduces reason as that which protects the noble features of human nature—called here humanity. In war, humanity is called to the test and, as Warren documents, is frequently found wanting. What she discovers is that while on the one hand, the extraordinary situation of the Revolution induces some people to abandon self-interest and choose honor, on the other, war produces rival value systems. In depicting the recapture of Stoney Point by American Gen. Anthony Wayne, Warren acknowledges the military honor he won with his bayonet charge, but adds that the action "was not altogether so consistent with humanity" (*H,* 2:151). In another episode, this time of British cruelty, she explains that "The courage which is accompanied by humanity, is a virtue; but bravery, that pushes through all dangers to destroy, is barbarous, is savage, is brutal" (*H,* 2:369).

For Warren, no situation exempts people from the obligation to assert humanity; although that obligation can be distorted either by life in a state of nature or by political or military oppression, one finally must honor it or suffer the consequences of moral condemnation. Even considering the conditions of the frontier, the historian cannot excuse slaughter. Some actions by a particularly loathesome band of British sympathizers she forbears to relate as "too painful to the writer, and too disgraceful to human nature to dwell on" (*H,* 2:115). Because the Revolution was not activated by revenge, its supporters did not as a rule indulge in the cruelties usually associated with violent upheavals (*H,* 3:428). The Revolution can be justified, then, if it produces that right balance of social obligation and individual freedom within the scientifically regulated rules of social intercourse (politeness) that allow humanity to flourish. In short, human nature exhibits itself most beneficially in a system of "rational liberty" (*H,* 1:141).[29]

Given the attributes Warren assigns to human nature, or humanity, she can support only one form of government: the republic. This word would be the cause of much conflict between Warren and John Adams, but we can draw some conclusions about what Warren believed. Again, there is a contradiction in her logic. She warns frequently about a natural tendency toward "supineness" in the people, "which generally overspreads the multitude, and disposes mankind to submit quietly to any form of government, rather than to be at the expense and hazard of resistance" (*H,* 1:40). That can be overcome when the specter of "slavery" pushes even the moderate to see that they need to resist. A republic, therefore, is that form of government which intrudes least on its citizens, but the implication is that it must also be that form of government which most activates a contrary tendency to the "supineness" that leads to loss of liberty.

In Warren's view, a republic is essentially a system whereby the people (though in real terms, white men) freely choose their representatives and leaders. It is maintained when the executive relies more on "the unanimity and affection of the people" than on "the dread of penal inflictions, or any restraints that might repress free inquiry, relative to the principles of their own government, and the conduct of its administrators!" (*H,* 1:vii). As other remarks clarify, Warren opposes the methods argued by Machiavelli in *The Prince.* Ideally, the republic supports the provisions for human rights, as outlined by John Locke in his *Essay on Civil Government,* and civil liberty, as described by William Paley in *The Principles of Moral and Political Philosophy* (1785) and quoted by Warren: "*that* people, government, and constitution, is the *freest,* which makes the best provision for the enacting of expedient and salutary laws" (*H,* 1:vii).[30] Whether a republic would work was, in Warren's time, an open question. As she notes, following Paley, the world watches as America is "experimenting" with this new form (Paley, 462; *H,* 1:vii). But for Warren, all world history goes to prove that a republic, in principle, should be the best system.

Three situations elsewhere in the world interest her in this regard. One is Poland, a country that furnished America with two noted supporters of liberty, Casimir Pulaski and Thaddeus Kosciusko. Though nurturing the desire for freedom in some of its citizens, Poland, through internal dissension, aristocratic maneuverings, and foreign oppression, had then lost any hope for a republic; as Warren remarks, "the ruin of Poland may be viewed as an example and a warning to other nations, particularly to those who enjoy a free, elective representative government" (*H,* 2:186). Geneva, in Switzerland, is a second example of lost liberty. There, spies and invitations for external military influence undo the republican model. Like Poland, Geneva is a model of how republics are "subverted": "This is generally done by the pride of a few families, the ambition of individuals, and the supineness of the people. Thus an undue authority is established by a select number, more mortifying to the middling class of mankind, and which has a tendency to render more abject and servile the mass of the people, than the single arm of the most despotic individual" (*H,* 3:73–74). With both, but especially Geneva, Warren urges special vigilance against the establishment of a powerful elite that achieves dominance by means other than free elections.

The third example—and the most troubling for Warren—is France. She initially supported the revolution of 1789 as akin to the American, and in the *History* follows Catharine Macaulay in chastising Edmund Burke for his attack on the French Revolution.[31] As word of republican excesses reached America, however, many turned on the French, and support for their Revolution was seen as evidence of political extremism. The failure of the French to establish a republic without mass hysteria and murder led to charges that republicanism is the refuge of the godless and that it leads to anarchy. These charges were serious threats to Warren's attempt to affirm the value of a republic for the United States.

Her answer sheds light on the quality of her thinking. First, she draws on an earlier point about human nature; that is, a people long suppressed, when given freedom, often react in violent, inhumane ways. The fault is not republican government or ideals but the originating oppression. Second, she claims that however much anticlerical thinking may have been unleashed in the resulting "pandemonium," one must not confuse genuine desire for freedom with skeptical license. If anything, the French Revolution shows that for a republic to work, one must not abandon religious thinking. There must always be cognizance of a higher power. Nevertheless, nothing in the French example warrants a questioning of the republican model for America (*H,* 3:402–9).

For Warren, the biggest threats to republican security come not from the examples without but from actions and statements within. As her letters from the 1780s make clear, she feared that the country would slide again into another form of despotic government. In the *History,* the sign for this was the formation of the Cincinnati, a group of Revolutionary officers who banded together in a postwar society to proclaim themselves as a new elite, a privileged order. This "self-created rank," a kind of "military knighthood," with hereditary privileges, struck Warren as inimical to a republic (*H,* 3:280, 281). Eventually, "The people were generally aroused from their supineness by the alarming aspect of these pretensions" and forced to retrench (*H,* 3:290). But for a republic to be successful, its members must be constantly vigilant against the depredations of the few. If anything, this is a major purpose of Warren's writing: to educate the young on the need to be aware.

Many aspects of American society come under scrutiny: the arts, education, history. There is not space here to detail them all. But Warren dwells on one topic: the wilderness and the people who live there. Like Crevecoeur in his *Letters from an American Farmer* (1782), Warren finds life in the wilderness both fascinating and horrifying. Her interest stems from the death of her son Winslow on the frontier, yet she manages to see the subject from a variety of angles. For instance, she often avers to the roughness of North Carolinians and uses their crude character as the basis for discourse on life in the backwoods. When the British under Colonel Ferguson are defeated at Kings Mountain, the Carolinian victors waste no time in executing some British prisoners. This action, contrary to Warren's idea of humanity in war, can be explained readily: "This summary infliction was imposed by order of some of those fierce and uncivilized chieftains, who had spent most of their lives in the mountains and forests, amidst the slaughter of wild animals, which was necessary to their daily subsistence" (*H,* 2:251). Thus, like Crevecoeur's frontiersmen who forego the plow and pick up the gun, Warren's backwoodsmen lean toward a justice more primitive than is allowed by polite society.[32] This would become a theme for James Fenimore Cooper, as well, particularly in his ruffian character Ishmael Bush of *The Prairie* (1827), a novel that, ironically, takes place in 1805, the publication date of Warren's *History.* The problem faced by Cooper in his creation of Natty Bumppo resembles that confronted by Warren: can one be at home in the wilds without exhibiting a fatal loss of humanity?

Although the story she tells in the *History* is largely that of conventional military campaigns in the eastern districts, she returns to the relationship of wilderness and civilized society several times. She worries about westward expansion; the encroachment on Indian territories will lead to violence, the eventual extermination of the natives, and the settlement of rough characters whose proximity to the more civilized people of the East can result only in upheaval (*H,* 3:206). She later cites as evidence the war of 1791. Continued British presence in the West, coupled with the "barbarity of the borderers," provokes a "horrid Indian war, in which . . . some of the flower of the American youth, perished in the wilderness" (*H,* 3:313)—including her son. Her solution is an unusual one: build "*a Chinese wall*" along the Appalachians at a "price" far less than that paid by "the lives of young heroes" (*H,* 3:314). In that way, the lives of both whites and Indians are spared—and the civilized districts might be preserved from the baneful influence of the borderers.

This is more an idle suggestion than a serious demonstration of her philosophy. Despite the several references in the *History* to Winslow and her evident preoccupation with his death, Warren shows a surprising liberality in her attitudes toward a people she might, following the prejudices of the time, charge with her son's murder. For one thing, her hostility to British policy supersedes all; the American Indians are seen in her view as but pawns of a wicked administration. This belief is made manifest in an earlier episode, the brutal killing of "Miss McCrea." Another of Warren's suffering women, Jane McCrea dies at the hands of the Indian allies of General Burgoyne in upstate New York. Burgoyne pardons the killers, fearing the loss of manpower should the Indians feel resentment at his punishment; thus when Warren writes, in true sentimental style, "The helpless maid was butchered and scalped, and her bleeding corpse left in the woods, to excite the tear of every beholder," she implies that Burgoyne, more than the Indians, is the one most to blame (*H,* 2:27).[33]

For another thing, Warren understands that the Indians are equally the victims of a general white depredation on their lands. When she describes how the American General Sullivan led an expedition against the Six Nations, she records that the incident "was replete with circumstances that must wound the feelings of the compassionate heart," for the people that Sullivan attacked were "enjoying domestic quiet in the simplicity of nature" (*H,* 2:117). Indeed, though she often speaks strongly against savagery, she respects simplicity, whoever practices it. She is enough of a providentialist to remain committed to the triumph of civilization as a desirable, if not absolutely inevitable, end, but enough of a compassionate realist to fear and lament the extermination of whole peoples. Her best hope, overtly written against her worst fears, is that the Revolution will lead to a softening of Indian manners and to opportunities for education. In Lockean fashion, she rejects the idea "that the rude tribes of savages cannot be civilized by the kind and humane endeavours of their neighbours" (*H,* 2:122). For Warren, equality means equality: "there is no difference in the moral or intellectual capacity of nations, but what arises from adventitious circumstances, that give some a more early and rapid improvement in civilization than others" (*H,* 2:123). In fact, she quotes Winslow Warren himself as evidence that the problems with Indians are to be laid most often at the feet of whites. There is no doubt in her mind that they have been "enveloped in darkness, ignorance, and barbarism," but she has equal faith that through "reason and humanity" they, too, can be brought into a state of "dignity" (*H,* 2:127). Although modern readers will see this remark as ethnocentric, it is crucial to her entire text: the Revolution is the path by which the noble principle inherent in all persons may be, for the first time in history, fully realized.

Does this mean political equality for all? That is less certain. It would seem from her discussion of the Indians that despite her reservations about their current life-style, education and civility would be sufficient to bring them in to the franchise. About the other sizable nonwhite minority, African-Americans, Warren says little, except to criticize southern colonies for having brought in "foreign slaves" in the first place, thus making themselves vulnerable to slave revolts or such British tactics as royal governor Dunmore's freeing of the slaves in Virginia (*H,* 1:92, 200–203, 297). We have seen, however, that Warren was quite taken with the poetry of Phillis Wheatley; if pressed to answer on the issue of political equality, she would have to grant the application of her principles to Wheatley's race as well. Regarding women, however, we have little evidence in the text of the *History* by which to judge whether Warren would assert overtly the political inclusion of her sex. The examples serve to show women as essentially helpless in war, yet in writing her text and advocating for female education, as well as in traveling frequently "out of the road of female attention" in the content of her correspondence, she suggests that her claim of equality in nations extends to gender. But because her text has as one of its aims a national reconciliation and avoidance of party spirit, she may have felt there would be no point in making, as one modern historian puts it, "a public display of one's sexual ideology."[34]

As a reader of providence, Warren shapes the story to reflect what Philip Freneau and Hugh Henry Brackenridge in their commencement poem of 1771 call "the Rising Glory of America." As the writer of a jeremiad, however, she cannot end without due warning to future generations. Like others in the postwar years, she and her husband James fretted throughout the 1780s about the increased social decay brought about by sudden wealth and a resistance to the ideals of sacrifice. In volume 3, she returns to that theme through her favored method of contrast. Should principles be lost and general weakness reign, then some future historian may take America to task "and hold up the contrast between a simple, virtuous, and free people, and a degenerate, servile race of beings, corrupted by wealth, effeminated by luxury, impoverished by licentiousness, and become the *automatons* of intoxicated ambition" (*H,* 3:337). The way to resist such error is through a strategy long known to the Puritans—vigilance. This applies to those in power as well as to the national character. In choosing a president, for instance, a people "cannot be too scrutinous on the character of their executive officers. No man should be lifted by the voice of his country to presidential rank, who may probably forget the republican designation, and sigh to wield a sceptre, instead of guarding sacredly the charter from the people" (*H,* 3:424). Despite these warnings, Warren sees full reason to hope that "this last civilized quarter of the globe may exhibit those striking traits of grandeur and magnificence, which the Divine Œconomist may have reserved to crown the closing scene" (*H,* 3:436).

With the curtain closed on her text as well, she also hoped that this, her longest and greatest work, would win her that portion of fame which a woman of her disposition might dare to gather about her. There were few reviews. An anonymous writer for a Christian periodical criticized the book on a number of grounds.[35] The style varies from "the polished period" to "the heavy sentence, rendered tedious" (*Panoplist,* 381); the author uses words improperly, such as "derelict" for a verb (*Panoplist,* 382); errors of fact dot her first chapter on the Pilgrims (*Panoplist,* 383); the narrative, while "both interesting and entertaining," delves into topics and images beyond its purview (*Panoplist,* 429). Beneath these remarks is doubt about the propriety of a woman to write history at all. In a wicked penultimate paragraph, the reviewer, agreeing with Warren on the duties of clergymen, remarks, "The advice . . . might have been extended to other classes of the community . . . even 'aged women' have a sphere of usefulness; and in his first epistle to Timothy [Paul] points out a part of the duty of women *generally*" (*Panoplist,* 432). The passage referred to—"Let a woman learn in silence with all submissiveness. I permit no woman to teach or to have authority over men; she is to keep silent" (1 Tim. 2:11–12)—rather obviates his final comment on the *History*: "we have no hesitation in acknowledging that we have derived considerable pleasure, and, we hope, some profit from a careful perusal of it" (*Panoplist,* 432).

The ever-politic James Freeman, hoping that "the shaft which this writer aims at your bosom will not wound you," assured Warren in a letter that she had always attended her duties fully and urged her to maintain a Christian forgiveness toward the *Panoplist* reviewer (12 March 1807, MWP2). Her patience would receive its reward nearly three years later. A seven-part review in the Worcester *National Aegis,* a Jeffersonian paper, effectively, if rather fulsomely, rebuts the points made in the *Panoplist.*[36] As for the matter of gender, for example, the *Aegis* writer finds a female historian a matter for national pride. The *History*

> at once exalts the character of the female and the human intellect. This work will evince to foreign nations that Americans, so far from imposing on woman the vile and degrading restrictions of the haram [*sic*] can adore her loveliness & personal graces, without enviously denying her the additional advantages of intellectual improvements. If indeed he [presumably a foreigner] should enter our literary circle, he would often hear the lessons of wisdom flow with accumulated charms from the lips of Beauty. (*Aegis,* 10 January 1810)

The reviewer, in between garrulous comments on matters not always related to the book, finds Warren's character sketches as well as her style worthy of praise. Her writing shows "the enlightened sensibility of the painter," and her observations "display all the strength of the masculine understanding and all the tenderness of the female heart" (17 January 1810; 28 February 1810). Most important, and in sharp contrast to the opinion of the *Panoplist* reviewer, she follows "the most sacred obligation of a historian . . . a strict adherence to every minutiae of truth" (28 February 1810). Unfortunately, few people in Boston read the *Aegis;* its words were better suited to salving the wound created by the misogynist review in the Christian monthly than to influencing public opinion.

She depended on friends for accolades—although she asked for genuine criticism—when reviewers fell short. Freeman, who had served as the *History*'s midwife, coyly praised the beauty of the binding and type in a letter to Warren (12 March 1807, MWP2). James Winthrop gave a more critical reading, but assured her in a letter that "It is a well digested and polished narrative, and gave great satisfaction" (4 February 1807,

WAL, 2:350).[37] In a telling sign, however, the husband of her friend Sarah Cary never bothered to read it. John Adams, her old friend, after receiving his copies in 1807, had much to say, none of it good.

In an exhaustive and withering series of letters, the former president blasted Warren for her characterization of him. Reflecting the coolness that had developed between the Adams and Warren households since the end of the war, the historian withheld her earlier and enthusiastic mode of address and praise for Adams—whose good opinion she once openly courted—and instead cut him to size with diminishing remarks or outright charges in her *History:* that Adams did not appear in political affairs before 1774; that while in foreign countries, but especially in England, taking part in government negotiations, he lost his republicanism and took a liking to monarchy; that he was too passionate a character "for his sagacity and judgment"; and that while president, Adams, as can be inferred from a passage quoted above (*H,* 3:424), threatened to bring the country to autocratic ruin (*H,* 1:131–32; *H,* 3:392–94). Other statements or omissions made by Warren—for instance, her assertion that while home between foreign trips Adams was "retired" or her failure to mention the full extent of his Dutch negotiations—Adams took as attacks.

To some extent, Adams had good grounds for complaint; Warren sometimes seems to go out of her way to tweak her old ally. In describing the Declaration of Independence, she praises Adams for his speech in favor, but follows with a comparison to John Dickinson's speech, the latter having "equal pathos of express, and more brilliance of epithet" than Adams's.[38] At the same time, Adams had access to experience and papers that were unavailable to Warren, though it must be said that she relied heavily on letters from Adams for much of her information throughout the *History.* Her omissions, or in some cases errors of fact, are genuine.[39]

Still, Adams flogged on for 10 letters, never responding directly to Warren's attempts to answer his charges. He says in his last, "I have received none of your favors since I began to write," which could mean that they had not arrived—or that he simply would not accept them when they did arrive (*CBAW,* 478). But as criticism, his attacks were devastating. She viewed them not as corrections—though Adams states that as his initial intention—but as personal and indelicate aspersions on her character and that of her family (as letter 10 from Adams most certainly is). Adams even likens the passages in the *History* about him to the effusions of the fishwife obloquy from Alexander Pope's poem in imitation of Spenser, "The Alley," accompanied by Slander, Envy, and Malice (*CBAW,* 478). For Mercy Warren, who thought in her fifth letter to have said the last word, this was too much to bear: "The lines with which you concluded your late correspondence cap the climax of rancor, indecency, and vulgarism" (*CBAW,* 490).

The one issue from their epistolary debate that has lasting substance is the question of what constitutes republicanism. Adams reads Warren's *History* as an attack on what he thought was his unwavering support for a republican system, and, indeed, Warren makes overt her reservations about what she sees as loss of support: "Mr. Adams's former opinions were beclouded by a partiality for monarchy," an act that produced "his lapse from former republican principles" (*H,* 3:394, 395). Beyond the personal dimension, however, the *History* and the subsequent exchange of letters show the rift that existed in the early republic over what or who carried the mantle of the Revolution. Adams leaps all over the map in trying to state his own principles, which are laden with suspicions of popular government and assemblies and directly include an odium for democracy. Though Warren herself was skeptical of popular opinion—had decried it when James Warren had been turned out of office in 1778—she believed that a genuine republicanism, a system without titles that kept the executive beholden to the franchise, was possible (MW to JW, 2 June 1778, *WAL,* 2:16–18).[40] But it is clear from the *History* and from the letters that neither Adams nor Warren was capable of defining republicanism in a consistent and practical way.[41]

In rebutting Adams's denigration of her *History,* Warren makes this remark: "Criticism, in order to be useful, should always be decent"; in her view, Adams's commentary, "more like the ravings of a maniac than the cool *critique* of genius and science," was not (MW to JA, 27 August 1807, *CBAW,* 489). In his pique, Adams wrote to Elbridge Gerry, the friend who effected the reconciliation with Warren in 1813, "History is not the Province of the Ladies" (17 April 1813, *WAL,* 2:380). Unfortunately for Warren, the nineteenth century seemed to agree. Her book was not reprinted until the twentieth century and its place in Warren's canon, as well as in those of history and literature, was minimized or ignored.[42] In recent years, new attention has been focused on the *History* that might have pleased Warren more than the extended and "vindictive" interpretation of her "ancient friend" John Adams (MW to

JA, 27 August 1807, *CBAW,* 486). Her major work is now taken seriously by many scholars as thoughtful if uneven, fully as valuable as any other history by her contemporaries—more so, perhaps, for its unique place as a full-length, comprehensive history of the Revolution by a woman and a republican.[43]

Afterword: Mercy Otis Warren, Woman of Letters

Reopening the American canon has given readers not only new writers to peruse but new eyes with which to see. The writings of Mercy Warren have sat a long time without getting their due. True, her style can be forbidding, and yes, her interest in philosophical more than material life prevents her work from being easily accessible. But for years her reputation as a writer has been held captive to a historiography that could only mock or diminish her achievements, not appreciate them. Literary critics followed suit, choosing not to read Warren in the context of her times but only as a relic, an antique about whom "quaint" would be the highest praise delivered. Her works and her reputation deserve better.

Feminist historians and critics as well as other readers sympathetic to new ways of looking at old texts have reopened the case of Warren; new studies have appeared in recent years that take Warren's thought and literary accomplishments as serious areas for study. Many projects remain, both biographical and critical, before we can fully know the scope of Warren's work and its impact. Despite the difficulty modern students may encounter at first meeting with her poetry and prose, Warren has left a body of material reflective of an original, striving mind at work. One of the bravest intellectual women of her day, Warren reached from her outpost in Plymouth to a nation and made people—many of them powerful—take notice of what she said. Passionate, contentious, satiric, and stoical, Mercy Otis Warren wanted most of all to teach future generations the commitment Americans must exercise if the republic is to thrive. Her words in many genres can still serve that office, and other offices, too, if we only listen to what she has to say.

Notes and References

Abbreviations used in text and in notes:

AA: Abigail Adams
JA: John Adams
MW: Mercy Warren
JW: James Warren (husband)
GW: George Warren (son)
HW: Henry Warren (son)
JW2: James Warren, Jr. (son)
WW: Winslow Warren (son)
AFC: Adams Family Correspondence
BPL: Boston Public Library
CBAW: Correspondence between John Adams and Mercy Warren
CFP: Cary Family Papers, Massachusetts Historical Society
DA: Diary and Autobiography (of John Adams)
DAB: Dictionary of American Biography
DLB Dictionary of Literary Biography
DNB: Dictionary of National Biography
HL: Houghton Library, Harvard University
MWP: Mercy Warren Papers, Massachusetts Historical Society
PDM/PP: *Plays, Dramatic and Miscellaneous*, in *The Plays and Poems of Mercy Warren*, edited by Benjamin Franklin V
PJA: Papers of John Adams
WAL: Warren-Adams Letters: Being Chiefly a Correspondence among John Adams, Samuel Adams, and James Warren

Chapter One

1. *Columbian Centinel,* 22 October 1814, 2.
2. Henry Warren to Mary Otis, 19 October 1814, Mercy Warren Papers, reel 2, Massachusetts Historical Society. This collection is hereafter cited as MWP, plus microfilm reel number.
3. Three book-length biographies have appeared: Alice Brown, *Mercy Warren* (New York: Scribner's, 1896); Katharine Anthony, *First Lady of the Revolution: The Life of Mercy Otis Warren* (Garden City, N.Y.: Doubleday, 1958); and Jean Fritz, *Cast for a Revolution: Some American Friends and Enemies, 1728–1814* (Boston: Houghton Mifflin, 1972), the latter a "collective biography" that makes MW the "central character." Shorter biographies include

Annie Russell Marble, "Mistress Mercy Warren: Real Daughter of the American Revolution," *New England Magazine* 28 (1903): 163–80; Maud Macdonald Hutcheson, "Mercy Warren, 1728–1814," *William and Mary Quarterly* 10 (1953): 378–401; Frank Shuffelton, "Mercy Otis Warren," in *Dictionary of Literary Biography,* vol. 33, *American Colonial Writers, 1735–1781,* ed. Emory Elliot (Detroit: Gale, 1984), 246–52; and Jean Fritz, "Mercy Otis Warren," *Constitution* 2 (1989): 58–63. *Dictionary of Literary Biography* hereafter cited as *DLB.*

4. Fritz claims the Copley portrait shows Mary Allyne Otis as "buxom, shrewd, severe, peasant-faced" (1972, 8).

5. Otis family genealogy derived from John J. Waters, Jr., *The Otis Family in Provincial and Revolutionary Massachusetts* (Chapel Hill: University of North Carolina Press, 1968), esp. 3–75, supplemented by Horatio N. Otis, "Genealogical and Historical Memoir of the Otis Family," *New England Historical and Genealogical Register* 2 (1848): 281–96, and 4 (1850): 143–65, and by Clifford K. Shipton, "James Otis," in *Sibley's Harvard Graduates,* vol. 9, 1741–1745 (Boston: Massachusetts Historical Society, 1960), 247–87.

6. Fritz 1972, 9; Paul Engle, *Women in the American Revolution* (Chicago: Follett, 1976), 48. Russell, the Otis family minister, married Mercy Otis, MW's aunt: Fritz 1972, 6; Anthony, 28.

7. Brown, 33; Fritz 1972, 23, Waters, 71. Fritz suggests possibilities other than the two mentioned for the meeting of JW and MW.

8. James Otis, Jr., to MW, 11 April 1766, in John Adams et al., *Warren-Adams Letters: Being Chiefly a Correspondence among John Adams, Samuel Adams, and James Warren,* vol. 1, 1743–77 (Boston: Massachusetts Historical Society, 1917), 1, 2. Vol. 1 and vol. 2, 1778–1814 (1925), hereafter cited as *WAL.*

9. Fritz 1972, 9. The house, privately owned, still stands. Though it has been modernized by recent residents, the old foundation and basic structure remain intact. In MW's time, the yard sloped to the river with an open view, and up from the house, at the crest of the hill, she could see Warren Cove and Cape Cod.

10. Barbara J. Berg, *The Remembered Gate: Origins of American Feminism: The Woman and the City, 1800–1860* (New York: Oxford University Press, 1978), 23–26.

11. Stephanie Coontz, *The Social Origins of Private Life* (London: Verso, 1988), 145.

12. From 6 April 1775, *WAL,* 1:46; the passage appears in a segment of the letter JW dated 7 April.

13. An excellent selection of poems by MW's contemporaries can be found in Pattie Cowell, *Women Poets in Pre-Revolutionary America, 1650–1775: An Anthology* (Troy, N.Y.: Whitston, 1981).

14. Nancy F. Cott, *The Bonds of Womanhood: "Women's Sphere" in New England, 1780–1835* (New Haven: Yale University Press, 1977), 200.

15. M. B. Norton, *Liberty's Daughters: The Revolutionary Experience of American Women, 1750–1800* (Boston: Little, Brown, 1980).

16. MW's religion has occasioned some confusion. Some writers refer to her as a "Christian Deist" (for example, Emily Stipes Watts, *The Poetry of American Women from 1632 to 1945* [Austin: University of Texas Press, 1977], 43). Cheryl Z. Oreovicz, in one of the best discussions on the subject, "Mercy Warren and 'Freedom's Genius,'" *University of Mississippi Studies in English* 5 (1987): 215–30, argues correctly that MW attacks the whole skeptical tradition on which Deism is a part and calls attention to the Calvinism in MW's republicanism.

17. MW to AA, 19 January 1774, *Adams Family Correspondence,* ed. L. H. Butterfield, et al. (Cambridge: Belknap/Harvard University Press, 1963), 1:92; volumes in this series hereafter cited as *AFC.*

18. MWP2 as separate untitled item. Conjectural readings of manuscript in brackets. According to a transcript note by JW2, the prayer was "made many years before her death, and kept in her Bible."

19. MW to Margaret Cary, 1 January 1814, Cary Family Papers 3, box 3; hereafter cited as CFP3. This letter is a transcript in an unknown hand, reflecting a pattern among some of MW's correspondents of making copies of her advice letters and passing them around.

20. Robert Middlekauff, *The Glorious Cause: The American Revolution, 1763–1789* (New York: Oxford University Press, 1982), 85.

21. Bernard Bailyn, *The Ordeal of Thomas Hutchinson* (Cambridge: Belknap/Harvard University Press, 1974), 39–62; Middlekauff, 83–88; Waters, 117–20.

22. Waters, 154–55; William Gordon, *The History of the Rise, Progress, and Establishment of the Independence of the United States of America,* 3 vols., 3d (American) ed. (London, 1788; New York: Samuel Campbell, 1801), 1:119–20.

23. The poem is "A Thought on the inestimable Blessing of reason, occasioned by its privation to a friend of very superior talents and virtues. 1770," discussed in chapter 3 of this volume. On the beating itself, see Hutcheson, 381; Page Smith, *A New Age Now Begins,* (New York: McGraw-Hill, 1976), 1:321–22; Middlekauff, 199–200; and Waters, 177. For a blow-by-blow description of the fight, as well as preamble and postscript, see Miller B. Zobel, *The Boston Massacre* (New York: Norton, 1970), 144–51.

24. Catharine Sawbridge Macaulay, *The History of England from the Accession of James I to the Elevation of the House of Hanover,* 3d ed., 5 vols. (London: Dilly, 1769–1772).

25. Lucy Martin Donnelly, "The Celebrated Mrs. Macaulay," *William and Mary Quarterly* 6 (1949): 174–77.

26. MW to JA, 14 July 1774, John Adams, et al., *Papers of John Adams,* ed. Robert J. Taylor et al., vol. 2, December 1773–April 1775 (Cambridge: Belknap/Harvard University Press, 1977), 108; volumes in this series hereafter

cited as *PJA*. What MW calls Liberty Square is today bounded by North Street to the north and Main Street to the west, where the Warren house still stands.

27. Mercy Otis Warren, "The Adulateur, a Tragedy," *Massachusetts Spy* 2, no. 56 (26 March 1772): 15; Middlekauff, 215. Andrew Oliver and Peter Oliver are others attacked in the play.

28. As for instance "Hazelrod"—Peter Oliver—in JA to JW, 9 April 1774, *PJA*, 2:83.

29. JA to MW, 3 January 1775, *PJA*, 2:209–10; letter is misdated 1774 by JA and so listed in *WAL*, 1:21–23.

30. See, for instance, Winthrop's description of the "Luxurious manner" in which British prisoners of war were housed after their surrender at Saratoga and movement back to Cambridge (Hannah Winthrop to MW, 4 February 1778, *WAL*, 2:4).

31. This is the implication of Shipton's entry on James in *Sibley's Harvard Graduates*, 11:584–606; see also Fritz 1972, 182–83.

32. JW to JA, 27 October 1783, *WAL*, 2:229: "I am quite contented with a private life, and my Ambition is quite satisfied by excelling in the perfection of my Composts."

33. MW to WW, 28 September 1781, quoted in Hutcheson, 390. JW2, a lieutenant of marines and sailing aboard the continental frigate *Alliance*, Capt. John Barry commanding, was wounded in the right knee during a battle with two British sloops of war, 28 May 1781. For information on the *Alliance*, its battles, its peculiar captains, and its marines, including JW2, see Charles R. Smith, *Marines in the Revolution: A History of the Continental Marines in the American Revolution, 1775–1783* (Washington, D.C.: History and Museums Division, U.S. Marine Corps, 1975), esp. 176, 223–24, 233–39, 257–60, 280, 391, 475.

34. Hutchinson, who had fled to England in 1774, died from stroke 3 June 1780 (Bailyn 1974, 373).

35. John S. Ezell, ed., *The New Democracy in America: Travels of Francisco de Miranda in the United States, 1783–1784*, trans. Judson S. Wood (Norman: University of Oklahoma Press, 1963), 174.

36. On the postwar American obsession with "luxury" and corruption, see Jeffrey H. Richards, *Theater Enough: American Culture and the Metaphor of the World Stage, 1607–1789* (Durham, N.C.: Duke University Press, 1991), 265–79.

37. On the near drowning, see Abigail (Nabby) Adams to Elizabeth Cranch, 1 January 1779, *AFC*, 3:144. Abigail (Nabby) Adams, daughter of John and Abigail Adams, spent the winter months of 1778–79 with the Warrens while her father was in France—a happy visit, apparently, by the evidence of MW's and Nabby's letters.

38. *AFC*, 3:359n1, 359–60n2; Charles Warren, "A Young American's Adventures in England and France during the Revolutionary War," Massachusetts Historical Society *Proceedings* 65 (1932–36): 234–67; Winslow Warren Papers (Massachusetts Historical Society), on which preceding article is based in part; Fritz 1972, 234.

39. On this battle, see Wiley Sword, *President Washington's Indian War: The Struggle for the Old Northwest, 1790–1795* (Norman: University of Oklahoma Press, 1985), 171–91; see also Fritz 1972, 264–67.

40. "A letter from a Gentleman in the Western territory," n.d. (c. late 1791 or early 1792), MWP2. Although nothing in MWP indicates the author of this piece, it is worth noting that Bostonian Winthrop Sargent, brother of Judith Sargent Murray, was with St. Clair's forces and wrote about the expedition and the battle.

41. JA to JW, 10 September 1783, *WAL,* 2:223, called the manner of death "happy and distinguished."

42. MW to Elizabeth Brown, 15 June 1783, Pilgrim Society. This transcript is not in MW's hand, but another draft of the letter can be found in MWP.

43. See JW to JA, 22 October 1786, *WAL,* 2:278–79; JW to JA, 18 May 1787, *WAL,* 2:291–92.

44. See, for example, MW to JA, 7 May 1789, *WAL,* 2:310–13; JA to MW, 29 May 1789, *WAL,* 2:313–14.

45. As is apparent, in MW to JA, 8 May 1789, MWP2; see also Anthony, 170–73, and David P. Szatmary, *Shays's Rebellion: The Making of an Agrarian Insurrection* (Amherst: University of Massachusetts Press, 1980).

46. Subscription list to *History,* MWP2; Judith Sargent Murray, *The Gleaner,* intro. Nina Baym (Schenectady, N.Y.: Union College Press, 1992), 727.

47. Janet Montgomery to MW, July 1788, Boston Public Library; hereafter cited as BPL.

48. Accounts of Sarah Cary's life have a number of inconsistencies, but many details can be gleaned from Caroline Gardiner Curtis, *The Cary Family Letters* (Cambridge: Riverside, 1891).

49. The alphabet is in MWP2, in two hands, one of which is JW2's. A descendant of Marcia Warren Torrey (her married name) later presented Harvard University with the manuscript of *History* now in the Houghton Library, suggesting she had some interest in preserving MW's writings.

50. Letters from the Warrens to Ebenezer Larkin are bound at the end of the third volume of the manuscript of the *History* at the Houghton Library, Harvard University.

51. Fulsome praise, partly in response to Adams's criticism, can be found in Charles Turner to MW, 3 October 1810, BPL.

52. JA to MW, 11 July 1807, *Correspondence between John Adams and Mercy Warren,* ed. Charles F. Adams (1878; New York: Arno, 1972), 321; hereafter cited as *CBAW.*

53. Shipton, 11:605. Fritz 1972, 309, gives the date as 27 November.

54. MW to Sarah Cary, 30 October 1809, CFP3, box 3. Sarah Cary's reply is drafted onto MW's letter. It should be noted that Sarah was mourning her own loss, a son, Edward, during the period of her silence.

55. Charles Turner to MW, 3 October 1810, BPL. Turner's son, Charles Turner, Jr., while serving as a congressman from Massachusetts at the outset of the War of 1812, had to flee to the Warren home in Plymouth to escape a Federalist mob that was opposed to his support for the war (Fritz 1972, 314; *Who Was Who in America,* historical volume, 1607–1896 [Chicago: Marquis, 1963], 541).

56. AA to MW, 30 December 1812, *CBAW,* 502; MW to AA, 26 January 1813, *CBAW,* 503; JA to MW, 24 November 1813, *CBAW,* 504, 505.

57. MW to JA, 10 July 1814, *WAL,* 2:395; JA to MW, 17 August 1814, *WAL,* 2:396; Anthony, 244.

58. MW to Mary Otis, 24 May 1814, MWP2. The quoted passages are from a section of the letter dated 25 May.

59. This lovely spot, only about 25 or 30 feet from the site of the original Plymouth fort, overlooks Plymouth Bay; a separate marker from the original headstone, erected in 1923, memorializes JW.

60. HW to Harrison Gray Otis, 23 October 1814, Harrison Gray Otis Papers (Massachusetts Historical Society), reel 5; these papers hereafter cited as HGOP.

61. Janis L. McDonald, "The Need for Contextual ReVision: Mercy Otis Warren, A Case in Point," *Yale Journal of Law and Feminism* 5 (1992): 183–215.

Chapter Two

1. Elizabeth F. Ellet, *The Women of the American Revolution,* (1848; Philadelphia: Jacobs, 1900), 1:94.

2. I am preparing a complete calendar of extent correspondence as well as a volume of selected letters.

3. Mercy Otis Warren, *The History of the Rise, Progress, and Termination of the American Revolution. Interspersed with Biographical, Political, and Moral Observations,* 3 vols. (1805; New York: AMS, 1970), 2:234; hereafter cited as *H.*

4. Linda K. Kerber, "The Republican Mother," in *Women's America: Refocusing the Past,* ed. Kerber and Jane Shennon DeHart, 3d ed. (New York: Oxford University Press, 1991), 87–95.

5. MW to JA, 15 October 1778, *PJA,* 7:142; also *WAL,* 2:55. Variations exist between versions in modern Adams editions and *WAL,* but most of these are likely the result of guessing at MW's script more than major editorial differences. Rarely is anything more than determining a capital or lowercase letter involved.

6. MW to James Otis, Jr., MWP1, 85. Although the "Letterbook" dates this as "Plymouth 1770," it was most probably written in September 1769, the month of the attack. MW's "seeing" is, of course, through the imagination of sympathy.

7. MW to Elizabeth Otis Brown, 15 June 1783, MWP1, and Pilgrim Society library.

8. "To a Very Young Lady," undated, MWP1, 113–14. See Judith Sargent Murray, "Desultory Thoughts upon the Utility of encouraging a degree of Self-Complacency, especially in Female Bosoms," *Gentleman and Lady's Town and Country Magazine* (Boston, 1784); "On the Equality of the Sexes," *Massachusetts Magazine: or, Monthly Museum of Knowledge and Rational Entertainment* 2 (1790); and "On the Domestic Education of Children," *Massachusetts Magazine* 2 (1790), all of which have been reprinted in the *Heath Anthology of American Literature,* vol. 1, ed. Paul Lauter et al., 2d ed. (Lexington, Mass.: D.C. Heath, 1994), 1,006–18. See also Vena Bernadette Field, *Constantia: A Study of the Life and Works of Judith Sargent Murray, 1751–1820* (Orono: University of Maine Press, 1931), 53–71. Another contemporary piece of advice literature to women with concerns similar to those voiced by MW is Hannah Webster Foster, *The Boarding School* (Boston, 1798). On Foster and other issues related to women in the 1790s, see my article, "The Politics of Seduction: Theater, Sexuality, and National Virtue in the Novels of Hannah Foster," in *Exceptional Spaces: Essays in Performance and History,* ed. Della Pollock (Chapel Hill: University of North Carolina Press, forthcoming 1996).

9. In the Mercy Warren Papers is a subcollection of more than 40 letters to Winslow, not all of them accurately dated, and some letters from WW, especially those written while he was en route to his fatal encounter in the West. A separate collection of his letters to MW and JW can be found in the Winslow Warren Papers.

10. Edmund M. Hayes reprints the published version and provides background on the editions in "Mercy Otis Warren versus Lord Chesterfield," *William and Mary Quarterly* 40 (1983): 616–21; quotations from Warren's letter are from this edition. The three published versions—*Independent Chronicle,* 18 January 1781; *Boston Magazine,* June 1784; and *Massachusetts Magazine* 2 (1790)—are virtually the same, but another version in MWP1 differs somewhat from the others.

11. Hayes 1983, 619–20. Not only was Abigail Adams the cause of the letter's 1781 publication and part of her cover letter the text of the headnote, but the 1790 publication carried a headnote signed "Constantia"—the pen name of Judith Sargent Murray. Lettered women saw in this production a measured, reasoned rebuff to a misogynistic worldview. As AA remarks, the style and judgment in the letter "would do honour to either sex, but . . . peculiarly distinguish this Lady" (Hayes 1983, 617n4).

12. C. Warren 1932–36, 251–52n31. Winslow was spared imprisonment in England largely as a result of MW's letters to him. Lord Hillsborough apparently told Winslow that his mother's letters "would do honour to the greatest writer that ever wrote. . . . I hope you will profit by her instructions and advice" (WW to MW, 28 April 1781, MWP2; quoted in C. Warren 1932–36, 252).

13. Most of these men are well enough known not to require any further word about them here, but two who will not be discussed later may need

to be identified briefly: Jabez Bowen (1739–1815), whom the Warrens visited in April 1775, was deputy governor of Rhode Island from 1778 to 1786 under Gov. William Greene and from 1785 until his death the chancellor of Brown University (originally Rhode Island College); extant letters include Bowen to MW, 6 September 1775, Schlesinger Library, Lutz Collection, and 20 April 1796(?), *WAL,* 2:329–30. James Lloyd, Jr. (1769–1831), was a U.S. senator from Massachusetts at the time of his letter to MW, 15 April 1812, BPL, Chamberlain Collection.

14. Letter of 10 January 1776, John Thomas Papers (Massachusetts Historical Society), reel 3. On Thomas's career and subsequent death in 1776 on a mission to Quebec, see *Dictionary of American Biography,* ed. Dumas Malone (1936; New York: Scribner's, 1964), 9, pt. 1:438–39; hereafter cited as *DAB.*

15. Mercy Otis Waren, *Poems, Dramatic and Miscellaneous* (Boston, 1790), iii, iv. A facsimile reprint of this book is available in *The Plays and Poems of Mercy Warren,* ed. Benjamin Franklin V (Delmar, N.Y.: Scholars Facsimiles, 1980). All future references to MW's 1790 book designated *PDM/PP* to indicate Franklin's edition.

16. George Athan Billias, *Elbridge Gerry: Founding Father and Republican Statesman* (New York: McGraw-Hill, 1976), 142–46.

17. C. Harvey Gardiner, ed., *A Study in Dissent: The Warren-Gerry Correspondence, 1776–1792* (Carbondale: Southern Illinois University Press, 1968), 151.

18. On Tuckerman (1778–1840), who was a minister in Chelsea before he turned to founding societies in Boston to aid the poor, see Joseph Tuckerman to MW, 8 April 1814, MWP2; Tuckerman, *The Principles and Results of the Ministry at Large* (Boston, 1838); *DAB,* 10:46; Daniel T. McColgan, *Joseph Tuckerman: Pioneer in American Social Work* (Washington, D.C.: Catholic University Press, 1940); Ann Douglas, *The Feminization of American Culture* (New York: Knopf, 1977), 152–53.

19. Ruth Bloch, *Visionary Republic: Millennial Themes in American Thought, 1756–1800* (Cambridge: Cambridge University Press, 1985), 151–52, 156. Winthrop later collected his works on prophesy and added to them in his *Appendix to the New Testament* (Cambridge: Hilliard and Metcalf, 1809).

20. Winthrop (1752–1821) was thought by some of his contemporaries to be an eccentric and a difficult personality; see *DAB,* 10, pt. 1:407–8.

21. An English speculative thinker, Faber (1773–1854) wrote on matters of religion, but at least two of his works by the time of MW's letter would have had direct relevance to the topic of prophecy: *Two Sermons before the University of Oxford, an attempt to explain by recent events five of the Seven Vials mentioned in the Revelations* (1799) and *A Dissertation on the Prophecies relative to the Great Period of 1,200 Years, the Papal and Mahomedan Apostasies, the Reign of Antichrist, and the Restoration of the Jews,* 2 vols. (1807); see *Dictionary of National Biography,* ed. Leslie Stephen and Sidney Lee (London: Oxford University Press, 1917), 6:975–76; hereafter cited as *DNB.*

22. John Adams, *Diary and Autobiography,* ed. L. H. Butterfield et al., 4 vols. (Cambridge: Belknap/Harvard University Press, 1961), 1:335, 2:64; hereafter as *DA.*

23. MW to JA, October 1775, *PJA,* 3:267. For a discussion of the date of this letter, see *PJA,* 3:271n1, n6, n7, n8.

24. JA to MW, 29 May 1789, *WAL,* 2:313, 314. Cf. AA to Mary Smith Cranch, 12 July 1789, commenting on the exchange of letters between MW and JA: "You cannot mistake who the Lady [who asked for patronage] was. I know no other equally ambitious, but I presume her pretentions & those of her Family will fail, as I think they ought to if one quarter part is true which has been reported of them." In *New Letters of Abigail Adams, 1788–1801,* ed. Stewart Mitchell (Boston: Houghton Mifflin, 1947), 16.

25. The issue of gender and discourse in the Warren and Adams letters, based in part on the research of Lawrence Kohlberg (*The Philosophy of Moral Development,* 1981) and Carol Gilligan (*In a Different Voice,* 1982), is the subject of Frank Shuffelton, "In Different Voices: Gender in the American Republic of Letters," *Early American Literature* 25 (1990): 289–304.

26. A few details about Janet (1743–1828) and Catherine (1752–1849), who in 1793 married itinerant Methodist Freeborn Garretson, can be found in Clare Brandt, *An American Aristocracy: The Livingstons* (Garden City, N.Y.: Doubleday, 1986).

27. Sarah (b. 1736) and Maria Walter (b. 1743), the second wife of MW's brother Joseph Otis (m. 22 February 1770), were daughters of Rev. Nathaniel Walter (1711–76), Harvard class of 1729. The name Hesilrige—there are many variant spellings—officially became Hazlerigg in 1818. C. Frederick Adams, "Pedigree of Walter," *New England Historical and Genealogical Register* 8 (1854), opp. 209; "Sir Arthur Hesilrige," *DNB,* 9:743–47; "Nathaniel Walter," in Shipton, 8:630–34.

28. The identity of Mrs. C is problematic, but leads into an important issue. I suggest Chapone for two reasons: the date of her book and evidence in a later Warren letter that MW had read *Letters on the Improvement of the Mind.* There are, however, several contingencies. If the book is poetry, as MW's letter hints, then either the author would have to be someone else—possibly Chapone's friend Elizabeth Carter, whose earlier book, *Poems on Several Occasions,* had been published in London in 1762—or the date of MW's letter is inaccurate, since Chapone did publish *Miscellanies in Prose and Verse* in 1775. One factor also suggests someone other than Chapone: MW inquires of Hesilrige about Mrs. C's stay in America before returning to England. I cannot find biographical evidence to link either Chapone or Carter to an American trip.

It should be noted, nevertheless, that both Chapone and Carter were friends of Elizabeth Robinson Montagu, to whom MW wrote a poem, and that MW's later friend Catharine Macaulay was often associated in the public mind with those women, even though her politics were more radical than theirs. All of these women were called bluestockings, after Montagu's literary discussion circle, and MW's interest in them suggests her own model for a literary discourse among women. On this group, in addition to *DNB* articles on individuals, see Sylvia Harcstark Myers, *The Bluestocking Circle: Women, Friendship, and the Life of the Mind in Eighteenth-Century England* (Oxford: Clarendon, 1990).

29. MW to Sarah Hesilrige, 1773, MWP1, 81–82. Roger Lonsdale, editor of *Eighteenth-Century Women Poets: An Oxford Anthology* (New York: Oxford University Press, 1990), says that Chapone is "adept in the polished mode" (xxxi). MW's poetry, as is later suggested, shows more similarity to Wheatley's.

30. MW to Catharine Macaulay, 29 December 1774, MWP1, 4. On parent-child imagery and its significance for the Revolutionary generations, see Jay Fliegelman, *Prodigals and Pilgrims: The American Revolution against Patriarchal Authority, 1750–1800* (Cambridge: Cambridge University Press, 1982).

31. MW to Catharine Macaulay, 1 February 1777, MWP1, 9; 15 February 1777, MWP1, 14–15. A note after these letters in the hand of James Warren, Jr., explains what can be observed by the reader of the *History:* "Several paragraphs in the two preceding letters were afterwards transcribed by the author into her annals of the American Revolution" (MWP1, 19).

32. MW, as a scholarly and literary woman, has sometimes been called a "bluestocking" (from Elizabeth Montagu's Blue Stocking Society in London). While the connotation of pedant or amateur sometimes attached to the term paints her unfairly with a broad—and sexist—brush, she deserves consideration for her efforts to foster a transatlantic "salon" of intellectually active women. On the implications of the term *bluestocking,* see Myers, 290–303.

33. It could be argued that AA's career as a letter writer begins with MW; see AA's first letter to MW, one that comes two years after any known letter by AA to anyone, and her statement of apology, "I have so long neglected my pen that I am conscious I shall make but a poor figure" (16 July 1773, *AFC,* 1:85).

34. There was a family tie as well, since AA's cousin Mary Smith Gray married MW's brother, Samuel Allyne Otis, in 1782.

35. MW to JA, 5 December 1773, *AFC,* 1: 89. From a section of the letter dated 11 December.

36. For a variant reading of this letter, see *WAL,* 1:228–30.

37. Sarah (b. 1753) was the daughter of Ellis Gray, Harvard 1734, and Sarah Brame. Her brother Edward Gray (c. 1750–79) married Mary Smith, AA's cousin, who, after Gray's death, married MW's brother Samuel Allyne Otis. Sarah married Samuel Cary on 5 November 1772 and had 13 children. MW elsewhere cites Sarah Gray Cary's mother as a friend. AA to JA, 20 October 1777, *AFC,* 2:356 and notes; *AFC,* 3:307n3; Augustus Thorndike Perkins, "Necrology of Edward Montague Cary," *New England Historical and Genealogical Register* 45 (1891): 322–24; Shipton, 9:30–32 (on Samuel Cary, Sarah's father-in-law), and 400–404 (on Ellis Gray); and Curtis, 10–70, passim.

Chapter Three

1. These include Rufus Wilmot Griswold, *The Female Poets of America,* 2d ed. (Philadelphia: Baird, 1853), and Caroline May, *The American Female Poets: With Biographical and Critical Notices* (Philadelphia: Lindsay and Blakiston, 1853).

2. Edward Clarence Stedman, ed., *An American Anthology, 1787–1900: Selections Illustrating the Editor's Critical Review of American Poetry in the Nineteenth Century* (Boston: Houghton Mifflin, 1900).

3. In addition to the facsimile reprint of Warren's *Poems, Dramatic and Miscellaneous* in *The Plays and Poems of Mercy Otis Warren,* ed. Franklin, selections of her work in the following have given MW's poems new currency: Edmund Hayes, "The Private Poems of Mercy Otis Warren," *New England Quarterly* 52 (1981): 199–224; Cowell, *Women Poets in Pre-Revolutionary America, 1650–1775;* and the *Heath Anthology of American Literature,* vol. 1.

4. Alicia Suskin Ostriker, *Stealing the Language: The Emergence of Women's Poetry in America* (Boston: Beacon Press, 1986), 23.

5. Additional poems are available in Cowell's *Women Poets.* The manuscript booklets at the Houghton Library and the Massachusetts Historical Society overlap considerably; I have cited the Houghton Library manuscript here (designated Am ms. 1354.1 by the library; hereafter cited as HL ms.) primarily because it contains more poems and for the sake of consistency (the poems reprinted by Hayes come from this collection as well). I have, however, sometimes verified readings by comparison of Houghton Library and Massachusetts Historical Society texts. Much work needs to be done in correlating versions since there are differences, many of them slight, among the manuscripts.

6. *PDM/PP,* 181; see also Cowell, 86. The poem is dated 10 July 1790, making it the last composed. "Mrs. Montague" is Elizabeth Robinson Montagu (1720–1800), whose animosity toward America is mentioned by AA in a letter to MW, 14 May 1787, *WAL,* 2:287. She wrote *An Essay on the Writings and Genius of Shakespeare* (1769). MW might have been attracted to Montagu for more reasons than gender. Like MW, Montagu criticized Voltaire, though more for his dislike of Shakespeare than for his skepticism.

7. First published in the *Boston Gazette,* 21 March 1774, under a different title, this poem is found in *PDM/PP,* 202–5, the source used here. A somewhat more satisfactory version can be found in *AFC,* 1:100–103, which I have used to confirm readings of words marked with dashes or misprints in *PDM/PP.*

8. "Tilans" in *PDM/PP.*

9. Thomas Bulfinch, *Bulfinch's Mythology of Greece and Rome with Eastern and Norse Legends* (New York: Collier, 1962), 171.

10. "N——— hills" in *PDM/PP;* see *AFC,* 1:103n3. Immediately after the Tea Party, Loyalist William Brattle met with Hutchinson at Milton to discuss strategy. In her play *The Defeat,* MW refers to Brattle as Proteus.

11. "Plutas" in *PDM/PP.*

12. HL ms., 39–40; another version, in MW's hand, is in MWP2.

13. HL ms., 39; another version in MWP2 was published in Brown, 189–90.

14. As noted in chapter 2, MW had read Wheatley's volume *Poems on Various Subjects, Divine and Moral,* in 1773, the year of its publication. It is possible that Wheatley's poem (originally written in 1767) exerted some influence on MW. James Warren, Jr., was also a student at Harvard at this time.

15. *PDM/PP,* 208–12. The original title in the 1774 publication is "To a Gentleman Who Requested a List of those Articles which Female Vanity has Comprised under the Head of Necessaries"; similar language was incorporated by MW in her headnote to the 1790 version (208).

16. Ducape is a variety of silk fabric.

17. *PDM/PP,* 188–94. In her headnote, MW erroneously states that the poem appeared first in 1774; it was originally published in the *Boston Gazette,* 13 February 1775.

18. Locke's *Two Treatises on Government* and Sidney's *Discourses Concerning Government* influenced many Whig political thinkers, including John Adams.

19. HL ms., 43.

20. *PDM/PP,* 246–52. Originally published in the *Boston Gazette* as "O Tempora! O Mores!"

21. *PDM/PP,* 206–7.

22. Ibid., 183–87.

23. Such letters of advice from the Adamses in America to John Quincy Adams abroad include one from Abigail Adams (daughter), 3 May 1782, *AFC,* 4:319–21, and from John Adams, 13 May 1782, *AFC,* 4:322–23. On the subject of whether Warren was in fact addressing her poem to young Adams, Oreovicz (1987) disagrees, identifying Torrismond as Winslow, but the evidence is against such a reading. WW was in Europe on business, not study.

24. *PDM/PP,* 221–27.

25. Hayes 1981, 206–7.

26. HL ms., 64; another text is in MWP2.

27. HL ms., 69.

28. *PDM/PP,* 213–15. It is entirely possible that MW knew Bradstreet's work, since the volume in which "A Letter to Her Husband" appears, first published in 1678, was issued in a Boston edition in 1758.

29. This reference and another to the coming of the spring strongly suggest the poem was written in the early months of 1776.

30. Cowell, 80–81; ms. versions in HL ms. and MWP2.

31. HL ms., 52–53; also in MWP2.

32. Hayes 1981, 215–17, 218. The information in these poems contradicts many statements by biographers and historians, especially on Eliza, who was thought to have died in infancy. See Fritz 1972, 68, and Hayes 1981, 215n12.

33. *PDM/PP,* 200–201.

34. HL ms., 55; also MWP2.

35. *PDM/PP,* 242–45.

36. Ibid., 235–39; originally published in the *Independent Chronicle,* 21 October 1779. Winthrop died on 3 May 1779.

37. See, for example, Wheatley's "To a Lady on the Death of Her Husband" and "On the Death of Samuel Marshall."

38. *PDM/PP,* 240–41.

39. Hayes 1981, 220–21.

40. Ibid., 219–20.

41. Ibid., 204–5.

42. Ibid., 208–9; *PDM/PP,* 219–20; *PDM/PP,* 198–99. None of these are dated, but all strike me as comparatively early, especially the first two. Anthony considers "Lines, Written" to be one of MW's best poems (80).

43. *PDM/PP,* 216–18.

44. Hayes 1981, 203–4.

45. Ibid., 213–14.

46. Hayes claims the presence of the compass conceit links the poem to the metaphysical tradition (1981, 213n11).

47. *PDM/PP,* 229–34. Called "To Mr. ———" in *PDM/PP,* the poem exists in an earlier version sent to Adams; the 1790 revision differs in several respects from the original, but the basic message remains the same. For the 1773 version, see *PJA,* 1:354–56.

48. *PDM/PP,* 229–34. The poem is preceded by a poetic introduction.

49. Hayes 1981, 222.

50. Ibid., 209–10. Hayes, 209n9, speaks of the poem as post-Revolution, but in the MWP2 ms. a copy of the poem in MW's hand dates it 1770.

51. Epictetus, *The Enchiridion,* 2d ed., trans. Thomas W. Higginson, intro. Albert Salomon (Indianapolis: Bobbs-Merrill, 1955), 22–23.

52. Hayes 1981, 211–12.

53. Ibid., 212–13.

54. Ibid., 210.

55. Ibid., 211.

56. Ibid., 207–8.

57. HL ms., 45–48; also in MWP2 poetry ms., 3–5.

58. Hayes 1981, 223–24. Hayes takes the reference generally, saying that MW wrote the poem "in her eighties" (203). It seems likely that she wrote it at the time of her eightieth birthday, two months before the death of JW and to whose loss she probably would have alluded had the poem been written later.

59. One of those involved the reprinting of her letter to WW on Chesterfield in the January issue.

60. *Massachusetts Magazine* 2 (1790): 198.

61. *Massachusetts Magazine* 2 (1790): 437. For a modern printing of

Morton's poem, see Cowell, 190. A correspondent of Morton's friend and fellow poet Joseph Dennie also remarked on MW's *Poems* in late 1790: "I think the old lady deserves praise, Joe. I believe she is no fool" (Roger Vose to Dennie, quoted in Harold Milton Ellis, *Joseph Dennie and His Circle: A Study in American Literature from 1792 to 1812* [1915; New York: AMS, 1971], 43).

62. Morton, 437. Writing under her newly altered signature name to distinguish herself from another and prior Constantia, Judith Sargent Murray, Morton must have seen at least some of the poems before the book was published in September and been asked to subscribe. With her husband and former Plymouth resident Perez Morton, MW's fellow poet lived in Boston, where MW's publisher was located. That there was a female literary subculture, as Cowell (12–16) describes, seems clear by the process of cross-praise and address in poems, but relations were not always harmonious. On the Morton-Murray conflict, see Emily Pendleton and Milton Ellis, *Philenia: The Life and Works of Sarah Wentworth Morton, 1759–1846* (Orono: University of Maine Press, 1931), 43–44.

63. Review of Mercy Warren, *Poems, Dramatic and Miscellaneous, Massachusetts Magazine* 2 (1790): 559–63, 628–30, 692–94; hereafter cited as *PDM* review.

64. The lines in question are the couplet beginning "Broke the firm union," *PDM/PP,* 191. Attribution to WW is speculative.

Chapter Four

1. Robert Munford's play is reprinted with a helpful introduction in *Dramas from the American Theater, 1762–1909,* ed. Richard Moody (Cleveland: World, 1966), 11–26. See also Rodney M. Baine, *Robert Munford: America's First Comic Dramatist* (Athens: University of Georgia Press, 1967). One character in the play, Ralpho, anticipates Mrs. Malaprop in Richard Brinsley Sheridan's *The Rivals.*

2. A modern edition with an authoritative introduction is [Forrest, Thomas], *The Disappointment: or, the Force of Credulity,* ed. David Mays (Gainesville: University Press of Florida, 1976).

3. For information on Hunter's play, see Walter J. Meserve, *An Emerging Entertainment: The Drama of the American People to 1828* (Bloomington: Indiana University Press, 1977), 39–41.

4. Vera O. Laska, *"Remember the Ladies": Outstanding Women of the American Revolution* (Boston: Commonwealth of Massachusetts Bicentennial Commission, 1976), 45.

5. G. Thomas Tanselle, *Royall Tyler* (Cambridge: Harvard University Press, 1967), 49–50.

6. Jean B. Kern, "Mercy Otis Warren: Dramatist of the American Revolution," *Curtain Calls: British and American Women and the Theater, 1660–1820,* ed. Mary Anne Schofield and Cecilia Macheski (Athens: Ohio University Press, 1991), 248.

7. Moses Coit Tyler, *The Literary History of the American Revolution, 1763–1783* 2 vols. (1897; New York: Barnes and Noble, 1941), 2:194.

8. *Massachusetts Spy* 2, no. 56, 15, and no. 61, 32. Never published as a complete play by MW, *The Adulateur* may not have been more than fragments when printed by Thomas in 1772. See below.

9. HL ms., 4. "Servia" could have several implications: (1) The character Rapatio is called "bashaw," a title used for officials in the Ottoman Empire and a word designed to evoke the stereotype of the scheming Turk; the once-independent state of Serbia was under Ottoman control at the time MW wrote the play. (2) In ancient Rome, the city wall in the days of the republic was called the Servian Wall, named after King Servius Tullius. (3) MW might be playing on the theme of servitude in that Boston—the Upper Servia of the play—is under the corrupt rule of the Loyalist government.

10. For a lengthy reconstruction of the play's development from periodical to pamphlet, see Gerald Weales, "*The Adulateur* and How It Grew," *Library Chronicle* 43 (1979): 103–33. Although Weales's article is the best piece on the play, it inevitably, like all such reconstructions, must use some speculation. Except as noted, I have followed my own inclinations as to what is MW's, relying more heavily than does Weales on the manuscripts as authorities.

11. Franklin, in his otherwise informative introduction to *The Plays and Poems,* unaccountably says that Brundo is a character "unknown to the reader" (viii). Since Rapatio's connection to Hutchinson is clear, readers would easily make the connection to Bernard. In the HL manuscript, MW makes the identification explicit.

12. *The Adulateur,* 26. A facsimile of the pamphlet version is printed in *Plays and Poems* (*PP*); unless otherwise noted, all page numbers refer to this edition.

13. The identity of Brutus is problematic. In the *Spy* version, he is called Cassius, but in both the pamphlet and in MW's manuscript he is called Brutus. The Cassius in the pamphlet is a different character, not identifiably Warren's. Weales, 115, claims that the Brutus of 1773 is Samuel Adams, but the HL manuscript clearly marks James Otis, Jr., as Brutus.

14. Clifford K. Shipton explains the name by noting that Oliver once sent a "report to [Ezra] Stiles, an ardent Whig, of his experiments with divining"; *New England Life in the Eighteenth Century: Representative Biographies from Sibley's Harvard Graduates* (Cambridge: Belknap/Harvard, 1963), 329.

15. Also spelled Limpet and Limput in various versions.

16. Weales (129–30, 126) protests the Montagu identification and says Bagshot is Colonel Dalrymple, Preston's superior.

17. In act 2, Cato speaking to Sempronius and Lucius the lines beginning, "Then let us rise, my friends, and strive to fill / This little interval, this pause of life." Joseph Addison, *Cato,* in *Eighteenth-Century Plays,* ed. Ricardo Quintana (New York: Modern Library, 1951), 25.

18. Some background to the play, with focus largely on the 1773 version, can be found in Arthur Hobson Quinn, *History of the American Drama from the Beginning to the Civil War,* 2d ed. (New York: Appleton-Century-Crofts, 1943), 34–38.

19. AA remarks on "the Dark designs of a Rapatio soul" in a letter to MW, 5 December 1773 (*AFC,* 1:88). In their note to this letter, the *AFC* editors, with their usual dismissal of MW, call *The Adulateur* "bombastic" (89n1).

20. Edmund M. Hayes, in the introduction to his edition of the play remarks that "[t]he play was prompted by the incriminating Hutchinson-Oliver letters." While the letters play a crucial role in the play's history, they may not be, as I intend to show, the actual "prompting" of the play. Except as otherwise noted, the Hayes edition of the play is the one cited here: "Mercy Otis Warren: *The Defeat,*" *New England Quarterly* 49 (1976): 440–58; quotation above here from p. 440. As a modern edition, the Hayes printing is easier to use than that in *PP,* which requires seeking out another page in another source. See Benjamin Franklin V, "A Note on Mercy Otis Warren's *The Defeat,*" *Early American Literature* 17 (1982): 165.

21. Bailyn 1974, 202–8; HL ms., 7. MW's note in the Houghton Library manuscript, referring to Rapatio's soliloquy in act 1, scene 1, is as follows: "This scene refers to Mr. Hutchinson's tedious and affrontive debate with the General Assembly on the right of Parliamentary taxation. This debate may be seen at length in the Journals of the House of Representatives 1773." See also *Speeches of His Excellency Governor Hutchinson, to the General Assembly of the Massachusetts-Bay . . . with the Answers . . .* (Boston, 1773).

22. Waters, 138, 140, 142; Bailyn 1974, 72; James H. Stark, *The Loyalists of Massachusetts and the Other Side of the American Revolution* (Boston: W. B. Clarke, 1910), 294–95; *PJA,* 1:252–56. See also David Hackett Fischer, *Paul Revere's Ride* (New York: Oxford University Press, 1994), 44–47.

23. The exchange of letters in the *Boston Gazette* between Adams and Brattle is printed in *PJA,* 1:256–309. Turning tail became a literal necessity for Brattle on 2 September 1774; after writing the new governor, British general Gage, about placement of munitions in Cambridge, an act that led to a military seizure of gunpowder, Brattle was forced to flee to British-occupied Boston ahead of bullets directed at him by outraged Cambridge Whigs (*PJA,* 2:170n3, 143n1; *AFC,* 1:148n3; Fischer, 47).

24. JA compares Brattle to the changeable god Proteus in a letter to William Tudor, 29 June 1774, a usage quite probably borrowed from MW's play. The editors of the *Papers of John Adams* suggest MW borrowed this usage from Adams or others for her next play, *The Group,* but the order of attribution seems to be otherwise (*PJA,* 2:105 and n4).

25. Bailyn 1974, 223–44. The pamphlet version was entitled *Copy of Letters Sent to Great-Britain, by His Excellency Thomas Hutchinson, the Hon. Andrew Oliver, and Several Other Persons, . . . Which Threatned Total Destruction to the Liberties of All America* (Boston, 1773).

26. In fairness to Warren, the linkage of the devil and Hutchinson had long been a part of popular mythology in cart displays and effigy-hangings.

27. Winthrop was negatived—that is, he was not allowed to take the seat he was elected to—the following year, 1774, but by the new governor, Gen. Thomas Gage (*PJA,* 2:96).

28. Philalethes published two pieces, 24 June and 1 July (Bailyn 1974, 245–46), thus dating Warren's scene as written in July, some time before the nineteenth.

29. *PJA,* 1:350; Bailyn 1974, 243. Phillips, called Deacon by contemporaries, had been part of a committee that appealed to Hutchinson to remove troops from Boston after the Massacre. He is not to be confused with British general William Phillips, part of Burgoyne's army at Saratoga.

30. In a series of letters by Humphrey Ploughjogger, Misanthrop, and other names, to Philanthrop (*PJA,* 1:174–210).

31. Two modern facsimiles of the Boston edition can be found in *The Group, 1779* [*sic*], intro. Colton Storm (Ann Arbor: William L. Clements Library, University of Michigan, 1953), and *PP,* the source cited here. Montrose Moses, in *Representative Plays by American Dramatists, 1765–1819* (New York: Blom, 1964), 1:209–32, prints the incomplete New York–Philadelphia version. On early publishing history, see Franklin's introduction to *PP,* xii–xiv.

32. For a general overview of satiric writing by women, including brief comments on *The Group,* see Jacqueline Hornstein, "Comic Vision in the Literature of New England before 1800," *Regionalism and the Female Imagination* 3, no. 2–3 (1977–78): 11–19.

33. See MW's terse response to JA's praise in her letter of 4 April 1775 (*PJA,* 2:413–14). On MW's reactions to presumed gender slights by JA, see Mary Beth Norton's *Liberty's Daughters,* 122–23.

34. All the speakers will be named in their turn, but two of the dramatis personae have no lines. Sir Sparrow Spendall is Sir William Pepperell the younger (1746–1816), the only American baronet (his lands were in Maine). His given name at birth was Sparhawk, but by terms in the will of his grandfather Sir William Pepperell the elder, he was required to take his mother's patronymic to inherit the estate (Stark, 207–8). Commodore Batteau is Joshua Loring (1716–81), commodore of naval forces of Lakes Champlain and Ontario during the French and Indian War, and prior to the Revolution a commissioner of revenue; during the Revolution, his son, also Joshua, entered the British army and served as "commissary of prisoners" with charges, perhaps not entirely warranted, of excessive cruelty to American patriots. Quinn confuses father and son in his remarks on *The Group* (*DAB,* 6: pt. 1, 418–20; Stark, 423–24; Quinn, 41).

35. Quinn calls her satires "conversations rather than plays" (46).

36. *AFC,* 1:251n3; Stark, 421. A few months after the appearance of the play, AA refers to Thomas as Simple Sapling in a letter to JA, 16 July 1775 (*AFC,* 1:248).

37. Murray (d. 1794), whose origins are obscure, is not to be confused with several others of the same name, including the Universalist minister who married Judith Sargent Stephens and the fourth earl of Dunmore, crown governor of Virginia. This one rose to wealth as a merchant and served in the General Court (House) for many years (Stark, 376–77). In 1763, after a fistfight with William Brattle over an alleged slight by the latter, Murray found himself the object of a suit by Brattle. The general, whom MW memorialized as Proteus in *The Defeat,* was represented by John Adams in a suit that occasioned JA's "U" essays against extralegal means of satisfaction for insults (*PJA,* 1:60–61, 72–76). Murray's short temper in this affair may be the source of his character name in *The Group*—a warrior quick to spring up but no more potent than a fungus. Like Brattle and some others represented in the play, Murray was a relative latecomer to the Hutchinson faction (*PJA,* 1:244). As a result, a mob gathered to prevent him from accepting the mandamus post; see, in addition to sources above, William Tudor to JA, 3 September 1774 (*PJA,* 2:141).

38. Quoted in Bernard Bailyn, *Faces of Revolution: Personalities and Themes in the Struggle for American Independence* (New York: Knopf, 1990), 241.

39. The incident is described in Carl Van Doren, *Benjamin Franklin* (New York: Viking, 1938), 467–76. For an interpretation of Franklin's response to Wedderburn's attack, see Michael Warner, *The Letters of the Republic: Publication and the Public Sphere in Eighteenth-Century America* (Cambridge: Harvard University Press, 1990), 91–96.

40. Stark, 325–27, 331; Shipton, 14:641–48; *PJA,* 2:xi, 217, 221–22. Leonard's identity as author was known to John Trumbull by 1775 and conveyed to JA through Trumbull's poem *M'Fingal,* but JA persisted throughout his life to believe Sewall to be Massachusettensis (*PJA,* 2:221–22). At Harvard, Leonard was also only one year behind MW's brother, Samuel Allyne Otis.

41. Boutineau (b. 1710), father-in-law to and attorney for John Robinson, the customs commissioner charged with the beating of James Otis in 1769; Gray (1711–94), treasurer of Massachusetts 1753–74 and father-in-law of MW's brother Samuel Allyne Otis; Browne (1737–1802), classmate of John Adams at Harvard (1755) and superior court judge from Salem; Erving (1727–1816), Harvard 1747, sometimes called Colonel (Stark, 448–49, 334–36, 449–51, 298–99; *DAB,* 2: pt. 2, 169–70). All were among the 10 who took the oath.

42. Carol Berkin, *Jonathan Sewall: Odyssey of an American Loyalist* (New York: Columbia University Press, 1974), 25–44.

43. Boston, 1775. The play begins in a barbershop as an inquiry among patrons as to the difference "between a *true whig* and an *honest tory*" (6) but ends up with a diatribe against the Whig position for being "treason" (32); see Berkin, 110–11, and Kenneth Silverman, *A Cultural History of the American Revolution* (1976; New York: Columbia University Press, 1987), 268–69. For a discussion of *Cure* in the context of other political plays about "blockheads"—including the play attributed to MW—see John J. Teunissen, "Blockheadism

and the Propaganda Plays of the American Revolution," *Early American Literature* 7 (1972): 148–62.

44. The "father" of Humbug is John Erving, Sr. (1693–1786).

45. A "publican" in the sense of a "tax" collector, but probably in the customs service, following his father Thomas Lechmere, 1683–1765.

46. On Gage's early sympathies for America, see Fischer, 30–43.

47. Kate is Bathsheba Bourne Newcomb Ruggles, a tavern keeper whose squabbles with husband her Timothy were the stuff of legend (Shipton, 9:201–2). In his sketch of Timothy, Shipton, who frequently displays his sympathies for Harvard Loyalists, rather testily and ridiculously says of Bathsheba, "Her social background was better than that of Mercy (Otis) Warren who lampooned her in her skits" (201). Shipton claims that MW portrays Kate as a "tavern slut," then rushes to defend the honor of Bathsheba Ruggles, but nothing in *The Group* supports the notion that MW means to impugn *her* at all, let alone as a sexual profligate. For a contemporary approval of MW's portrayal of Hateall and Kate, see Samuel Swift to JA, 31 March 1775, *PJA,* 2: 410.

48. *PP* includes a reprint of the Boston 1776 edition, the source cited here. Another modern printing can be found in Norman Philbrick, ed., *Trumpets Sounding: Propaganda Plays of the American Revolution* (New York: Blom, 1972), 149–68.

49. P. L. Ford, *Some Notes towards an Essay on the Beginnings of American Dramatic Literature, 1606–1789* (1893; New York: Burt Franklin, 1971), 15–16, 18, 24–25; M. C. Tyler, 2:207–8; Quinn, 46; Anthony, 109–16; Philbrick, 137–47; Meserve, 71–72.

50. *PP,* xvii–xx; Kern, 247–59; Krystan V. Douglas, "A Question of Authorship: Mercy Otis Warren and *The Blockheads,*" *Theatre Survey* 30, no. 1–2 (1989): 85–92. Franklin, whose reasoning Douglas and Kern generally second, uses internal evidence and alleged parallels of imagery and situation between *The Blockheads* and the three earlier MW plays to make his case. None of these items alone, such as the presence of characters who "incriminate themselves," or even the reasons in aggregate, can do more than suggest that the author of *The Blockheads* had some surface familiarity with one or more of MW's first three plays.

51. W. C. Ford, 20–21; Hutcheson never mentions *The Blockheads* or *The Motley Assembly;* Fritz 1972, 318–19.

52. Kern says the characters are the same as those in *The Blockheads,* but that cannot be supported, even if there is some overlap in the historical figures being satirized.

53. Other characters not otherwise named can be identified as follows: Captain Bashaw is British Rear Admiral Molyneaux Shuldham; Puff is General William Howe, Gage's replacement as overall commander of British forces; L——d Dapper is Brigadier General Hugh Percy, commander of the British relief brigade at Lexington; Dupe, a name assigned to Loyalist Thomas Flucker in earlier plays, is here marked as a British officer, "Who you please." See W. C. Ford, 20.

54. A facsimile edition is reprinted in *PP,* the source of citations here.

55. M. C. Tyler, 2:227n1. Others writing in support of the attribution are Anthony, 112–13; Laska, 50; Meserve, 72–73, though with reservations; and Franklin, in *PP,* xx–xxiii.

56. Although, as Franklin remarks, a male persona could simply be a cover for a female—a typical strategy for women writers of the time—Warren never identifies herself as male in other published works (*PP,* xxi). Murray, on the other hand, uses several male personae in her *Gleaner* writings.

57. W. C. Ford prints two lists from marked copies of the play to identify characters (21). The lists do not agree, and one has to wonder anyway how closely the playwright meant to denominate particular persons. Mr. and Mrs. Bubble are indicated as being James Swan and his wife, persons also thought to be satirized in *Sans Souci.* But Swan (1754–1831), while wealthy, had a long record in Whig activities, including the Boston Tea Party, Bunker Hill, and other official posts (*The Letters of Joseph Dennie,* ed. Laura Pedder [Orono: University of Maine Press, 1936], 3n5). Miss Doggrel in one copy is suggested to be Sarah Wentworth Morton, who, with her husband Perez, was friends with the Swans in Boston (Pendleton and Ellis, 26). While Sarah's family, the Apthorps, were generally Loyalist and she seems to have maintained conservative political connections, her husband was a staunch Whig. One last identification of interest: Miss Flourish in one version is Elizabeth Deblois, who turned down the passionate entreaties of Benedict Arnold, then an American general, to be his wife (W. C. Ford, 22; Clare Brandt, *The Man in the Mirror: A Life of Benedict Arnold* [New York: Random House, 1994], 116, 118, 143–44, 147).

58. All references are to the 2d ed. of *Sans Souci* (Boston: Warden and Russell, 1785); hereafter cited as *SS.*

59. Charles Warren, "Samuel Adams and the Sans Souci Club in 1785," Massachusetts Historical Society *Proceedings* 60 (1926–27): 332–33.

60. Some of these letters can be found in Gordon S. Wood, ed., *The Rising Glory of America, 1760–1820* (New York: Braziller, 1971); see esp. pp. 138–42.

61. See Pendleton and Ellis, 29–30.

62. In saying this, I differ markedly from Franklin, who claims in *PP* that "her literary reputation correctly rests on the best of her early, technically flawed plays" (xxv). On the contrary, the later verse dramas deserve a critical rehearing.

63. Although some events occur in Toledo, further to the south, most of the action takes place in the vicinity of Valladolid, including Segovia, Tordesillas, Toro, Villalar (Villabar in *Ladies*), Torrelobatan (Torbolatan), Villapando, and Medina de Rio Seco (site of the first battle between rebels and Royalists).

64. Charles's territory is described as running from "Tagus to the Scheld," rivers in Spain and Belgium, respectively (*PDM/PP,* 139).

65. The story of Sulayman and Roxalana appeared on the London stage

in Isaac Bickerstaff's *The Sultan; or, A Peep into the Seraglio,* 12 December 1775. It is possible MW knew of this play, although the text was not published until 1787, three years after MW had finished *Ladies.* A production in the United States, entitled *The American Captive,* took place in 1794. See Valerie C. Rudolph, "Isaac John Bickerstaff," *DLB,* 89:12–13, 22.

66. William Robertson, *The History of the Reign of the Emperor Charles V* (New York: Harper, 1838). George Washington owned a set of the four-volume 1782 edition.

67. Robertson, 160–72; 95–119. To give one example of her use of Robertson, MW extracts sentiments expressed in two letters by de Padilla (as translated by Robertson, 170–71) and puts them in his speeches, notably that in act 4, scene 4 (*PDM/PP,* 156). Still, the essential phrasing and emphases are MW's.

68. The son of Velasco is called either Haro or de Haro in the play; Robertson has de Haro.

69. Linda K. Kerber, *Women of the Republic: Intellect and Ideology in Revolutionary America* (Chapel Hill: University of North Carolina Press, 1980), 269–71. See also Kern, 254–56.

70. Cheryl Z. Oreovicz, "Heroic Drama for an Uncertain Age: The Plays of Mercy Warren," in *Early American Literature and Culture: Essays Honoring Harrison T. Meserole,* ed. Kathryn Zabelle Derounian-Stodola (Newark: University of Delaware Press, 1992), 201–6. Oreovicz, however, mistakenly labels Donna Maria as "pseudo-historical," an observation that undercuts her argument that Warren was writing a different kind of literature for women than the usual historical-model readings for men (201n27).

71. Facsimile in *PDM/PP,* 9–96, the source cited here.

72. Historical information on this period is from N. G. L. Hammond and H. H. Scullard, *The Oxford Classical Dictionary,* 2d ed. (Oxford: Clarendon, 1970); Michael Grant, *History of Rome* (New York: Scribner's, 1978), esp. pp. 423–36; Edward Gibbon, *The Decline and Fall of the Roman Empire,* vol. 1 (Chicago: Encyclopedia Britannica, 1952), esp. pp. 477–582; and other sources as noted.

73. In addition to the Huns and their leaders, Attila and Bleda, and the Vandals and their rulers, Genseric and Hunneric, Warren mentions the following tribes and individuals: the Alans, a nomadic people originally from Southeastern Russia; the Visigoths ("the Goths"), who threatened the empire from the area of the Danube; the Burgundians, a Germanic people once routed by Aetius and the Huns, one of whom kills Petronius Maximus in his flight (Gibbon, 573); the Scythians; the Germanic Suebi or Suevi and their leader, "Ricemar" (Ricimer), a general working for the Romans; and the Quadi (MW uses the phrase "Quadian lakes," 46), a subtribe of the Suebi. Traulista is called "mighty prince of Hermannic's line" (46), corrected in the Errata to Hermanric, a Suebian king of the fifth century. MW's Romans regularly excoriate the non-Romans in terms perhaps unintentionally like those used against American

Indians by the early English settlers: "savages," "infernal fiends," and the like (46).

74. Gibbon's book appeared in several volumes beginning in 1776, in time for MW to have seen the ones relevant to her story. Recall that James Winthrop sent her later volumes in 1791.

75. Gibbon never gives the name of Petronius's wife.

76. See, for instance, the various laments by Maria in Royall Tyler's play *The Contrast* (1787).

77. The historical Eudocia, elder daughter of Eudoxia, did in fact go with the Vandals in company with her mother and sister (Gibbon, 573; Grant, 434). Placidia and Eudoxia "were honorably restored" after payment to Genseric from the eastern emperor, but Eudocia remained "the reluctant wife of Hunneric" (Gibbon, 582).

78. The historical Eudoxia was the daughter of Emperor Theodosius II and great-granddaughter of Theodosius I (the Great). Since Valentinian was a grandson of Theodosius I, each could claim equal lineage.

79. MW follows Gibbon in making much of Petronius's wealth as a member of the Anician line (Gibbon, 497–98, 572); the character of Edoxia, however, is largely MW's interpretation.

80. This actress spoke an unusual "Apology for the Author" between acts during a production of Murray's play *The Traveller Returned* (Meserve, 154).

Chapter Five

1. For publication dates and locations of these articles, see Charles Warren, "Elbridge Gerry, James Warren, Mercy Warren, and the Ratification of the Federal Constitution in Massachusetts," Massachusetts Historical Society *Proceedings* 64 (1930–32), 115n22. This article (143–64) establishes MW's authorship (there are also many internal clues, including references to her hero from *Ladies,* de Padilla) and reprints letters from MW to Catharine Macaulay on the subject matter of Warren's essay *Observations.*

2. On the Massachusetts convention, see Jackson Turner Main, *The Antifederalists: Critics of the Constitution, 1781–1788* (Chapel Hill: University of North Carolina Press, 1961), 200–9. Main also mentions MW in several places (114, 140, 169, 186, 235).

3. A summary of MW's ideas in *Observations* and their translation into her *History* can be found in Raymond Pollin and Constance Pollin, "Mercy Otis Warren: Patriot Founding Mother," *Daughters of the American Revolution Magazine* 123 (1989): 104–5, 150–51.

4. *Observations* (Boston, 1788), 4. A modern facsimile reprint can be found in Richard Henry Lee, *An Additional Number of Letters from the Federal Farmer to the Republican* (Chicago: Quadrangle, 1962).

5. On the influence of Sidney on American Whigs, see Caroline Robbins, "Algernon Sidney's *Discourses Concerning Government:* Textbook of

Revolution," *William and Mary Quarterly* 4 (1947): 269–96, and H. Trevor Colbourn, *The Lamp of Experience: Whig History and the Intellectual Origins of the American Revolution* (Chapel Hill: University of North Carolina Press, 1965), 9, passim.

6. As *Observations on the Government and Laws of the United States of America* (Amsterdam, 1784) and as *Remarks concerning the Government and the Laws of the United States of America* (London, 1784). On JA's personal knowledge of the abbè, see AA to Mary Smith Cranch, 5 September 1784, *AFC,* 5:440. Royall Tyler, the future playwright and disappointed suitor of John and Abigail Adams's daughter, wrote to JA to request a copy of the translation, with which JA complied (Tyler to JA, 15 October 1785, *AFC,* 6:430; JA to Tyler, 12 December 1785, *AFC,* 6:493).

7. Mably's *Remarks* is a curious book, full of seeming contradictions. How well MW knew this is not entirely clear, but if she read it thoroughly she must have been repelled by one sentence in which he expresses his hope to Adams that "your laws maintain a prudent distrust of women, by whom corruption is introduced through all republics whatsoever" (214). Mably's conservatism was exposed by another foreign commentator, the Italian Jeffersonian Philip Mazzei, in 1788; see *Researches on the United States,* trans. Constance D. Sherman (Charlottesville: University Press of Virginia, 1976), 115–204. On Mably's thought in general, see Ira O. Wade, *The Structure and Form of the French Enlightenment,* vol. 2, *Esprit Révolutionnaire* (Princeton: Princeton University Press, 1977), 337–51.

8. On the main features of Helvétius's thought, see John Herman Randall, *The Making of the Modern Mind: A Survey of the Intellectual Background of the Present Age* (1926; New York: Columbia University Press, 1976), 316–18; Irving Louis Horowitz, *Claude Helvétius: Philosopher of Democracy and Enlightenment* (New York: Paine-Whitman, 1954); and Wade, 262–95.

9. Boston, 1791. Macaulay's *Observations* originally appeared in London in 1790. Burke's *Reflections on the Revolution in France* was first published in 1789, then in several editions beginning in 1790.

10. The printing must have occurred in the fall of that year, as Winthrop notes to MW that hers is the only copy he's seen (3 August 1791, *WAL,* 2:327).

11. The printer's manuscript, bound in three volumes and written in the hand of James Warren, Jr., rests at Houghton Library, Harvard University; included with it are final changes and a set of 15 letters sent by the Warrens to Ebenezer Larkin, the publisher, that contain complaints about slowness and other details. Other and earlier manuscripts of *History* are deposited in the Library of Congress. Letters from Rev. James Freeman are found in MWP2. A summary of the problems faced by Warren in publishing is in Fritz 1972, 298–300.

12. An account sheet, showing costs of printing and binding, is included with the Warren-Larkin letters in volume 3 of the manuscript. Letters in that

series that discuss subscribers include MW to Ebenezer Larkin, 11 and 18 December 1805; JW2 to Larkin, 18 December 1805; JW2 to Larkin, 19 February 1806.

13. Michael Kammen, *A Season of Youth: The American Revolution and the Historical Imagination* (New York: Knopf, 1978), 43.

14. Lester H. Cohen, "Explaining the Revolution: Ideology and Ethics in Mercy Otis Warren's Historical Theory," *William and Mary Quarterly* 37 (1980): 205.

15. Sacvan Bercovitch, *The American Jeremiad* (Madison: University of Wisconsin Press, 1978).

16. Whether the committees were actually the idea of JW, Sam Adams, even MW, or some combination is in dispute; see Anthony, 77–78. In his *History of the Rise, Progress, and Establishment of the Independence of the United States,* William Gordon, a supporter of the Revolution who served as a minister in America during the war and collected documents and anecdotes from participants, credits James Warren with the proposal (1:207).

17. The matter of providential thinking in MW's history is a complex one. On several occasions, she evokes providence as an overseeing guide to human affairs, moving America toward its revolutionary end. As Lester H. Cohen notes, however, appeals to providence do not square with the doctrine of self-determination that MW's and others' histories affirm. Cohen argues "that the providential language of the histories was a strategic language that no longer reflected its theological origins"; nevertheless, MW's interests in millenialism, as evidenced by her letters in the 1790s and early 1800s to James Winthrop, a writer on the biblical book of Revelation, suggests she means providence as something more than rhetorical enhancement. See Cohen, *The Revolutionary Histories: Contemporary Narratives of the American Revolution* (Ithaca: Cornell University Press, 1980), 53.

18. Following providence, however, also means accounting for chance, which MW does with some equivocation; this gives some weight to Cohen's remarks in *Revolutionary Histories* that providential language is largely a dramatic intensifier, while the matter of causation is left "as a complex problem," not properly declared one way or the other (Cohen, 67, 83). But the fervency of MW's religious views, particularly as expressed later in her life, must always be kept in mind.

19. As Cohen notes throughout his article "Explaining the Revolution," Warren's providentialism is obviated by the evidence of corruption in the postwar period; as long as the *History* points to the end of the war itself, however, it bears a progressive, providential stamp.

20. See James Winthrop to MW, 26 August 1788, regarding Federalist attitudes toward North Carolina, whose representatives, it was reported, had just voted against the Constitution: "They [the Federalists] immediately began to vilify that State as being originally peopled by outlaws and convicts, who were driven from the more civilized parts of the world into the wilds of

Carolina, where they had formed a settlement but little superior in morals to the infernal world" (*WAL,* 2:303).

21. For example, see MW to JA, 10 March 1776, *PJA,* 4:51.

22. An early draft of the Hutchinson material had been sent to James Winthrop, a member of a staunch patriot family, who in his comment to MW identifies politely her tendency to paint Hutchinson in one color: "Though we cannot form a very high opinion of the political talents of a man who has made the establishment of a particular system the pursuit of his whole life, and is disappointed in the attainment of his object: yet would it not be better to give him, on the credit of his own party, a little undeserved praise, to procure their judgment in favor of the work?" (Winthrop to MW, 26 February 1787, *WAL,* 2:282–83).

23. Kerber 1980; Lester Olsen, *Emblems of American Community in the Revolutionary Era: A Study in Rhetorical Iconology* (Washington, D.C.: Smithsonian Institution Press, 1991).

24. Nina Baym, "Mercy Otis Warren's Gendered Melodrama of Revolution," *South Atlantic Quarterly* 90 (1991): 531–54.

25. Royall Tyler, *The Contrast* (1790), act 1, scene 2. Reprinted in the *Heath Anthology of American Literature,* vol. 1. In another episode in MW's text, the author says of the officers' wives who visit Valley Forge, "Nothing but the inexperience of the American ladies and their confidence in the judgment of their husbands, could justify this hazard to their persons, and to their feelings of delicacy" (*H,* 1:389n).

26. One part of MW's style that reflects her consciousness of herself as a woman writing is her turning away from scenes of violence or using a phrase such as "the pen wearies" to describe her refusal to continue to depict the horrors of war (see, e.g., *H,* 1:370–71). A similar strategy, though in a very different context, is used by Harriet Jacobs when describing the sexual depredations by slave owners on slave women in her narrative *Incidents in the Life of a Slave-Girl* (1861). The implication is, for nineteenth-century females, that a woman may enter a man's sphere—writing history—but she may not exercise the prerogatives of men to depict uncensored brutality without forfeiting her womanhood. This problem of graphic depiction by women writers is one of the themes in Virginia Woolf's 1931 talk, "Professions for Women," in *Current Issues and Enduring Questions: A Guide to Critical Thinking and Argument,* ed. Sylvan Barnet and Hugo Bedau, 3d ed. (New York: St. Martin's, 1993), 63–67.

27. In "Explaining the Revolution," Cohen claims that Warren's thinking on the place of good and evil in human nature is "unclear" (206). Though she is quite explicit that the noble principle is original, Cohen sees throughout the *History* a tension between "virtue and avarice," in which Warren finally calls for a necessary, extrainstitutional vigilance against the corruptions instigated by environmental factors.

28. On the matter of perverted ambition and the "favorable circumstances" for its appearance, see especially *H,* 1:2, and the discussion of MW's

terms in Merle Curti, *Human Nature in American Historical Thought* (Columbia: University of Missouri Press, 1968), 52–53.

29. The larger context of American thinking on human nature in MW's time is discussed in another book by Merle Curti, *Human Nature in American Thought: A History* (Madison: University of Wisconsin Press, 1980), 70–136.

30. William Paley, *The Principles of Moral and Political Philosophy* (London, 1785), 448.

31. On this matter, in addition to Macaulay's *Observations,* see *H,* 1:43; MW to Macaulay, 31 May 1791, MWP1, 29–31; James Winthrop to MW, 3 August 1791, *WAL,* 2:327.

32. J. Hector St. John [Michel-Gillaume Jean] de Crevecoueur, *Letters from an American Farmer* (1782; New York: Dutton, 1957), 35–82 (letter 3).

33. Baym compares Warren's version of this story—which had become and would remain famous for a century or more—with that of David Ramsay in his history, and sees the former's treatment as offering, particularly in the sentence I have quoted, "sado-erotic additions" (545). Paintings on the subject include John Vanderlyn, *The Death of Jane McCrea* (1803–1805), reproduced in Kammen, opp. p. 102, and Asher B. Durand, *The Murder of Jane McCrea* (1839). Kammen also notes a poem by George P. Morris, "Janet McRae [*sic*]" (80). Vanderlyn's painting highlights the native menace from two brawny attackers and the kneeling McCrea's eroticized vulnerability. Ironically, the actual woman was a Tory (Silverman, 330–31).

34. Lawrence J. Friedman and Arthur H. Shaffer, "Mercy Otis Warren and the Politics of Historical Nationalism," *New England Quarterly* 48 (1975): 210. For a contrary view on the matters of race and gender in Warren's scheme, see Baym, 545–51. Joan Hoff Wilson claims that based on an alleged interchange between AA and MW, in which MW declined to argue for a liberalized law for women that AA urged her to support, "there is no evidence that her liberal politics included even as much moderate concern and commitment to civil rights for women as that demonstrated by Abigail Adams" (178). As evidence she cites (182n28) a letter from AA to her sister, Mary Cranch, dated 4 July 1797, in as printed in Mitchell, 102–3. Neither this letter nor any other letter to Mary Cranch during the 1790s has anything to do with this issue.

35. *The Panoplist; or the Christian's Armory* 2, no. 8 (1807): 380–84; no. 9, 429–32; hereafter cited as *Panoplist.* The review in this publication and in others cited below contradict the statement by Elaine Crovitz and Elizabeth Buford that "not even one review of Mercy's book can be found in archives today" (*Courage Knows No Sex* [North Quincy, Mass.: Christopher, 1978], 48).

36. Worcester *National Aegis,* 10 January 1810, 4; 17 January 1810, 4; 24 January 1810, 4; 31 January 1810, 4; 7 February 1810, 4; 21 February 1810, 4; 28 February 1810, 4; hereafter cited as *Aegis.* See also JW2 to James Winthrop, 10 March 1810, BPL.

37. After MW had apparently reacted with some sensitivity to Winthrop's mention of factual errors, he assured her that, as he had told her son

Henry in person, "if I was about to review the book, for the public eye, such a minute criticism I should be ashamed to insert" (11 March 1807, *WAL,* 2:355).

38. See JA's complaint on this point (17 August 1807, *CBAW,* 466–69).

39. Most of JA's biographers take his side in the matter. For a more balanced discussion of the affair that demonstrates how MW's comments hit home, see Peter Shaw, *The Character of John Adams* (Chapel Hill: University of North Carolina Press, 1976), 287–94. MW made many changes in the passages on Adams from manuscript to print copy, often omitting qualifying phrases that would have lessened the impact of her remarks (Brown, 224–26).

40. William Raymond Smith, *History as Argument: Three Patriot Historians of the American Revolution* (The Hague: Mouton, 1966), 104–5, lists 4 "principles" and 15 "precepts" that describe MW's definition of a republic.

41. MW claimed that she could not define republicanism for someone so intemperate, but that she would have done it gladly 20 years earlier and that JW still could (MW to JA, 15 August 1807, *CBAW,* 450–51).

42. For a comprehensive look at how MW has been minimized as a historian well into the twentieth century, see Judith B. Markowitz, "Radical and Feminist: Mercy Otis Warren and the Historiographers," *Peace and Change* 4 (1977): 10–20. Markowitz is one of the first historians to credit MW with a thoroughgoing, well-conceived, radical political philosophy. In this vein, too, see McDonald.

43. For modern commentaries on the history other than those already mentioned, see M. C. Tyler, 2:419–23; Alma Lutz, "Early American Women Historians," *Boston Public Library Quarterly* 8 (1956): 85–99; and Cecilia Tichi, "Worried Celebrants of the American Revolution," *American Literature 1764–1789: The Revolutionary Years,* ed. Everett Emerson (Madison: University of Wisconsin Press, 1977), 286–90.

Selected Bibliography

Under primary sources, I have listed only some of the manuscript sources, printed collections of letters that have significant pieces by Mercy Warren, and essential editions of her work. I have omitted many anthologies and other reprintings of letters or poems, although some of those not listed here are mentioned in the notes. For list of manuscript sources, researchers are urged to consult J. Albert Robbins et al., eds., *American Literary Manuscripts: A Checklist of Holdings in Academic, Historical, and Public Libraries, Museums, and Authors' Homes in the United States,* 2d ed. (Athens: University of Georgia Press, 1977).

For secondary sources, I have included, with few exceptions, only those works that devote some significant attention to Warren but have excluded doctoral dissertations. She is mentioned in many other works, and to find these mentions investigators are encouraged to use citation indexes or such reference tools as Eugenie Andruss Leonard, Sophie Hutchinson Drinker, and Miriam Young Holden, *The American Woman in Colonial and Revolutionary Times: A Syllabus with Bibliography* (Philadelphia: University of Pennsylvania Press, 1962).

PRIMARY SOURCES

Butterfield, L. H., et al., eds. *Adams Family Correspondence.* 6 vols. to date. Cambridge: Belknap/Harvard University Press, 1963–. Significant source of letters by and to Warren, with focus on Abigail Adams.

Franklin, Benjamin, V. "A Note on Mercy Otis Warren's *The Defeat.*" *Early American Literature* 17 (1982): 165. Prints passage that did not copy clearly in Franklin's edition of *Plays and Poems.*

_____, ed. *The Plays and Poems of Mercy Otis Warren.* Delmar, N.Y.: Scholars Facsimiles, 1980. The most complete modern edition, this volume provides facsimile versions of the three political plays, plus *The Blockheads* and *The Motley Assembly* and the complete *Poems, Dramatic and Miscellaneous* (see below). Introduction by Franklin.

Gardiner, C. Harvey, ed. *A Study in Dissent: The Warren-Gerry Correspondence, 1776–1792.* Carbondale: Southern Illinois University Press, 1968. Some letters between Warren and Elbridge and Ann Gerry.

Hayes, Edmund M. "Mercy Otis Warren: *The Defeat.*" *New England Quarterly* 49 (1976): 440–58. Most usable text of that play, with introduction.

_____. "Mercy Otis Warren versus Lord Chesterfield, 1779." *William and Mary Quarterly* 40 (1983), 616–21. Annotated version of letter to Winslow that was published at the behest of Abigail Adams.

_____. "The Private Poems of Mercy Otis Warren." *New England Quarterly* 54 (1981): 199–224. Large selection of previously unpublished poems from Houghton Library manuscripts at Harvard University.

M. O. Warren, Drama and Poems; History of the American Revolution. Houghton Library, Harvard University. Manuscripts of *The Adulateur, The Defeat, The Group,* and poems unpublished in the author's lifetime; a separate three-volume final manuscript of *History* with publication letters bound in. All major items in the handwriting of James Warren, Jr.

Mercy Otis Warren Papers. Library of Congress. Several manuscript versions of *History.*

Mercy Warren Papers. Massachusetts Historical Society. Largest single collection of manuscript material; includes so-called "Letterbook" as well as other letters, poems, and family documents. Available on two reels of microfilm. Warren materials housed in several collections.

Taylor, Robert J., et al., eds. *Papers of John Adams.* 8 vols. to date. Cambridge: Belknap/Harvard University Press, 1977–. Many letters between Warren and Adams.

Warren-Adams Letters: Being chiefly a correspondence among John Adams, Samuel Adams, and James Warren. 2 vols. Massachusetts Historical Society *Collections* 72–73 (1917, 1925). Warren's letters amply represented, but many in truncated form; among her correspondents are Martha Washington and Hannah Winthrop.

Warren, Mercy Otis. *History of the Rise, Progress, and Termination of the American Revolution.* 3 vols. Boston: Larkin, 1805. First edition. More recent editions include a facsimile reprint of above (New York: AMS Press, 1970), and the slightly modernized version with an excellent introduction by Lester H. Cohen, 2 vols. (Indianapolis: Liberty Classics, 1988).

_____. *Observations on the New Constitution, and on the Federal and State Conventions. By a Columbian Patriot.* Boston, 1788.

_____. *Poems, Dramatic and Miscellaneous.* Boston: Thomas and Andrews, 1790. Includes two verse dramas and poems of several types.

SECONDARY SOURCES

Anthony, Katharine. *First Lady of the Revolution: The Life of Mercy Otis Warren.* Garden City, N.Y.: Doubleday, 1958. This biography helped bring Warren back into the public eye; remains useful, but new research dates author's critical judgments.

Bauer, G. Philip. "Mercy Otis Warren." In *Dictionary of American Biography,* vol. 10, pt. 1, 484–85. Early (1936) application of the term *feminist* to Warren's views.

Baym, Nina. "Mercy Otis Warren's Gendered Melodrama of Revolution." *South Atlantic Quarterly* 90 (1991): 531–54. Major literary critical perspective on gender codes in *History.*

Bloomfield, Maxwell. "Constitutional Values and the Literature of the Early Republic." *Journal of American Culture* 11, no. 4 (1988): 53–58. Brief mention of Warren in context of uncertainty over Constitution and her eventual endorsement.

Brown, Alice. *Mercy Warren.* New York: Scribner's, 1896. First book-length biography, by a fellow playwright. Lively and opinionated.

Cohen, Lester H. "Explaining the Revolution: Ideology and Ethics in Mercy Otis Warren's Historical Theory." *William and Mary Quarterly* 37 (1980), 200–218. Significant look at philosophical underpinnings in *History* by one of the best-informed of Warren commentators.

_____. "Mercy Otis Warren: The Politics of Language and the Aesthetics of Self." *American Quarterly* 35 (1983), 481–98. Examines problematic aspects of Republican Mother concept in relation to Warren's writing.

_____. *The Revolutionary Histories: Contemporary Narratives of the American Revolution.* Ithaca: Cornell University Press, 1980. Mentions of Warren appear throughout this excellent comparative study.

Cowell, Pattie. *Women Poets in Pre-Revolutionary America, 1650–1775,* esp. 71–86. Troy, N.Y.: Whitson, 1981. Valuable as an anthology that includes several poems by Warren, this book also has an excellent introduction to her verse.

Crovitz, Elaine, and Elizabeth Buford. *Courage Knows No Sex,* 47–72. North Quincy, Mass.: Christopher, 1978. Appreciation of Warren in context of other great women, such as Teresa of Avila and Florence Nightingale, but to be used with caution.

Curti, Merle. *Human Nature in American Historical Thought,* 52–54. Columbia: University of Missouri Press, 1968. Looks at the view of human nature in Warren's *History;* best read together with Cohen's "Explaining the Revolution"; see above.

Douglas, Krystan V. "A Question of Authorship: Mercy Otis Warren and *The Blockheads.*" *Theatre Survey* 30, no. 1–2 (1989): 85–92. Ingenious, if unsuccessful, attempt to make *The Blockheads* fit the Warren canon.

Ellet, Elizabeth F. *The Women of the American Revolution,* vol. 1, 91–126. 1848; Philadelphia: Jacobs, 1900. Most important of the attempts in the middle of the nineteenth century to recover Warren as part of American women's history.

Engle, Paul. "Mercy Otis Warren." In *Women in the American Revolution,* 45–70. Chicago: Follett, 1976. Serviceable introduction to Warren for a general audience.

Ford, Paul Leicester. *Some Notes towards an Essay on the Beginnings of American Dramatic Literature, 1606–1789,* 15–16, 18, 24–25. 1893; New York: Burt Franklin, 1971. Important early work on Warren's authorship and place in American literature, but not to be relied on for facts.

Ford, Worthington C. "Mrs. Warren's *The Group.*" Massachusetts Historical Society *Proceedings* 62 (1928–29): 15–22. Discusses identities of historical figures in Warren's political satires.

Friedman, Lawrence J., and Arthur H. Shaffer. "Mercy Otis Warren and the Politics of Historical Nationalism." *New England Quarterly* 48 (1975): 194–215. Takes a serious look at Warren's political theory in *History,* but contains some factual errors.

Fritz, Jean. *Cast for a Revolution: Some American Friends and Enemies, 1728–1814.* Boston: Houghton Mifflin, 1972. Useful biography of Warren as central figure in context with others, including John Adams, Samuel Adams, and Thomas Hutchinson.

_____. "Mercy Otis Warren." *Constitution* 1, no. 2 (1989): 58–63. Lively summary of life and career.

Haverstick, Iola S. "Three Lively Ladies of the Overbury Collection." Columbia Library *Columns* 21 (1971), 20–27. Concerns collection at Barnard College relating to American women authors, including Warren.

Hornstein, Jacqueline. "Comic Vision in the Literature of New England Women before 1800." *Regionalism and the Female Imagination* 3, no. 2–3 (1977–78): 11–19. Brief, general survey of female humorists (Bradstreet, Knight, Murray, Rowson), including Warren.

Hutcheson, Maud Macdonald. "Mercy Warren, 1728–1814." *William and Mary Quarterly* 10 (1953): 378–402. Remains one of the best biographical works. An excellent starting point for researchers new to Warren.

Kerber, Linda K. *Women of the Republic: Intellect and Ideology in Revolutionary America.* Chapel Hill: University of North Carolina Press, 1980. Definition of "Republican Mother"; includes a reading of Warren's verse dramas in female and political terms.

Kern, Jean B. "Mercy Otis Warren: Dramatist of the American Revolution." In *Curtain Calls: British and American Women and the Theater, 1660–1820,* edited by Mary Anne Schofield and Cecilia Macheski, 247–59. Athens: Ohio University Press, 1991. Introductory commentary on Warren's plays, but without serious attention to authorship of attributed works.

Laska, Vera O. *"Remember the Ladies": Outstanding Women of the American Revolution,* 35–60. Boston: Commonwealth of Massachusetts Bicentennial Commission, 1976. Readable summary of life and work.

Lutz, Alma. "Early American Women Historians." *Boston Public Library Quarterly* 8 (1956): 85–99. Discusses Warren in context of others, including Hannah Adams and Emma Willard (Lutz's collection of letters and materials by American women writers is at the Schlesinger Library, Harvard).

McDonald, Janis L. "The Need for Contextual ReVision: Mercy Otis Warren, A Case in Point." *Yale Journal of Law and Feminism* 5 (1992): 183–215. Article in form of discovery of Warren that critiques previous views of her and her work; calls for fresh approach.

Marble, Annie Russell. "Mistress Mercy Warren: Real Daughter of the American Revolution." *New England Magazine* 28 (1903): 163–80. Warren emerges as a "sensitive" woman in this appreciation; article valuable for its illustrations, including photos of Warren's two Plymouth homes.

Markovitz, Judith B. "Radical and Feminist: Mercy Otis Warren and the Historiographers." *Peace and Change* 4 (1977): 10–20. Important article reviving the notion of Warren as feminist; useful for a look at previous historians' assessments of her.

"Mercy Otis Warren." *National Cyclopedia of American Biography,* vol. 7, 177. 1892; Ann Arbor: University Microfilms. 1967. Brief notice of her life, citing John Neal's approval of Warren.

Meserve, Walter J. *An Emerging Entertainment: The Drama of the American People to 1828,* esp. 65–75. Bloomington: Indiana University Press, 1977. Successor to Quinn, below, Meserve's is a basic, historical study.

Norton, Mary Beth. *Liberty's Daughters: The Revolutionary Experience of American Women, 1750–1800.* Boston: Little, Brown, 1980. Warren as one of intellectual women of period; excellent overall study.

Oreovicz, Cheryl Z. "Heroic Drama for an Uncertain Age: The Plays of Mercy Warren." In *Early American Literature and Culture: Essays Honoring Harrison T. Meserole,* edited by Kathryn Zabelle Derounian-Stodola, 192–210. Newark: University of Delaware Press, 1992. One of few articles to take verse dramas seriously; puts Warren's in context with Addison's *Cato.*

______. "Mercy Warren and 'Freedom's Genius.'" *University of Mississippi Studies in English* 5 (1984–87): 215–30. One of the best descriptions of Warren as poet; argues contra Cohen that her providentialism is intentional, not just rhetorical.

Ostriker, Alicia Suskin. *Stealing the Language: The Emergence of Women's Poetry in America,* #23 and passim. Boston: Beacon Press, 1986. Warren in context of female poets—early and more recent.

Polin, Raymond, and Constance Polin. "Mercy Otis Warren: Patriot Founding Mother." *Daughters of the American Revolution Magazine* 123 no. 2 (1989): 104–5, 150–51. An attempt to look at her political principles using *Observations* and *History.*

Quinn, Arthur Hobson. *A History of the American Drama from the Beginnings to the Civil War,* 33–46. 2d ed. New York: Appleton-Century-Crofts, 1943. Solid discussion of *The Adulateur* and *The Group,* but somewhat dismissive of works as plays.

Richards, Jeffrey H. "Providential Actor: The Example of John Adams." In *Theater Enough: American Culture and the Metaphor of the World Stage,*

1607–1789, 230–44. Durham: Duke University Press, 1991. Warren and John Adams as users of theater tropes.

Schofield, Mary Anne. "The Happy Revolution: Colonial Women and the Eighteenth-Century Theater." In *Modern American Drama: The Female Canon,* edited by Jane Schlueter, 29–37. Madison, N.J.: Fairleigh Dickinson University Press, 1990. Survey of subject, including short discussion of Warren.

_____. "'Quitting the Loom and Distaff': Eighteenth-Century American Women Dramatists." In *Curtain Calls: British and American Women and the Theater, 1660–1820,* edited by Schofield and Cecilia Macheski, 260–73. Athens: Ohio University Press, 1991. Helpful introduction to topic.

Shaffer, Arthur H. *The Politics of History: Writing the History of the American Revolution, 1783–1815,* esp. 146–51. Chicago: Precedent, 1975. Warren's place as republican historian among many others; should, however, be read in light of Markovitz, above.

Shipton, Clifford K. "James Warren." In *Sibley's Harvard Graduates,* vol. 11, 584–606. Comments on Mercy Warren show grudging respect and persistent denigration; Shipton mentions her in many of his biographical sketches in this series.

Shuffelton, Frank. "In Different Voices: Gender in the American Republic of Letters." *Early American Literature* 25 (1990): 289–304. Warren and John Adams are examined as correspondents.

_____. "Mercy Otis Warren (25 September 1728–19 October 1814)." In *Dictionary of Literary Biography,* vol. 31, 246–52. The best of the most recent summaries of Warren's life and work.

Silverman, Kenneth. *A Cultural History of the Revolution: Painting, Music, Literature, and the Theatre in the Colonies and the United States from the Treaty of Paris to the Inauguration of George Washington, 1763–1789.* 1976; New York: Columbia University Press, 1987. Essential background.

Smith, William Raymond. *History as Argument: Three Patriot Historians of the American Revolution.* The Hague: Mouton, 1966. Ground-breaking analysis of Warren's historiographic method.

Teunissen, John J. "Blockheadism and the Propaganda Plays of the American Revolution." *Early American Literature* 7 (1972): 148–62. Assumes Warren's authorship of *The Blockheads* as a convenience; puts that play in context with Sewall's *Cure* and an anonymous 1782 play also called *The Blockheads.*

Tichi, Cecelia. "Worried Celebrants of the American Revolution." In *American Literature 1764–1789: The Revolutionary Years,* edited by Everett Emerson, 275–91. Madison: University of Wisconsin Press, 1977. Presents Warren as one of the historians who saw much in America to be concerned about after war.

Tyler, Moses Coit. *The Literary History of the American Revolution, 1763–1783.* 2 vols. 1897; New York: Barnes and Noble, 1941. Warren gets several mentions for her works in this first major study of Revolutionary literature.

Ulrich, Laurel Thatcher. "Of Pens and Needles: Sources in Early American Women's History." *Journal of American History* 77 (1990): 200–207. A call for new studies on American women, including Warren, and a discussion of some resources available.

Warren, Charles. "Elbridge Gerry, James Warren, Mercy Warren, and the Ratification of the Federal Constitution in Massachusetts." Massachusetts Historical Society *Proceedings* 64 (1930–32): 143–64. Essential article, establishing Warren's authorship of *Observations.*

_____. "Samuel Adams and the Sans Souci Club in 1785." Massachusetts Historical Society *Proceedings* 60 (1926–27): 318–44. Provides historical background for the play *Sans Souci* and demonstrates Warren's connection to the real-life Tea-Assembly episode while showing the play not hers.

_____. "A Young Man's Adventures in England and France during the Revolutionary War." Massachusetts Historical Society *Proceedings* 65 (1932–36): 234–67. On Warren's son Winslow and her correspondence with him.

Watts, Emily Stipes. *The Poetry of American Women from 1632 to 1945,* esp. 39–44. Austin: University of Texas Press, 1977. One of the first modern studies to take Warren's poetry seriously.

Weales, Gerald. "*The Adulateur* and How It Grew." University of Pennsylvania *Library Chronicle* 43 (1979): 103–33. Essential article on the background and versions of this play.

_____. "The Quality of Mercy, or Mrs. Warren's Profession." *Georgia Review* 33 (1979), 881–94. Sees Warren as the first American woman author to be "an amateur who became a professional."

Wilson, Joan Hoff, and Sharon L. Bollinger. "Mercy Otis Warren: Playwright, Poet, and Historian of the American Revolution (American, 1728–1814)." In *Female Scholars: A Tradition of Learned Women before 1800,* edited by J. B. Brink, 161–82. Montreal: Eden Press, 1980. One of the several rediscovery articles from this period surveying Warren's work.

Zagarri, Rosemarie. *Mercy Otis Warren and the American Revolution: A Woman's Dilemma.* Wheeling, Ill.: Davidson, Harlan, 1995. Biography.

_____. "Morals, Manners, and the Republican Mother." *American Quarterly* 44, no. 2 (1992): 192–215. Although not mentioning Warren specifically, provides a supplementary view to Kerber, above, in terms of intellectual background to the Republican Mother concept.

Index

The Author

Jeffrey H. Richards is a professor of English at Old Dominion University, specializing in early and nineteenth-century American literature. He is the author of *Theater Enough: American Culture and the Metaphor of the World Stage, 1607–1789* (1991).

The Editor

Pattie Cowell received her Ph.D. from the University of Massachusetts at Amherst in 1977. Her research has been directed by combined interests in early American literature and women's studies. She has published *Women Poets in Pre-Revolutionary America* (1981) and several related articles and notes on individual colonial women writers. Additionally, she has coedited with Ann Stanford *Critical Essays on Anne Bradstreet* (1983) and prepared a facsimile edition of Cotton Mather's *Ornaments for the Daughters of Zion* (1978). She is currently at work on a second edition of *Women Poets in Pre-Revolutionary America* and on a cultural study of early New England women poets. She chairs the English department at Colorado State University.